The Life and Diary of
JOHN P. WADDILL

The Life and Diary of
JOHN P. WADDILL

THE LAWYER WHO FREED SOLOMON NORTHUP, 1813–1855

CHARLES A. RIDDLE III

2019
University of Louisiana at Lafayette Press

© 2019 by University of Louisiana at Lafayette Press
All rights reserved
ISBN 13 (paper): 978-1-946160-20-1

http://ulpress.org
University of Louisiana at Lafayette Press
P.O. Box 43558
Lafayette, LA 70504-3558
Printed on acid-free paper

Library of Congress Cataloging-in-Publication Data

Names: Riddle, Charles A., III, 1955- author.
  Title: The life and diary of John P. Waddill : the lawyer who freed Solomon Northup, 1813-1855 / Charles A. Riddle III.
  Description: Lafayette, LA : University of Louisiana at Lafayette Press, [2018]
  Identifiers: LCCN 2017057193 | ISBN 9781946160201 (alk. paper)
  Subjects: LCSH: Waddill, John P., 1813-1855. | Lawyers--Louisiana--Biography. | Northup, Solomon, 1808-1863? | Louisiana--Politics and government--1803-1865. | Louisiana--Social conditions--19th century. Classification: LCC F374.W33 R53 2018 | DDC 976.3/05092 [B] --dc23
  LC record available at https://lccn.loc.gov/2017057193

To my wife, Margaret Susan Noone Riddle
b. June 25, 1955 - d. July 14, 2018

TABLE OF CONTENTS

FOREWORD xi
INTRODUCTION xv
PROLOGUE
Yellow Fever, September 1855 xix

BOOK I
THE EARLY LIFE OF JOHN P. WADDILL, 1813–1838

CHAPTER 1: The Beginning, 1821 to 1832 1
CHAPTER 2: Augusta College, 1836 7
CHAPTER 3: Life at Augusta 11
CHAPTER 4: Theories in Education 17
CHAPTER 5: Professor Joseph Tomlinson 21
CHAPTER 6: Debates as Education Tools 25
CHAPTER 7: Church Life 29
CHAPTER 8: The Beauty of Augusta and Thoughts of Waddill 31
CHAPTER 9: Issues in America 37
CHAPTER 10: Sadness at Augusta College 41
CHAPTER 11: End of Term 49
CHAPTER 12: Beginning of Another Term at Augusta College 55
CHAPTER 13: Classmates Departed 63
CHAPTER 14: The Return of George R. Waters
 and Thoughts on Politicians 69
CHAPTER 15: Late Enrolling in Class 75
CHAPTER 16: Continuing Debates 83

Book II
The Early Legal Career and Entry into Politics of John P. Waddill, 1838–1847

Chapter 17: Leaving Augusta College and
John P. Waddill's Law Career, 1838 91
Chapter 18: The Courtship and Marriage
of John P. Waddill and Julia Barlow................................. 101
Chapter 19: Physicians in Avoyelles 103
Chapter 20: Spring Creek Academy... 109
Chapter 21: The Reality of the Slave Trade 113
Chapter 22: Joseph Barton Elam, Born June 12, 1821........................... 115
Chapter 23: Waddill Grows in Popularity 117
Chapter 24: News From *The Villager*, September 23, 1843 125
Chapter 25: The Mexican War, 1846 131
Chapter 26: The Mexican War Continues... 143
Chapter 27: The Browder Family Cousins 147
Chapter 28: Challenging Decisions in the Practice of Law.................... 153

Book III
The Later Legal Career and Entry into State Politics by John P. Waddill, 1847–1852

Chapter 29: Election to State Senate, September 22, 1847 159
Chapter 30: Politics 1848, Senator Waddill 165
Chapter 31: Faith Challenge, May 1848 181
Chapter 32: Politics, Business, and Temperance, August 10, 1848 189
Chapter 33: The Mail Fail and Patronizing the Press............................. 201
Chapter 34: Politics, Mail, and Death.. 205
Chapter 35: The Senate in 1850 and Back Home 211
Chapter 36: Teaching William Wallace Waddill the Law...................... 217

Chapter 37: Politics Heat Up 227
Chapter 38: John P. Waddill and William W. Waddill Practice Law 231
Chapter 39: Deadly Politics 235
Chapter 40: Christmas 1851 241
Chapter 41: The Lodge, May 1, 1852 245

Book IV
The Constitutional Convention 1852, Samuel Bass, and the Freeing of Solomon Northup, Death of John P. Waddil

Chapter 42: The Constitutional Convention of 1852 253
Chapter 43: The Trial for the Murder of A. B. Coco, 1852 259
Chapter 44: Charles Étienne Arthur Gayarré 265
Chapter 45: Samuel Bass and John P. Waddill 269
Chapter 46: Politics, November 1852 271
Chapter 47: Meeting with Solomon Northup 273
Chapter 48: Relationship with Samuel Bass
and the Freeing of Solomon Northup 275
Chapter 49: A. G. Pearce 285
Chapter 50: Life in the 1850s 291
Chapter 51: Education of Waddill's Children 299
Chapter 52: Sale of Land, 1853 303
Chapter 53: Business Decisions 305
Chapter 54: William Waddill Leaves Avoyelles 309
Chapter 55: The Last Legal Filing and Death of John P. Waddill 313

Epilogue
New Orleans, April 12, 2014 317

Appendix 321
Index 355

FOREWORD

This well-researched volume, *The Life and Diary of John P. Waddill, the Lawyer Who Freed Solomon Northup, 1813–1855,* provides a rare glimpse into the experiences and thoughts of a reflective antebellum Southern man. In the decades before the Civil War, John Waddill became an attorney, politician, planter, and family man at Marksville, Louisiana. His adopted home, a modest-sized town and seat of Avoyelles Parish (county), contained no more than a few thousand residents during Waddill's time. Although a considerable distance from New Orleans, this part of the lower Red River Valley developed into a vital component of the Gulf South's agricultural economy. From 1830 to 1860, the parish shared characteristics with the rest of the Deep South, mainly its thousands of acres of farmable land, lush bayous, and in this case a flat, broad grassy plain called the Avoyelles Prairie. This fertile landscape gave rise to both cotton and sugar plantations on the Red River and its tributaries. In addition, plenty of smaller farms, an extensive slave population, and brisk riverboat traffic helped integrate this place into the wider American economy.

It was into this Louisiana place that Waddill walked during the last year of the 1830s. He had been born in 1813 just outside of Nashville in Williamston County, Tennessee. He was one of nine children in a household where, not long after his birth, he lost both his father and mother. His employment began at an early age on farms in Tennessee and eventually for relatives who owned land in Louisiana. As a farmhand, Waddill learned the value of hard work and understood very well the strains of being a small farmer. His life's trajectory changed dramatically when a relative and patron secured for him a place at a college in Kentucky. He matriculated at Augusta College in northern Kentucky. This Methodist school near the Ohio River drew students from both the free state of Ohio and slave state of Kentucky. There, in the flower of his adolescence, Waddill began recording observations and musings, which were meticulously kept in a handwritten diary.

These personal experiences, kept for the rest of his adult life and then passed down through the generations, have been brought to light. With careful transcription and a tremendous amount of biographical research and notes, this volume provides a magnificent history of a young man's coming of age, entry into the legal profession, and common life in Avoyelles Parish. The first entries are filled with fascinating discussions and debates he enjoyed with fellow college students. There in the middle of the 1830s, the United States had slipped into a period of intense partisanship. The presidency of Andrew Jackson provided much of the subject matter for Waddill to reflect upon. From the start, he sympathized with President Jackson. His political leaning toward the new Democratic Party came through clearly. The college years of his life were also a time of intellectual curiosity, and the diary contains numerous mentions of both literary and scientific topics. Waddill proved to be a very smart and contemplative young man. Reading through his early thoughts is one of the most interesting parts of this whole account.

Following college, the new scholar moved to Marksville and became a lawyer there. He mentions all his clients and cases he worked on, some in more detail than others. He joined the Democratic Party during the 1840s, and the diary provides excellent information on antebellum Louisiana politics. Waddill would serve on the first municipal council of his town, as a delegate to the Louisiana Constitutional Convention of 1852, and win election as a state senator. There is no greater source for information about Avoyelles politics during the 1847–1855 time periods than within this volume. The information flows from Waddill's keen mind right to the page. He covers both local and national issues. When war broke out on the southern border of the United States, he rallied his community as a fervent supporter of the Mexican War, 1846–1848. He made speeches at Marksville, helped raise volunteers for the venture. He followed the news coming out of Mexico and made comments about all he heard and read. Antebellum Louisiana's history is richer because we now have many details about important events such as the war that Waddill wrote about in the diary.

Waddill's life also intersected one of the most extraordinary stories of the time. He became the attorney who completed the legal work to free Solomon Northup. Northup had been a free African American in upstate New York before being tricked, drugged, and kidnapped in 1841. Northup found himself sold into slavery at Washington, D.C., and then brought to Central Louisiana via a slave market at New Orleans. For twelve long years, Northup remained enslaved in both Rapides and Avoyelles Parishes. He became free at long last at the courthouse in Marksville on January 4, 1853.

The 2013 Academy Award-winning motion picture *Twelve Years a Slave* has raised awareness of this amazing story in the twenty-first century. Yet Northup's own written and published account from the 1850s, following his freedom, brought the reality of a slave's life along the Red River to the attention of a national audience. Due to its unique perspective of someone not born a slave, Northup's book has been an invaluable source on American slavery. Waddill enters into the story when he learned of Northup's plight from Samuel Bass, a Canadian carpenter who worked for and befriended Waddill. Bass was certainly an abolitionist and recognized Northup's dilemma from his first encounter with him. Once Northup's family knew of his fate, when Bass wrote a letter to them, the legal wheels started turning.

With compassion and after much hard work lasting late into the night, Waddill presented a strong case for Northup's freedom. Research done for this volume has uncovered all the documents related to the case and they add much to what we know already. Without Waddill's personal devotion to righting the wrong, Northup would have remained a slave for a lot longer and perhaps the rest of his life. The effort was not done out of an altruistic abolitionist impulse at all. Waddill facilitated Northup's manumission instead as a way to banish injustice in the slave system which he supported wholeheartedly. Waddill himself owned slaves and assisted other planters in property cases related to land and slaves. This Marksville lawyer did his part in sustaining the integrity of the chattel institution that formed the whole basis of the economy and culture of Louisiana. Waddill could, however, examine the facts objectively, see the merits of the legal issue, and because of his extensive education, remain unbiased by a slave regime mentality.

This volume does an excellent job of explaining Waddill's involvement and presenting exactly what happened in the story of Northup's freedom. Readers will want to explore every page to learn more about how Waddill came to be the lawyer who freed Northup. This book is a satisfying account of this episode and much more in the life and times of John Waddill.

This volume's author/editor, Charles Riddle, is an accomplished lawyer in his own right and is well-respected in Avoyelles Parish. He served as a legislator, district attorney, and private practice lawyer. He knows legal procedure quite well and has done extensive research in the courthouse records, scattered biographical sources, newspapers, and other libraries and archives to help everyone better understand the man and context behind this great diary. Through the research added to the volume, readers will arrive at a better understanding of one Southern man's life journey. That man became successful in the legal profession, in politics, and without question was vital to the story of Solomon Northup. I applaud the appearance of this book as a signal that sources are still to be found that can give new information about Louisiana's storied past.

Henry O. Robertson, Ph.D.
Louisiana College

INTRODUCTION

The diaries of John Pamplin Waddill provide a firsthand account of the effects that education, religion, slavery, and politics had on life in the antebellum South. They also take us on travels to rural Tennessee, Kentucky, and Waddill's home in central Louisiana.

Waddill loomed large in Avoyelles Parish, Louisiana. He served as a state senator in the Louisiana Legislature, a delegate of the 1852 state constitutional convention, and a member of the first Marksville City Council. He was a leader in his community and a fervent patriot.

Although not a plantation owner, he did own slaves that worked his several separate farms and various tracts of land throughout the parish. Ironically, we remember him for his role in freeing the wrongly enslaved Solomon Northop. Of course, many would agree that this was his greatest accomplishment, particularly as he undertook the task knowing that this would not be popular in his home in the antebellum South. John P. Waddill was a principled man, however. In his family and church life and as an attorney and a politician, he lived by those principles and was well respected in his day.

Later observers have pointed to Waddill's role in Northup's case for freedom and judged the lawyer to be an example of how insidious the institution of slavery was at the time. One reviewer of the 2013 film version of Northup's *Twelve Years a Slave* wrote:

> Rare and emotionally powerful, as first-person narratives of free blacks abducted into bound servitude were, they also exposed a central contradiction in the abolitionist attempt to present the slave narrative as Exhibit A in their case before the court of public opinion. Depicting an actual "crime," such anomalous accounts risked *affirming* the legitimacy of American slavery. The danger was that the reader might adopt the view of the Louisiana "legal gentleman of distinction" [Waddill] who facilitated Northup's liberation. Learning of the kidnapped black man's predicament, Judge [*sic*—Waddill

a lawyer, not a judge] John P. Waddill's "emotions of indignation" were "aroused by such an instance of injustice." Crucially, his sense of justice arose not from any principled opposition to slavery but, conversely, from an abiding respect for "the title of his fellow parishioners and clients to the property which constituted the larger proportion of their wealth," and which in turn "depended upon the good faith in which slave sales were transacted." By their very circulation, counterfeits threaten the value of legitimate commodities, weakening the market as a whole.[1]

Whether or not Waddill's "sense of justice" lacked proper motivation by today's standards, at the time he acted as he saw fit. His diaries help us to understand why he would do so.

Having access to the unpublished diaries of John P. Waddill grants insight into Waddill's beliefs and feelings on the events and national debates of his time. Diaries provide an excellent source of how we experience history, especially when other sources verify the statements in them—as they do here.

Waddill's first entry dates to March 1837. He labeled it "Diary of a Misanthrope." This book references notations to Waddill's diaries in two ways. Direct quotations from his writings come directly from the diary and are footnoted or set in block quotes. The other method cites one of the four volumes, each transcribed from images of the diaries that Elizabeth Brazelton, Waddill's great-great granddaughter, provided me. When discussing certain events on specific dates, the reader can be assured that Waddill noted them when there is a citation to the diary. The original volumes are fragile, so a transcription of the diaries was made from PDF scans of them that are saved on CDs. The numbering, or citations, is done by volume on the disc to match the page numbers of the transcription. The dates are noted also for easier finding of the source.

Every character mentioned and named in the book is an actual figure in history. Most of the names came from seven main sources: (1) Waddill's diaries; (2) *The History of Avoyelles Parish* by Corrinne L. Saucier; (3) *Three Pioneer Rapides Families—A Genealogy* by George Mason Graham Stafford; (4) *Twelve Years a Slave*, by Solomon Northup, edited by Sue Eakin and

---

1. Jeannine Marie DeLombard, "Why did *12 Years a Slave* Get the Hollywood Treatment, Not Frederick Douglass's Autobiography?," History News Network—George Mason University, October 28, 2013.

Introduction xvii

Joseph Logsdon; (5) legal records in the Avoyelles Parish Clerk of Court Archives; (6) *Biographical and Historical Memoires of Northwest Louisiana* (1890); and (7) original newspapers from Marksville, including the first newspaper published in the town, *The Expositor*, which ran from December 1842 to August 1843. Waddill advertised as "Attorney and Counselor at Law" in the paper throughout its life. The early newspapers were written in both French and English. *The Expositor* was followed by *The Villager* (*Le Villagois*), which began in August 1843 and ran for several years. No diary has been found that covers parts of the period from 1839 to 1845, so these newspapers proved to be invaluable sources for the events of those missing years. All of these newspapers have been microfilmed and are available through the LSU Library Newspapers Archives.

The lawsuits mentioned in this book are referred to in Waddill's diary or found in the Avoyelles Parish Clerk of Court Archives. These lawsuits produced interesting information about Waddill, who practiced law for seventeen years though he lived for only forty-two. All of the lawsuits mentioned with suit numbers are from the records of the Avoyelles Parish Clerk of Court Archives. From 1839 to 1845, they provide a record of what young Waddill did in his law practice during the missing diary years.

Ultimately, this story is about John P. Waddill and his context. It includes his family, friends, enemies, associates, and others. My goals have been to remain true to the facts and give the reader a view of the time period written herein. As an attorney, I focused on legal proceedings and documents. As an elected official of the community in which Waddill lived, I focus on the frustrations officials experience with the political process. As a former history major, I attempted to capture the thought, policies, and politics of the southern United States in antebellum times, with the primary focus being Waddill's point of view.

PROLOGUE

Yellow Fever
September 1855

John P. Waddill sat at his desk, admiring the quality of the work it took to construct it. He lit two candles for light just sufficient for reading. He opened one of the newspapers that he had received late the afternoon before and began to read. He felt a little strange and began to reflect on his past.

Waddill thought about his seventeen years of practicing law in Louisiana and his successes in the political realm. He felt a little light-headed as he looked at the two candles. "I must remember to order more candles." He thought about lighting one of his lanterns, but the smell was not pleasing to him.

Waddill left his office early that day after feeling feverish the previous two days. It was September 18, 1855. He had not eaten much since the day before and was sore in his back. He began to notice chills with his fever. His wife had asked him to stay home, but John had work to do and was committed to it. Now he could not stand, so he had someone drive him home in his carriage.

When he got home, he lay down but began to suffer from nausea and headaches. They sent for Dr. Donat MacEnery, who came on the nineteenth in the early morning. This was the fourth day of symptoms with no sign of relief. On the fifth day, the fever reached higher levels.

On the eleventh day of his fever, September 26, Waddill began vomiting quite a bit more than before. He wondered where it came from, since he had not eaten anything except a small amount of soup.

Doctor MacEnery recognized that Waddill had reached the second, final phase of yellow fever. All he could do was make him comfortable. He recommended that Julia keep the children and others away from him. The cause of yellow fever was unknown.

MacEnery wanted to try Peruvian bark, but he could not find any soon enough. Julia went to her husband with a wet, cold washcloth to sit by him. Her touch was soothing, and he briefly reminisced about the past.

But his face was yellow and his body jaundiced. He told Julia in a weakened voice that his stomach was in great pain. His eyes began to seep blood, and his vomiting increased, black with blood. Julia knew now why they called it the "black vomit."

It was hard for Julia to imagine the loss of her beloved husband and an unknown future. He was such a handsome and fine man. Love had struck the first time she saw him at the River Landing; she had hoped he noticed her. He had not. Why would he notice such a young girl? It was not until that day in town that he finally noticed her as a sixteen-year-old young lady. She had thought she would be the first to leave this world. She was the one who had been sickly. Now, she had to remain strong for the children. She would care for him until he was gone, losing hope for recovery each day.

Waddill continued to have blood in his urine and was extremely thirsty and dehydrated. Julia tried many remedies, lots of water, calomel, quinine, and nitre. Soon there would be nothing more to do than administer laudanum. The pain was too great, and the delirium was even worse.

Drifting in and out of consciousness, Waddill had moments of coherence, and he began to think of sad times. He drifted in a semi-concious state.

BOOK I

The Early Life of John P. Waddill
1813–1838

CHAPTER 1

The Beginning
1821 to 1832

John Waddill was born October 8, 1813, in Williamson County, Tennessee. His father, Samuel D. Waddill, had been a merchant but, finding those efforts unprofitable, had turned to farming by the time John was born. The family of Samuel's father, John Waddill, had lived in what was once the western part of North Carolina and later became Tennessee, (today's Washington County) along the Nolichucky River. In 1808, Samuel moved from Washington County to Williamson County. There he met Elizabeth Blagrave Browder, and on February 22, 1809, the two married. Her father, Frederic Browder, and mother, Elizabeth Pamplin, had come to Tennessee from Virginia some ten years earlier.

Samuel and Elizabeth had nine children: Frederick Browder Waddill, born on December 8, 1808; Seth Quee Waddill, born in 1812; John Pamplin Waddill, born on October 8, 1813; Samuel Rittenhouse Waddill, born in 1814; Martha Jane Waddill, born in 1816; Rachel Elizabeth Waddill, born in 1819; Mary Ann Waddill, born in 1821; Narcissa Browder Waddill, born in 1824; and William Wallace Waddill, born on September 5, 1829. Samuel D. Waddill never saw his last-born child, dying less than two months before William Wallace's birth. His wife, Elizabeth, followed him one year later.

In the fall of 1820, Samuel Waddill had purchased a farm and moved his family to an area of western Tennessee that would become Madison County in 1821. The farm at the time of Samuel and Elizabeth's deaths had four families living on it, sharing the work and the fruits of their labor. The four families also shared one female slave. At the time of their parents' passing, the Waddill children were all still very young. John and six of his siblings were under eighteen at the time of their mother's death. They had no kin nearby, so the older brothers helped to raise the others. When John's younger sisters were able to begin helping his older brothers, Frederick and Seth, take care of the the youngest siblings, Narcissa and William, he decided to strike out on his own and further his education.

John Waddill recalled the move to this part of Tennessee, which took place when he was seven, in his diaries. The only things he remembered were:

> …interminable and heavy forests, filled with bears, deer and other wild game in abundance. No schools were there until I was some ten years of age and that was in the fall of 1823.
>
> Then one of our neighbors who could read, write, and cypher a letter, and who was a pioneer farmer, set up a school and taught in it for four months. His name was Jeremiah T. Rust, and he was a native of Wake County, North Carolina. He was a sprightly good man, but unfit for a teacher.
>
> I received but little aid from schools until the year 1827, at which time an excellent teacher was employed by my father and some four other farmers, at the salary of six hundred dollars a year, which was at the at time considered an enormous price. His name was James T. Bledsoe—and he had a classical education. I studied English and Latin Grammar, Rhetoric, Arithmetic, and Payley's Philosophy under him. He taught in the same place until after the death of my mother.

This educational opportunity inspired John Waddill. After one year, he discussed at length with his father how much it meant to him. Mr. Bledsoe inspired him but John wanted to be a lawyer. He needed more education as Bledsoe gave him incentive to seek more.

Samuel Waddill was aware of John's intelligence. Education strained the finances of the communal families. John's father encouraged John to seek more, but he knew that he did not have the finances to give John a formal education.

Before his father's death, John Waddill, at the age of only fifteen, began the preliminary study of law, but his training for that profession was very limited.

Not long after this, however, Waddill's father died. The death of his father crushed John's spirit. The two had been close, and Samuel served as an inspiration to John. For days, John could not speak and tried not to cry. At age sixteen, he did not consider it manly to cry. After several weeks, he came out of his shell. He began to study again, and his desire to become a lawyer increased. His mother committed to their share of the instructor to allow the continued education.

A year later, nearly to the day, Waddill's mother died. This event caught John completely off guard. He had barely recovered from the loss of his father, and he now had no parent left. He cried. He confided in his brother, Frederick. His beautiful sweet mother left a one-year-old son and a six-year-old daughter, in addition to the other seven children. Frederick was in charge and was a great older brother. He had ambitions also but was devoted to his younger siblings. It was he who was able to reassure John after the death of their mother.

John wondered how they would make without their mother, who was the glue of the family for the short time after their father had died. The resources of the farm, cattle, milk cows, chickens, hogs, and the small farm would supply them with the necessities.

The farm had to be managed. Though wild game was their main source for meat, they would have to plant and harvest crops—corn for harvest during the summers, winter wheat for feed for the cattle, hogs, and chickens, and flour and grain. The corn allowed them to produce corn oil and syrup—enough to survive on and use for medicinal purposes. They also had a small amount of cotton because it was so marketable. Their father had constantly cleared the land to allow better production.

The youngest children handled the easiest chores on a daily basis. Those who were too young to work the fields collected eggs from the chickens and fed the animals. The hogs provided a good source of protein and were generally butchered and shared with the other three families trying to survive. Without salt, there would be much waste due to spoiling, so hog lard would be spread on the bottom of a barrel, and salt would be generously applied to both sides of the pork meat. Then the process began again: hog lard, salt on meat, and so forth until the barrel was full. The meat would last for months that way, sometimes more if it was smoked. Smokehouses were a necessity for survival. Beef was made into jerky or preserved in the same manner, though one would have to par boil it, which made it very tough. Pounding prior to par boil was a necessity. One benefit was that the meat did not have to last as long due to more than twenty individuals eating from the hog or cow.

Generally, the female children combined their efforts to milk cows, churn butter, and haul the milk and butter. They all helped except for the two youngest. It was a group effort on the part of all four families.

There were injuries on the farm, and doctors were scarce. The family used sap from a pine, which had some medicinal value, to treat cuts and wounds.

They boiled and then cooled the bark of pine to serve as a poultice to help cover wounds and possibly prevent infection, although not much was known about infection in the 1820s. The frequency of fevers elicited great care when a person fell ill.

All the while John's education continued, though it was soon coming to an end. John therefore approached his older brother and told him of his dreams to leave and get an education. Frederick did not hold him back and gave him the freedom to leave. Frederick and John were aware that William would join John wherever he lived after he turned sixteen.

Frederick could see how excited this nearly eighteen-year-old young man was to be set free from the burden he had taken on. The middle children were helping much more, and the family would be fine. Frederick also had a desire to move on, yet he was the oldest and would stay as long as it took.

Although relieved, the death of his mother continued to haunt Waddill. Frederick gave him comfort about being able to leave, but he could not wrap his mind around the loss, in quick succession, of both parents. He had trouble focusing on the studies at which he desired so much to excel. Mr. Bledsoe, a circuit-riding Methodist preacher, noticed John's troubles and spent extra time with him, not only helping with his studies, but also in a personal way. This proved to be a great comfort to Waddill as he committed to God that he would never give up the faith.

So, John P. Waddill began to ponder where he would go and how he would continue his education. He left in 1831, and five years later, Frederick would leave, heading for Texas. The rest of the family stayed on the farm until grown or married. In 1837, William was nine and Narcissa was thirteen. The rest of the family could take care of themselves and the farm. So began the early stages of John P. Waddill's adult life.

Rather than going directly to college in 1831, Waddill began the journey to Louisiana. His cousins, part of the Elam family, lived in western Louisiana. If needed, he would end up there for his start. He walked to Memphis from his home in a journey that took longer than he thought it would. It was a distance of about eighty miles as the crow flies, but there was no direct path then. He had jerked beef and a musket for hunting and protection. Just as he did when on long hunts for food with his father, he packed his possibles bag. Knowing that he would probably not need everything, but realizing that much could go wrong, he packed his flint, with steel to strike it, a rag, extra gun powder, a straight razor, fish hooks and string, and other items he might need. Before a hunt, his father would check the bag to make sure he had packed appropriately. Waddill thought of his father as he packed his bag.

The family could not afford to let Waddill take one of the horses shared by the four families, nor a mule to pack his belongings. Later that January in Tennessee, temperatures dropped below zero, reaching record lows. Through the cold, he traveled light. After four days, he arrived in Memphis.

Once there, Waddill waited two days for a steamboat from St. Louis to stop on its way to Louisiana. He purchased a ticket for passage on the *Yellow Stone*, which was heading south to work the Louisiana bayous for the winter. He got off in Washington, Louisiana, on the banks of Bayou Courtableau, which fed into the Atchafalaya River.

Waddill then continued his journey by traveling north to Rapides Parish, where he eventually met Thomas J. Hickman. Hickman was a planter and owned a plantation in an area that later became Grant Parish after the Civil War. The three Hickman brothers had moved from Missouri to the central part of Louisiana to purchase and work land on the east bank of the Red River, immediately south of the Randolph Colomb Plantation. Records show that they reached Louisiana in about 1835.[2] Peter and Terry Hickman (father and son) purchased property they called New Hope, Thomas J. Hickman purchased land and called it Flag Land, and William P. Hickman became owner of Fairmount, also known as Grand Bend, North Bend, and Bellevue.

Due to Waddill's knowledge of farm work, Thomas Hickman offered him a job to work his land. The two developed a strong relationship. By 1850, Thomas J. Hickman had 900 improved and 1,500 unimproved acres valued at $30,000.00; he also had livestock worth $3,000.00. Flag Land produced 10,000 bushels of corn; 42 bales of cotton; 400 hogsheads of sugar; and 200 gallons of molasses.[3] This was a large operation.

Waddill also worked for William P. Hickman, when his land was known as Bellevue, and did some work for his cousin J.P. Elam, who had property in Catahoula Parish.

---

2. See the Hickman-Bryan Papers, 1796–1920, at the State Historical Society of Missouri f. 89–94, Western Historical Manuscript Collection, University of Missouri-Columbia, Elllis Library, Columbia, Mo.

3. "Some Large Landholders of Rapides Parish, 1850," *Louisiana History: The Journal of the Louisiana Historical Association* 29, no. 4 (1988): 388.

CHAPTER 2

Augusta College, 1836

After working for Thomas Hickman and J. P. Elam during the early 1830s, John Waddill shared with Hickman his desire to continue his education and his goal of becoming an attorney. In fact, he talked incessantly about his desire. John shared with Thomas Hickman his desire to go to school in Kentucky. Specifically, he wanted to attend Augusta College. Thomas Hickman pledged his support with finances.

Hickman's inspiration and funding helped Waddill in his tireless effort to get there. Waddill would never forget this. With fervent desire, Waddill began this journey.

Augusta College

The Methodist Conferences of Kentucky and Ohio joined together to found Augusta College at Augusta, Kentucky, and the Legislature of Kentucky chartered the college on December 7, 1822.[4] John Waddill had a Protestant upbringing in Methodist churches. He never wavered in his faith, despite his struggles to cope with the loss of his parents and raise the family.

When Waddill arrived at Augusta in the spring of 1836, he found another Louisiana resident (who would later cross paths with Waddill in the Louisiana state legislature), Edward White Robertson. Robertson was ten years younger than Waddill and lived in Iberville Parish. He became a lawyer in 1850 after finishing his studies at the University of Louisiana (today's Tulane University).[5]

---

4. Thomas Nicholson, ed., *The Christian Student* 15, no. 3, (August 1914): 88–90. Bishop Joseph Soule was a Trustee.

5. "Edward White Robertson," https://en.wikipedia.org/wiki/Edward_White_Rob-

In the 1820s and 1830s, American higher education was undergoing a series of transformations. One new concept was the Lyceum Movement. The technical definition of a lyceum is a lecture hall, but the movement itself became more of a pedagogical experiment. Lectures would involve the latest scientific or sociological concepts, such as phrenology or slavery issues.[6] Students would be required to take notes and later declaim, or proceed with declamation, and debate the issues discussed by taking the concept posited, for or against, to further expand their personal view of the world. Augusta would bring in many lecturers and use their own professors to introduce this Lyceum concept of education.

A history of the Methodists in Kentucky includes the following description.[7]

> AUGUSTA COLLEGE The most important and far reaching event in Augusta's early history was the merger by the trustees of the Bracken Academy with Conferences of the Methodist Church of Ohio and Kentucky to found the Augusta College. The year was 1822. The Conference from Ohio appointed a committee consisting of Martin Ruter, John Collins and David Young to confer with a like committee from the Kentucky Conference. This committee appeared at the session at Lexington. The Kentucky Conference was favorable to the proposition and appointed Charles Holliday, Henry B. Bascom and Alexander Cummins to consider the matter with the Ohio committee. Their report heartily endorsed the proposed union, and a commission consisting of Marcus Lindsay, H. B. Bascom and William Holman was appointed for the Kentucky Conference, to carry forward the negotiations. They went to Augusta and succeeded in effecting an agreement with the trustees of the Bracken Academy. Such was the genesis of the Augusta College.

---

ertson. Robertson was elected to the Louisiana House of Representatives at the time Waddill was elected to the Senate, and again in 1853. That connection created a bond between the two of them. He was also a Democrat.

6. Josiah Holbrook, considered the father of the American Lyceum movement, published his article "The American Lyceum, or Society for the Improvement of Schools, and Diffusion of Useful Knowledge" in October 1826 in the *American Journal of Education*. Reprints are available through Amazon, printed by Forgotten Books, copyright 2015.

7. Walter H. Rankins, *Augusta College: Augusta, Kentucky, First Established Methodist College 1822–1849* (Frankfort, Ky.: Roberts Printing, 1957).

By 1825 the Augusta College was ready to receive more students and the trustees thought it advisable to spread some information about its plan, curriculum, staff of professors and achievement. An advertisement about the College in a Cincinnati, Ohio, newspaper for 1825 is quoted here:

"The Trustees of Augusta College, having been appointed to the superintendance of an institution intended expressly for the liberal education of youth in the various branches of useful science, take this method to communicate to the public some information respecting its situation and prospects. In December 1822, an act of incorporation was obtained from the Legislature of Kentucky, and a handsome brick building, pleasantly situated upon a three-acre lot of ground, has been commenced, and nearly completed. It already affords ample accommodations for a large number of students, and will be in a short time entirely finished. The present course of instruction is academical, including Latin, Greek, and the higher branches of English education; and is conducted by the Rev. John P. Finley, A.M. (Preparatory Department). It already affords ample accommodations for a large number of students, and will be in a short time entirely finished. The prices of tuition are, for Latin and Greek languages, $3.00 per quarter, and for higher branches of English, $2.00. — The prices for boarding in respectable families are from one dollar, to one dollar and fifty cents per week. The College is now open for the reception and instruction of students in the above branches, and careful attention will be paid to their morals. The Trustees and friends of the institution are determined to do all in their power to promote its prosperity; and when the moderate price of tuition and boarding, together with the various advantages of the establishment are considered, they matter themselves that it will receive its full share of public patronage.

Signed in behalf of the Trustees,
John Armstrong, Pres't. Martin Marshall, Sec'y."[8]

The first building constructed at Augusta College was 80 by 42 feet. On the first floor was a 40-by-30-feet chapel and two recitation rooms, each 30 by 18 feet. On the second floor were six rooms. The third story

---

8. W. E. Arnold, *A History of Methodism in Kentucky* (Louisville: 1936), II: 62–63.

was divided into seven rooms. Students were expected to board with local families for fees.[9]

Waddill arrived at Augusta College on March 27, 1836. One year later, in March 1837, he began keeping a detailed diary.

---

9. *The Christian Student* 15, no. 4 (August 1914): 89.

CHAPTER 3

LIFE AT AUGUSTA

Tuesday, March 28, 1837—The Wandering Piper

During John Waddill's first week of college, Augusta sponsored the "Wandering Piper," a rather famous bagpipe player, for a performance at the chapel. Although Augusta College didn't require students to learn music, it encouraged and supported its performance by inviting visiting musicians from diverse backgrounds. The Wandering Piper exicted Waddill, as both the music and the man were unique.

The piper met the attendees at the door and each received a list of mostly Scottish tunes, suited to the bagpipes. This intrigued Waddill. The piper wore plaid traditional Scottish garb, something Waddill had never seen. Also, he wore a sword with a sheath of silver. The sight of this mysterious, beautiful outfit consumed Waddill's imagination. He thought that the piper must be from one of the many warlike clans of the Grampian Hills of the Highlands.

Waddill became more intrigued when he found that the piper's family name was Stuart. He knew the history of this famous family who had once ruled over England, Scotland, and Ireland, and he thought of all the glory and honors that had then become almost extinct. Waddill noted:

> The civilized world has sympathized with their unfortunate race; and many noble spirits have bled and died in their cause, but all in vain! Misfortune's brightest cup has been held to their lips; they have drained it to the very dregs; yet their misery continues, and their fallen fortunes lie, still buried beneath the maps that first crushed them to the earth.
>
> In our speculation upon the claims which the wandering piper may hold to noble titles, we are at liberty to give it tis full scope, and launch into the fields of speculation; yet we must keep this before

our eyes, that the truth may never find its way into our surmises, and after wasting our time and paper, we may be forced to come to the conclusion that we have toiled in vain![10]

Waddill thought about the new things that he would be experiencing at Augusta. His thoughts turned to his mother and father and his family members. He had not seen any of his siblings in five years. It would not be easy to travel to visit them. This saddened him. From correspondence that came to him occasionally, he knew that they were in good condition. Despite his sadness, he knew that he was living his dream of furthering his education. He was determined to become a lawyer and practice in his new home, the State of Louisiana. He was fortunate to have others support his efforts, and he knew he would love his studies. He slept well that night.

Friday, March 31, 1837

John received a letter from Thomas J. Hickman, his benefactor. Waddill alone could never have afforded this type of education, and Hickman provided him with the means and sent money to allow him to live and not have to work while studying.

Saturday, April 1, 1837

Waddill and George R. Waters commenced rooming together. Thus began a long-lasting relationship that extended well beyond college. Waters had been acquainted with Thomas J. Hickman and the Hickman brothers in business transactions through the clerk's office. At 9:00 a.m. on Saturday, April 1, 1837, Waddill attended the declamation and realized that 190 students attended Augusta. Seventy had enrolled with him and, since there was no precise day to begin the academic session, students kept arriving.

That night, in candlelight, Waters and Waddill stayed up late, talking about their pasts and their plans for the future. Waters had attended Transylvania University (also referred to as Morrison College) in Lexington. Waddill liked George, but he did not see the desire or motivation in his life. George R. Waters would later offer Waddill his first job, in January 1838, but it was a job that did not really exist, and Waddill ended up disappointed in Waters.

---

10. Diary of John P. Waddill [hereafter cited as DJW], March 28, 1837, vol. 1, pgs. 2–3.

The next day, church met at 11:00 a.m. The preaching lasted about an hour. Mr. Joseph Tomlinson, president of the college, used the Lord's Prayer as his text. The congregation enjoyed it and seemed well-pleased. Tomlinson made these remarks:

> That we need not let the government of creation disturb our repose; for the hand, and wisdom that created all things, governed all things in their proper spheres; but that it was necessary for us to continually beseech that being to forgive our accumulating sins or the wrath of the Almighty would be made manifest to us, by consigning us to an everlasting punishment.

He continued:

> How if the Almighty made all things, and governed all things in the manner best suited to his wisdom, how can the human race be an exception to the mighty plan? How can we add anything to the glory and honor of the being who created us; by supplicating his mercy for crimes committed, either through our ignorance or weakness? Is it not more rational to suppose that God formed us in such a manner, that it would be impossible for us to do anything that would not answer the end for which we were created? Is it not directly charging God of love and mercy with an oversight in creation of man in such a manner that he does not answer the purpose for which he was created, or else with malicious design for omitting to make him perfect, if an everlasting torment in fire is to be the consequences of his misdeeds? The answers to these questions are obvious: God must either be wanting in wisdom and power, or else he is a malicious being, if we believe the doctrine taught concerning him.

The sermon inspired Waddill. He could not believe how enlightening this man was in presenting his points. The commitment to his faith Waddill made after his mother died held true and fast, and he knew he would like this college, which proved to be challenging and invigorating.

Tomlinson continued:

> The Christian religion, which is founded more upon philosophical principles than any other, and is better calculated to ameliorate the condition of man than any other, now in practice on the earth; yet it

is evident that it is far from being perfect; indeed in many instances it is frequently childish, and inculcated doctrines contrary to reason, and the happiness of men.

It is also contradictory in its tenets; for in the Old Testament, in one place we find an express command from God, saying 'Thou shalt worship no other God than me: for I am a jealous God.' And on turning to the New Testament we find a new code of doctrine entirely; for then we are commanded to worship the Son of God as well as the Father. Now if both of these commands are true we are truly left in a disposable, and we have no chance of salvation from any quarter.

Now, this perplexed Waddill. He had much to mull over and wonder. The preaching ended with the following:

All nature attests, that there is a creating and directing power, that has created, and now directs all things: that power is known to us by the appreciation of God. And it is contrary to reason to believe, that God is not an all wise being, and that the things that he has created, does not answer the purpose for which they were designed. This being the case, this question then presents itself: Is God a benevolent or malevolent being? If he is a benevolent being, he will to the extent of his power, render all created objects happy, if we exist in a future that is. But, if he is malevolent, we may expect the contradictory of bliss.[11]

At first, Waddill did not know whether to be sad, scared, or blessed, though he had no trouble sleeping that afternoon. He wanted more study, more talk, and more discussion. He hoped his roommate would be able to discuss these complex spiritual issues.

He knew that President Tomlinson was anti-slavery from a moral perspective, not as a political view.[12] Waddill was ambivalent toward the issue. His family was poor, but with other families they had owned a female slave for the shared farm. She was generally treated as part of the extended family, yet they still considered her their property. He would have to consider this view. It seemed that Waddill's perspective might have been biased since he lived around a slave from birth.

---

11. DJW, April 2, 1837, vol. 1, pg. 4.

12. Rankins, *First Established Methodist College*, 48.

The next day, April 4, 1837, it snowed nearly four inches. Waddill was up at 6:00 a.m., and after pondering all day, he wrote in his diary:

> Study is the main-spring of all human excellence. By it the various organs of the brain are filled with the exertion and display of all their energies. To the individual, be his natural power of the strongest order, can pour forth the energies of his mind to such advantage to himself and the world; if he applies himself not to study, as he could provide his mind and has been enlightened by a good education.

Cynicism already, Waddill thought and continued:

> In the eyes of the wise and enlightened their distinguishing badges. Indeed, with the enlightened, and truly wise, nothing but intrinsic worth can ennoble man. When honors, handed down from sire to son, through a long line of princes, fall upon a hereditary descendant, who is unworthy the distinction thus guaranteed to him by the custom of the nations, he is, and should be considered as an usurper of the rights of man, and the glories of natures nobility, by every noble and enlightened spirit of the world. If he be a hereditary King, the scepter and crown should be taken from him, and bestowed upon one whose abilities or moral qualifications gives him preference, above all others of his nation, to the honors and dignities of the executive power; and the ignorant lord, or pollutes wretched, from whom the soon reign sway has been wrested, live upon his personal property, if he possesses any, and if he is poor, let him learn to gain a sustenance, by digging the soil, over which he found to be incompetent to rule.[13]

---

13. DJW, April 4, 1837, vol. 1, pg. 4.

CHAPTER 4

THEORIES IN EDUCATION

Wednesday, April 5, 1837 – Phrenology

It was a gloomy day when Waddill woke up early that morning. He had to prepare and mediate a debate on the philosophy, or science, of phrenology. He had to be ready to either defend it or refute it, so he would study it well that day. Phrenology, which based estimates of intelligence and character on the size and shape of an individual's head, was a relatively new theory that, despite much controversy, American colleges promoted heavily in the 1820s and 1830s.

Waddill had hoped he could defend the position. It was always easier to defend a point in debate when his personal feelings were the same as his defense—as was the case this time. He began the discussion with his roommate, George Waters. His roommate asked for his defense of it. Waddill stated:

> We know that the old system of mental philosophy is very unsatisfactory; and beyond all doubt, wants a thorough purgation. Now if phrenology lays bare to the eyes, the effects of the old system of mental philosophy, by excoriating it of its smooth metaphysical skin; this truth is the evident; there must be a system of facts incorporated into the science of phrenology, that are worthy of our profound investigation: If we, in our observations on the human family, find them to differ widely in talents, genius, and natural bent of mind, it is then obvious that they cannot all possess souls alike, that is the soul and mind be the one, and the same thing.

George wondered if Waddill was proving this theory by logic, not by using any scientific facts. Waddill continued:

That the brain is the organ of mind, and that thought, and every mental power is the result of the organization of the brain, appears, in my opinion, as evident as any axiom, or result in Euclid's Elements of Geometry; and can be demonstrated as easily.

For a demonstration of the position, let us take a man who is laboring under a powerful disease such as a fever in the head, which is so violent that it completely dethrones reason; then to what cause do we attribute the mental derangement of the man? Is it not to an affection of the organization of the brain, brought about by a powerful tendency of the blood to that part? Or can we by any process of reasoning attribute it to anything else? I think that the conclusion is self-evident, that it can be attributed to nothing else but the affection of the phenol organization. Then if we invariably find it the cause, that the mind is disorder when the brain is affected, must not the combined principles, which designated by the affection of mind be the result of phenol organization? The conclusion is inevitable, it must be so—

Waddill continued his argument, with passion, as he was convinced of his thought process.

If it were otherwise, that is, if mind is an immaterial thing, it would follow of course, that it could not be affected by disease, and whether the brain be in a sound or diseased state, the mind would at all times act with the same energy, and effect as though it were not attached to the brain; and that when the brain is affected, the medium, through which this immaterial being acted is destroyed and consequently, the intelligence of the mind is totally debarred from developing itself. If this be the case it proves conclusively that mind cannot act correctly unless the brain is in a perfect state of organization, and consequently when the brain is entirely disorganized by death, that the powers of the mind are totally suspended, and must remain so, until a reorganization of the brain. How when the powers of my animated body become totally suspended, and when by no process of human agency they can be again put in motion, we say that body is dead. Consequently, according to the theory, that the brain is the medium of action for the mind, and that when the brain becomes disorganized the mind cannot act. This conclusion becomes inevitable, that the thinking and reasoning principle, that is, the mind dies with the brain.

> If it lives while the body is in a state of disorganization by death, it is evident, from our experience, concerning the mental faculties, that its powers are totally suspended. From that conclusion it would appear that if the soul, at the moment of death takes its departure for heaven or hell, it must be a principle distinct from mind. But if the soul and mind are the same, it follows that when reason, and the physical system, are suspended or disorganized by death, that the resurrection of the body is antecedent to the reorganization of the mind: and that when one is freed from the thralldom of death the other is also.[14]

Waddill loved the many new theories he was learning and was very happy with how his education was progressing. He was anxious to begin the study of law, but he enjoyed the lectures and debate at Augusta.

---

14. DJW, April 5, 1837, vol 1, pgs. 5–6.

CHAPTER 5

Professor Joseph Tomlinson

John Waddill's First Recitation of Lessons to the President

The president of Augusta College, Joseph Tomlinson, was a brilliant man who could be quite intimidating. Known as the "ablest debater in America,"[15] Professor Tomlinson examined as many as eight classes in a day.[16]

Part of Waddill's lessons at Augusta included memorizing readings or teachings and then reciting them to one of the professors. After hearing lessons, Waddill had to know the subject matter as taught. It would be acceptable to divert or give a slant on the lessons, but only if posited in a manner the student could support. Waddill tried to memorize the lessons, but sheer memorization was not what the faculty expected. Instead, they wanted students to use the memorization as a basis for expanding their knowledge of a subject. The professors could sense it was not coming from knowledge but instead memory. If that would happen, and the student was interrupted, it was hard to get back on point.

Waddill figured out quickly that the recitations of lessons, the art of declamation, required intense knowledge of the subject matter. That occurred only by paying attention in the Lyceum Method, writing copious notes and reviewing them as soon as possible after the lessons finished, and staying on point. This method did not accept diversions. Female companionship and interaction were rare. There was too much to study.

On April 6, 1837, Waddill recited Virgil to Tomlinson. After he finished, the president looked at him sternly, quiet for a moment. He was pleased with Waddill. John felt tolerably well-satisfied with the manner in which he acquitted himself and waited impatiently, but quiet.

---

15. Rankins, *First Established Methodist College*, 26.

16. Ibid., 41.

Finally, Tomlinson stated in his sonorous voice, "That was very good, Mr. Waddill. I am well pleased. Continue your studies with passion."

Waddill breathed a sigh of great satisfaction. "Thank you, Sir."

The Circus, April 6, 1837

On this night, a circus performed in town, and many students attended for the diversion. Waddill found the circus a disgraceful exhibition. An absurd folly, which men commit, is paying a vagrant to act a fool. He thought that by men not only paying the performer to act the fool, but also by showing him great deference, courting his acquaintance, and treating him, in every respect, as if he were skilled in the most enriching science that has ever enlightened the minds of men, they simply proved that the human race needed reforming. He felt that it showed that certain men were animals, void of some of the practical faculties that others possessed.[17]

Waddill felt that the circus and all it entailed was beneath him. He believed that man had two choices when it came to how society could function. Either it would be one possessed of moral and highly sought intellectual feelings or one in which the animal propensities predominated. Moral propensities would remove man from impressions of pleasure. It followed that man owed a duty to put down every species of immorality and that human development, through examinations, could teach the erring brethren to seek happiness in virtuous deeds and honorable employments.

Waddill decided to attend merely to support his thoughts and views and to make certain he was correct in this opinion. After attending, he felt out of humor with himself. He expected to be entertained, or that he would possibly see something novel, but he was disappointed. The talk from the master of ceremonies before each act seemed to be a pretense. In fact, some of the scenes were, in Waddill's mind, vulgar in the extreme—such as a clown who, after having danced with a young man dressed in woman's clothes, embraced him, and then kissed him with gusto. It was a scene suitable only to the lascivious revels of a brothel, Waddill thought. Since many ladies attended the exhibition, he thought that if they had any claim to morality or modesty, they would never attend another.

After the kissing scene, Waddill left the circus, disgusted, and promised he would never attend another. He wrote in his diary that evening:

---

17. DJW, April 6, 1837, vol. 1, pg. 6.

Morality with companions, whose actions declare to the world that thou art their guide, I would live in the herbless desert, surrounded with sterile rocks, and arid wastes of sand, in preference to dwelling in the regions, bedecked with natures most verdant beauties, where thou art not! Men may raise their impious arms against morality, may by precept and example endeavor to inculcate libidinous principles; yet, when they, and their wretched, and their accursed acts lie moldering in the tomb of the forgotten meanness, morality will continue to have motive and cleanse the most discordant foul principles of the human character.[18]

Such sentiment drove Waddill throughout his college days. He was determined to be of a higher order, and he lived with that determination and self will. In fact, when groups such as the Royal Society (formed in honor of Sir Walter Scott) hosted gaudeamus events somewhat as a jovial jest, Waddill generally would steer clear of them.

Friday, April 7, 1837

On April 7, Waddill observed a debate at the meeting of the Jefferson Literary Society[19] on the question, "Should the surplus revenue be appropriated to internal improvements or education?" This would be a good subject, he thought. He ended up disappointed with the debate in that it was highly animated but not logically argued. The participants seemed to be more interested in speech-making than substance. Although disappointed in its execution, the debate led Waddill to think that this must be why some politicians performed better than others. Never mind substance, always entertain the listeners, and that may sway them all, or most.

Waddill set his mind on learning all he could from different points of view, to round and sharpen his thought process and ability to argue. Debates and speeches were the cornerstone of this Augusta College's method of teaching. Along with recitations and attending church for spiritual teachings, little remained for the world to hear, but there was plenty to read. He enjoyed reading and in any spare time tried to find new books to peruse.

---

18. Ibid., April 6, 1837, vol. 1, pg. 7.

19. The Jefferson Literary Society was founded in 1825 by sixteen disgruntled members of the Patrick Henry Society. This became the Literary and Debating Society. http://www.jeffersonsociety.org/.

Waddill read George Combe's *The Constitution of Man*, which promoted phrenology.[20] He read Laurence Sterne's *Tristram Shandy*[21] and some of Swift's work. Much different from the work he had done almost his entire life, the intellectual labors allowed Waddill to find respite in studying.

20. *The Constitution of Man*, written by George Combe and published in 1828, was a phrenological theory popular at this time attempting to connect anatomy of humans with evolution of man by studying the brain. The focus was on the neurological basis of behavior and sickness being subject to natural laws. It was controversial and also very popular in the 1830s and 40s, especially in colleges worldwide. http://www.historyofphrenology.org.uk/constindex.html.

21. A humorous nine-volume work full of graphic devices, double entendre, digression, and similes, as other metaphysical poets. It was written over a period of years in the mid 1750s. The character Tristram would never explain anything simply, always digressing with his explanatory diversions.

CHAPTER 6

Debates as Education Tools

Saturday, April 8, 1837
Reflections and Debate with his Roommate, George Waters.[22]

This debate required Waddill to take an opposite view of his previous private debate over phrenology with George Waters. That would be a challenge, but Waddill believed he had a good argument.

> One principle objection to the science of phrenology, is that the brain cannot be that portion, or faculty of man which retains knowledge. The reason is that the brain is in a continual state of change, and, that in every three years, the brain, as well as the other parts of the corporal system, is entirely renewed, consequently any other impression upon the brain must be erased as the particles of matter which constitutes the mass at the time the impression was made, give place to the new materials. Now, that the impressions made upon the mind, will be erased by time, unless constantly recurred to admit of little doubt; and this one fact, is one of the strongest argument in favor of phrenology. Every man is a living witness of the truth of this position; for it is impossible to retain any impressions on the mind, unless we recur to it at times and renew it, by thus making it the subject of our thoughts. When we have once learned a thing, a slight reference to it is sufficient to bring it all before the mind, without any difficulty, if we do not let it sleep in forgetfulness too long. But if we learn it, then bury it into the oblivion of forgetfulness for three or four years, we will find that it has been totally eroded from the memory, and that nothing remains but a vague dream, as it were,

---

22. DJW, April 8, 1837, vol. 1, pgs. 7–8.

that we have known it; and this knowledge is retained, only by a reoccurrence to the fact that we upon a time learned such a science, or beheld such a transaction, and that is all.[23]

Waters countered:

My opponent's position is untenable. Considering that it takes three years for the brain to reform, or replace itself, that the process of this happening is so gradual, that the brain never loses its thoughts or memories. The gradual transformation allows the brain to reformat its memories and knowledge. To argue otherwise would mean that knowledge that is based on memory would have to be relearned every three years. That is living proof by thinking of our own lives and what we have learned.

While Waddill wondered about his theory, Waters continued this argument. Waddill, quick on his feet, responded to the counterpoints:

If the immaterial part of man received and retained the impression of knowledge, it would be impossible for us to forget anything, if once recorded there. This position is tenable, on this simple reason, because the immaterial soul of man, or mind of man, admits of no change at all, and remains immutable, according to the best writers of that subject, throughout eternity: It follows then that knowledge once imprinted on the soul would remain as legible after an age had elapsed, as it was at the time it was first registered.

Who can say that this has been the case with him, her, or it? Not one of all the human families will assert it. They may indeed say: that at 80 years of age may recollect the scenes of their boyhood more distinctly, than they do things of but a year's date; Now, that is easily accounted for; the scenes of boyhood, have been to as the sweetest scenes of our lives, they were impressed before our minds were embittered by deeds, of folly, and of vice, and therefore, our minds delighted to recur to, and to dwell upon them at all times; and by this means keep them forever bright and glowing in our memories. But, if the immaterial part of man received the impress, as above

---

23. Ibid., pg. 7.

states, scenes passed through and actions performed in old age would remain indelibly impressed upon the memory, as that of boyhood—

Waddill could not help but remember the great pleasures of his boyhood in the wilderness of Tennessee. Farm living and wild game always brought pleasant thoughts to him. Of course, the sad loss of his mother and father tempered these memories and experiences that shaped his life. Waddill's life had very much been shaped by his experiences.

April 9, 1837

On a cold, gloomy day, John Waddill began to focus more intensely on politics. His membership in several "societies" helped sharpen this focus. On April 9, 1837, he began to write on national issues of the time. President Andrew Jackson had requested Congress to expunge disparaging comments about him from the official journal. This "Expunging Resolution," as it was known, caused quite a stir.

Waddill thought that the supporters of the resolution were selfish and not thinking about the general good of the country. He saw this as a "the violent workings of the party spirit." Yet, he realized that the documentation of the criticism of Andrew Jackson went through the same motions that caused its erasure.

Senator John Calhoun of South Carolina had criticized President Jackson, while the president had his supporters expunge the comments. In his argument against the resolution, Calhoun argued:

> No one not blinded by party zeal can possibly be insensible that the measure proposed is a violation of the constitution. The constitution requires the Senate to keep a journal; this resolution goes to expunge the Journal. If you expunge a part you may expunge the whole; and if it is expunged, how is it kept? The Constitution says the journal shall be kept; this resolution says it shall be destroyed. It does the very thing that the Constitution declares shall not be done. That is the argument, the whole argument. There is none other."[24]

---

24. "On the Expunging Resolution, John Caldwell Calhoun (1818–1865) (1837)," in *The World's Famous Orations*, ed. William Jennings Bryan, vol. IX, *America: II (1818–1865)* (New York: Funk and Wagnalls Company, 1906). Accessed on http://www.bartleby.com/268/9/8.html.

Waddill was intrigued yet discouraged by the partisan politics of Congress. The discouragement inspired him, however, to resolve that one day he would be involved in the political process. He wrote passionately:

> This being the case it behooves the enlightened minds of the nation to denounce the degrading outrages perpetrated by each party, with all the bitterness and content due such transactions. Then our citizens in whom we have reposed the welfare of the nation are activated, in their Legislative capacity, by views other than to the honor and welfare of the country. They should be made to feel the contempt and ignominy, with which their conduct authorizes their fellow citizens to treat them by hurling them from their elevated stations, down to the dirtiest parts of oblivious degradation, there to fume and sweat in their own corruption.[25]

This marked the beginning of Waddill's interest in politics. He never abandoned his fervor in the political process.

---

25. DJW, April 9, 1837, vol. 1, pg. 8.

CHAPTER 7

CHURCH LIFE

Sunday, April 9, 1837

Church attendance was important to students of Augusta. Waddill attended the Methodist Church on a regular basis and found John Wesley's order in his life and work ethic inspiring. Always reading and studying, Wesley had tight schedules to improve his abilities in every area. Discipline was a priority.

Not all sermons proved good or stimulating. Mr. Savage's sermon, which started at 11:00 a.m. on this date, perplexed Waddill. He believed in God but listened to preachers of the Gospel with a cynical view, searching for errors.

Savage's assertion that Pharaoh would have to render an account of his actions before the bar of Heaven and that the children of Israel would array themselves against him, condemning him to hell forever, bothered Waddill greatly. Waddill thought of the unresolved conflict:

> This is a remark, that no man in his sober senses can admit; for according to the Bible, in which the story of the Pharaoh and Moses is told, we are bound to believe that God hardened Pharaoh's heart, so that he could not be prevailed upon to let the children of Israel go.
>
> Now God was as much the Maker of Pharaoh and consequently by Pharaoh's life would have been as sacred in the eyes of Almighty wisdom, as Moses was: Furthermore God conversed with Moses and informed him of everything that was to happen; he revealed himself to Moses in such a manner, that no doubt remained that he was not the Almighty himself; but to Pharaoh he revealed himself not, but secretly hardened his heart, and gave him a disposition to resist to the utmost of what Moses might say; thus, bearing every means of repen-

tance, and handing him over with a resisting power to be punished for deeds that God himself had cause him to commit.[26]

Hearing the story preached and the underlying doctrine caused Waddill to form his own beliefs. He wrote:

> This was the doctrine preached to us today. A doctrine said to be divine, and, also, the only law by which man should be governed; Is there a man, in whose bosom dwells the love of God, but what feels shamed and mortified when he hears such horrid tales as these preach as the acts and divine decree of God? Could an earthly tyrant wear his head among an enlightened community if he presumed to act with his subjects, as is thus related to the God of Love and Mercy? NO! Common sense says no! Why all nature repeats the answer. Then does it follow that we must take a look that contains such odious doctrine as the Bible, for our only guide through life; and the only means by which we can be saved from eternal fire? The reason with which the great God of the universe has gifted us teach us to reject it—[27]

Waddill would never stop searching for the spiritual meanings of the Bible. He also never stopped questioning those who claimed divine knowledge of the Bible's teaching.

---

26. DJW, April 9, 1837, vol. 1, pgs. 8–9.

27. Ibid.

CHAPTER 8

THE BEAUTY OF AUGUSTA
AND THOUGHTS OF WADDILL

Monday, April 10, 1837

Waddill found it difficult to describe the beauty of Augusta College in the spring. The Ohio River was lovely at sunset. The current flowed gently and appeared calm and unruffled, as if a plane of transparent crystal. Nothing broke its mirrored dish except a few light skiffs that skimmed the beautiful flood, loaded with youthful students who sought refreshment on the glassy surface.

John Waddill watched as he walked in reflection. As usual, he attended to his college exercises, with the exception of geometry and recitation, which he had missed due to the professor of mathematics' absence.

Waddill had more time to think on the national political scene. He kept up with the issues of the day, as Augusta College made sure that current periodicals stayed available to the students. One such contemporary matter centered on what to do with the surplus revenue of the United States.

Many members of Congress felt that it should be returned to the states according to their congressional representation, with the promise that Congress would distribute it only as a loan and may recall it at any time it may think proper. Waddill opined, "If our Government was out of debt, that the surplus should be given back to the citizens of the nation, (from whom it came), as their rightful property; but since it would be impossible to give each individual their separate due, that it should go irrevocably to the different states according to their census, to be used to that purpose which may result in the greatest benefit of all."

Waddill argued with other students that:

The central government should not have it in their power to demand the payment of its money back again. That would be in direct opposition to the good of the community. The central government had no right to lay claim to any money that may remain after the liquidation of its debts. This would allow the government to lock up the circulating currency and by this means put a check on the happiness and prosperity of the country.

This concept would make our government a moneyed oligarchy to have it under its power to bring under its control the commerce and agriculture of the nation, and thus render itself absolute.

Other students rambled on with their arguments as they ate their lunch and prepared for the afternoon lectures and lessons. The varying degrees of opinions surprised Waddill. He honestly thought his belief the correct one. He asked if he could speak. His classmates silenced themselves as he began:

It may be said that Congress would not permit such things to be accomplished. But a little reflection by the nearest novice in political knowledge will find that such an argument, can have no foundation. We have the truth before our eyes, that the executive department has acted for itself in many cases already, entirely independently of Congress.

When we see this fact proved to our senses, beyond a doubt, it behooves us, to curtail, as much as possible to the executive privileges; for, instead of their remaining as they were first intended. They are continually on the increase, there can be felt but little doubt, as to their imperial tendency; and a nation jealous of its liberties and proud the many of being free; should exert all its energies to check the destruction of its rights, by bringing it to narrower limits that power, that portends death to civil liberty.

Our government is yet young, and we may expect a total extinction of civil liberties yet, for a while; but if encroachments begin so early in our career, as we find that they have; the time will come, and that are long, when you shall have to struggle for our liberty, as arduously as we did in '76. We should not let our own self-interest be our only care, we should also toil for our posterity, that they may enjoy the blessing which, their progenitors so nobly purchased, and secured as a legacy to them.

That man is not a patriot, who cares alone for his own age. He should be considered, as criminally traitorous to the interest of his country, as if he had battle upon the side of her enemies; If he does not endeavor to bless future generations with his deeds, when he has it in his power to accomplish it: The statesman should protect and labor for his country, as if he expects it to slam the vicissitudes of fortune injured through eternity itself.

Then, and only then can he be truly considered his country's friend: and his reward will be while living, and an honored deathless name, when he lives no more.[28]

When Waddill stopped, he noticed that he had attracted a crowd. They listened in silence, with intense looks as though they were all convinced. Waddill realized that he may actually be capable of leading others and even holding positions in the political realm. He looked forward to that day.

Waddill faced the typical difficulties of college students almost daily. On one particular day when he was supposed to recite Virgil before the school's president, he looked at his watch and believed he was on time. He had other recitations that day, but he was particularly prepared for this one due to the respect he had for President Tomlinson. He remained unprepared for the others, but he did well.

As Waddill walked into the room to recite Virgil, the president offered a pained look of disappointment. Waddill was fifteen minutes late. He looked quickly at his pocket watch, a cheap timepiece that had fallen fifteen minutes behind the college's clocks. Embarrassed and quite nervous, he practically stuttered through the recitation.

Tomlinson let him know that Augusta expected all students to keep proper time. He reminded him that John Wesley taught the necessities of discipline and order. Tomlinson rescheduled.

Head hung low, Waddill walked to his room. He looked up and noticed a day more beautiful than any he had seen since autumn. He thought, "The sun had dispensed its blessings with a wild, and enlivening influence. The grass, and forest herbs begin to spring forth into life, and spread a charm

---

28. DJW, April 9, 1837, vol. 1, pgs. 9–10.

over the hitherto break hills, and naked valleys, that is grateful to every feeling of the soul." His steps livened, and he kept his head high. He would redeem himself.

Politics continued to be the topic all students wanted to debate. It was as though most students seemed inclined to be involved in the political world. They would even debate outside of their studies, often gathering after the evening meal. One frequent topic was corruption in politics. At one particular discussion, a Mr. Miley and a Mr. Sheppard seemed to take opposing views on corruption, with Sheppard less inclined to accept Miley's theory that those serving in office were purer and not corrupt.

Waddill held much more cynical views. The more he kept up with political stories in periodicals and newspapers, the more cynical he became. Waddill looked directly at Miley and spoke: "Our governmental institutions want a change badly. Corruption, with all its concomitant curses, begins to show itself in our country, and unless checked it will ultimately corrode the very vitals of our boasted liberty, and pull down the edifice of our freedom, under which we now shelter."

Waddill continued, then listed to the others and thought for a moment, before adding:

> But before we reform our institutions, it becomes necessary for us to find where the evil lies: and when found extract that part which is infected, from that which is sound. The task of arriving at the defected point is easy, and requires but little investigation, by those, at all acquainted with any part of our political history. From the nature, and organic constitution of man, he, nine times out of ten, is desirous of being distinguished, this desire leads him to put forth the energies of his mind and body for the purpose of gaining his ends; and when becoming fully engaged, he cares not for consequence so long as his own personal enterprises succeed.

The discussion ended without solutions. Waddill, however, could not sleep without continuing his thought process on this issue of corruption in government. He wrote:

> Neither country, nor friends find favor in his sight; ruin, and unending woe may follow him his wake; yet he heeds them not, nor turns aside to alleviate, but pushes forward to the goal of his desires. Wherever he sees a situation, which he thinks may favor his designs,

his inventive genius commence operations, for the purpose of securing it to himself; nor is he satisfied until he is master of it, and upon it founds his system for further operations. Wealth, power, and fame and the grand objects of his wishes, and when he finds them centered in one point, then desperate is the onset he makes to secure them for his ambition. This being the case, we marvel not, that the corruption is making its way into our noblest institutions. The Chief Magistracy of the United States is a situation calculated to satisfy the ambition of a Caesar or Napoleon. To it power is attached, to conduct the affairs of one of the greatest nations of earth; power to raise men to office who are to govern, and conduct our political relations with all nations; and it lies within his own breath, whether the laws that are passed by our national assembly, or to go into operation without a reconsideration or not: This is the power granted to the president—a power almost absolute, and independent. But few monarchs from Europe have such privileges granted them by their subjects, and as we think but few would dare to exercise such powers—

How under the present mode of election, the aspirant is unlimited, as to the number of times that he may be elected precedent who's fixed upon twice: but as there is no bounds set by law, to such limit we may conclude that this precedent will be dispensed with and that some ambitious individual will be elevated to that station who will establish himself for life: Besides the importance attached to this office; the love of lordly rule and unbridled power is a sufficient fate to draw into the contest for the peace, all who are ambitious, and grasping by dissolution. When men of such character aspire into office, their whole aim is to accomplish their election, whether by fair or foul means. If intrigue can be of service to them, they unhesitatingly call in its services, and thus steal into authority, by stooping to the basest deeds that can tarnish the glory of a name.

And in the present mode of election, there is the greatest scope left for the operations of intrigue. He, once elected into office, has it in his power to extend his influence throughout the union, by means of his dependent office holders. They, although professing to he of the firmest mold of patriotism, are, nevertheless bound up so thoroughly in self-interest, that they use their whole influence to further own views—

What is dependence? Tis' the bane of all that makes man noble. Pain, privation, sorrow, toil, and all of woes that mankind can fall, is sweet compared with that dread cup which the dependent wretch must suffer. Can friends, with all their love, allay the agonizing thoughts, which prey upon the hearts of those who feel they live but on another's will? Can words or deeds give ease and rest, to him, not him whose fiery breast there lives a soul whose only boast is to be free, or ever lost?[29]

---

29. Ibid., April 11, 1837, vol. 1, pgs. 9–10.

CHAPTER 9

ISSUES IN AMERICA

Saturday, April 15, 1837

In the lecture hall, Mr. J. Lancanshire of Natchez, Mississippi, gave a declamation that John Waddill thought was a very good original speech. Afterwards he retreated from the crowds to write a letter to his older brother Frederick in Tennessee. John had received a letter from Frederick two weeks earlier, on March 31, in which he told John that the family was doing well and he was no longer needed. Frederick was starting a new beginning and moving to Texas, a state where many people in the country were going because of plentiful and cheap land. Frederick moved to the Austin area and there married his wife, Susan. They had four children together: Samuel, in 1839; George, in 1841; Martha, in 1844; and William, in 1847.

John contemplated all of this. He missed his family greatly and was especially sad that his mother and father had died while he was so young. He was pleased that they were all doing well and could not wait for the day when his younger brother William Wallace could join him. William had even expressed interest in the law, perhaps fueled by John's encouragement in his letters home.

John responded to Frederick, thanking him for everything. He wrote of his excitement for his studies and his certainty, now more than ever, that he wanted to be an attorney. John Waddill now knew that it had not been a mistake to leave Tennessee, go to Louisiana, and then attend college. He wished Frederick well on his move to Texas and hoped he could somehow see him on his way south. He posted the letter the next morning.

The Importance of Increasing the Standing Army of the U.S.

One controversial issue of the day (a continuation from the earliest days of the United States Constitution) remained: How large should the United States professional army be in times of peace?

According to a 2005 military history of the United States:

> John C. Calhoun was convinced that the American frontier ought to be protected by regulars rather than by the militia. Calling the militia into active service, he wrote Brig. Gen. Edmund P. Gaines, was "harassing to them and exhausting to the treasury. Protection is the first object, and the second is protection by the regular force." But providing a regular force capable of protecting the frontiers north, south, and west, as well as the seacoast, was another matter. In 1820 the Congress called upon the Secretary of War to report on a plan for the reduction of the Army to 6,000 men. Calhoun suggested that the reduction, if it had to come, could be effected by cutting the enlisted personnel of each company to half strength. In time of war the Army could be quickly expanded to a force of 19,000 officers and men. This was the start of the "expansible army" concept. Did our country need a large army?
>
> On March 2, 1821, Congress passed the Reduction Act that cut the enlisted strength of the Army by half (from 11,709 to 5,586) but cut the size of the officer corps by only a fifth (from 680 to 540). Thus, even though the Congress had cut the end strength of the Army overall, its limited reduction of the officer corps confirmed that the idea of an expansible Army was beginning to achieve a measure of acceptance. Calhoun, although concerned with the drastic nature of the cuts, pronounced himself reasonably satisfied. The retention of a proportionally larger officer cadre would allow the Army to expand more rapidly upon the approach of war. This was a key milestone on the road to recognizing that the Regular Army and its officer corps was the first line of our nation's defense rather than relying totally upon the militia or hastily raised, equipped, and trained volunteer units.[30]

By 1836, there were just fewer than ten thousand men in the standing army and, that same year, only forty-nine graduates from West Point.[31] The

---

30. "Toward a Professional Army," in *American Military History*, vol. 1, *The United States Army and the forging of a Nation, 1775–1917*, ed. Richard W. Stewart, U.S. Army Center Of Military History, http://www.history.army.mil/Books/amh-v1/ch07.htm. Last updated July 10, 2006

31. Edward M. Coffman, *The Embattled Past: Reflections on Military History* (University Press of Kentucky, 2014): 16.

army later grew to about twelve thousand due to the Indian Wars. The United States fought the Second Seminole War (1835–1842) with forces made up of half regulars and half volunteers.[32] As a result, the debate continued about the size of the regular army needed to keep the nation's coasts and wilderness safe. Those who lived in the Midwest were more concerned about Indian attacks than those who lived farther east.

The students at Augusta debated the cost of the professional military versus the state militias, which far outnumbered the regular army. Militias were not made up of professional soldiers and, in many cases, were undependable.

Issues such as this allowed the students to practice their recitation and debating skills. The school encouraged debate among the students to help them prepare for better declamations and recitations. Of course, no one had to encourage Waddill. His propensity for thinking through issues and debating were becoming well known to his fellow students.

Before a group of them, Waddill began to state his long-winded, yet well thought out, opinion on the subject:

> From the extent of territory which we possess; from the long line of frontier, and seacoast, with which the cultivated part of our country is bordered, we find it absolutely necessary to station troops at the most exposed points of our country, as much to maintain the dignity and honor of our country, with regard to other nations, as to protect the adventurous backwoodsmen from the tomahawk and scalping knife of the warlike savages with whom we are partly surrounded. We have stationed small parties of soldiers along our frontier, for the purpose of securing the repose of the hardy pioneer; and we have also posted some few in our most commercial cities, for the purpose of enforcing payment of the duties on foreign articles of commerce. But, is it the number of soldiers, thus disposed of adequate to perform the duties enjoined upon them? Is our frontier at all times free from danger, and invasion? And are our great cities sufficiently protected from mobs, and riots which threaten the dissolution of the bonds of polite and refined society; which make null and void the most efficient laws of the nation? There is not a man who would venture to say yes to these interrogations.

---

32. Ibid.

It is plain to those who investigate this subject, that whose standing army, which numbers about nine thousand soldiers, would barely be sufficient for the seacoast service; and if thus disposed of would leave about 2,500 or 3,000 miles of our border settlements exposed to the most bloody scenes of savage warfare. Now it may be argued that the pioneer being endowed with a bold and adventurous spirit is capable and goes prepared to defend himself against the Indians. This may be, but be it remembered, that Indian wars are conducted in such a manner, that the forces opposed must always be on the alert, and must be ready to fight at a moment's warning. This being true, the backwoodsmen would be induced to embody themselves into armies for the purpose of protecting their lives, and consequently, it would be impossible to improve, or settle any exposed portion of our country, when those whose adventurous spirits had lead them in those regions for such purpose, were obliged to organize themselves into a standing army for self-preservation.

This shows conclusively, that if the U.S. as a government, do not protect the frontier inhabitants of the nation, with standing armies adequate for the occasion; the pioneers themselves must make up the deficiency by incorporating themselves into ranks into the defensive forces; and by so doing rob the nation of the benefits arising from the proceeds of a fertile, and well cultivated country. There are often features of the subject of higher moment still, and amongst them, the inhuman hunches of our fathers, brothers, and dearest kindred, which are continually taking place, in those districts adjacent to the different Indian tribes.[33]

Each of the students listening almost chuckled at the length of his speech, yet several of them were so entranced that they could not help but look on in wonder. Waddill seemed a natural spokesman for exploration and settlement of the frontier. In general, he was developing a good reputation, doing well in his studies, and even writing poetry when he felt inspired by any person, thing, or concept.[34]

---

33. DJW, April 15, 1837, vol. 1, pgs. 11–12.

34. Ibid.

CHAPTER 10

Sadness at Augusta College

There were not many pleasures available for students at Augusta, but the Ohio River did provide one source of recreation. Students used it for boating, rowing, and even fishing, though not John Waddill, who spent his time studying and preparing recitations.

On Tuesday, April 19, 1837, John A. Leake, Robert Wickliff, and Samuel I. Humphreys went out on a skiff for a pleasure ride. The trio was but half way across the Ohio when a gust of wind leaned the skiff, and Leake, attempting to manage the sail by means of a rope held in his hand and fastened to the sail, fell overboard.

The other two men threw Leake an oar in an effort to save him, leaving them with only one. Leake managed to grab the oar, but the current pulled him downstream almost one hundred yards, and the oar could not keep him afloat. As the wind blew them upstream, his companions had little control. Another skiff sailed close by, but those in it could not reach Leake, although the unfortunate man had sunk only a few yards distant them. They procured a large fishing seine and dragged it through the river for the purpose of finding Leake's body, but without success.

Leake's loss deeply affected those who knew the young man from Shelby County, Tennessee. The students would remember him as a well-beloved man of admirable-disposition. His death shocked them; no one would go near the river for several weeks, despite the mild and warming weather.

The students of Augusta College held a meeting in the chapel on Wednesday, April 20, for the purpose of passing resolutions relating to the death of John A. Leake. They appointed a committee and adopted resolutions suitable for the occasion.

Patrick Henry Junto

Students at Augusta joined various groups to continue their debating skills and increase their knowledge. One such group, the Patrick Henry Junto, became one of Waddill's favorite clubs. Benjamin Franklin started the Junto Society in approximately 1727 (called the Junto Club by 1743). "Junto" was Spanish loosely for "to join."

In *The Autobiography of Benjamin Franklin*, he wrote: "I should have mentioned before that in the autumn of the preceding year [1727], I had formed most of my ingenious acquaintances into a club of mutual improvement, which we called the JUNTO."[35]

Junto clubs sprouted up all over the nation, especially in colleges, and most were named for the founders of the United States, such as Patrick Henry. They provided an opportunity for thinkers and those desirous to learn and challenge each other to get together to discuss books and issues facing society. The Junto Club later transmuted into the American Philosophical Society.[36]

John Waddill hoped that the club would feed his mind and imagination. His first meeting did not disappoint. The discussion revolved around the actions of Henry Clay as related to his criticism of President Jackson and the motives that laid the foundation for such criticism. Each of the students in the Junto Club had an opinion. They were courteous not to interrupt, but gave no breath to begin their own spoken words of opinion.

Waddill pointed out that:

> The spirit that animated the bosom of Mr. Clay, and his supporters, in adopting a resolution, denouncing the conduct of A. Jackson President of the U.S. relative to moving the Public deposits, was, today the least of it, anything, but that, of Patriotism. Mr. Clay, as is well known, is a disappointed office seeker: Having been beaten once or twice, in the election for president; to which he aspired: And in both political contests he was the opponent of A. Jackson. In his first struggle, finding that it was likely that he would be left further behind, than was at all agreeable to the feelings of such an aspirant,

---

35. "Becoming American: The British Atlantic Colonies, 1690–1763," National Humanities Center Resource Toolbox, http://nationalhumanitiescenter.org/pds/becomingamer/index.htm.

36. Karl Baedeker, ed., *The United States : With an Excursion into Mexico: A Handbook for Travelers, 1893* (Dacapo Press, 1971).

he withdrew in favor of John L. Adams, but previous to his withdrawal he came to an agreement with Mr. Adams, as the conditions of which were these: That he, (Clay) would throw his influence into the hands of Adams, provided, if elected, Adams would make him Secretary of State: Thus selling himself, and the votes of his constituents for an office.

George Waters would not let his roommate speak unchallenged. As soon as Waddill paused to take a breath, he uttered: "John Quincy Adams is as fine a man and patriot of this country as any. He is a man of principles and would not do anything that would shame the country. If he had appointed Clay as Secretary of State, it would have brought honor to this country. We know their Whig tendencies, but put aside party politics. Let us put the country first."

Waddill knew that George liked to get his blood boiling but still spoke:

The conduct of Mr. Clay was ensured by the friends of Jackson, as also by many influential men of the opposite side. And it was from their circumstances, together, which his defeat in two subsequent elections; that he became an enemy to the late president. He ransacked his imagination to find plans by which he could thwart the measures of the administration. He has done everything that lay within his power to render the president, and his administrations popular with the citizens of America and, in such men endeavored to triumph over his successful opponent at the hazard of his country's welfare. When Jackson moved the deposits, just upon the expiration of his first presidential term: Clay's joy grew to raptures, thinking that he had his opponent now, completely in his power. He did not, probably assail his conduct, personally at that time, as he has done since, by set speeches in the Senate; yet insidiously gave the trumpet into the hands of his partisans, who sounded the tocsin with broken lungs, until it was heard in the deafening blast throughout the continent of America.

Another Junto member chimed in: "Are you suggesting that Clay wanted Jackson to do something controversial, just to allow him to align supporters and those who did not like Jackson in an effort to discredit him? This is preposterous."

Waddill defended:

But his schemes were defeated by the wisdom and patriotism of an enlightened people; and at the conclusion of his experiment, he found himself at the point, where he sets out, without having accomplished anything. This failure goaded him to the soul. And after having endeavored in vain to get up an impeachment, in the House of Representatives; he then stooped to the degrading refuge of instituting, and adopting a resolution in the Senate, denouncing the conduct of the President; meanly to gratify, his own, wounded self-esteem.[37]

The young men talked until they tired. Waddill felt energized but knew that he needed sleep. School, though exacting, still made him feel as though he was living the dream. Of course, he was.

Courting and The Arts

Augusta was a liberal arts college that not only taught the classics but also encouraged young men to experiment and make great efforts in different kinds of art. The professors felt that studying art expanded students' minds and promoted creativity. Waddill was interested in art, but he and the other students had other passions common to young men as well—women. The lack of feminine companionship grew tiresome. The faculty kept the students so busy that there was not much time to waste on courting women. It did not stop the young men from some creative endeavors in the art of pursuing the opposite sex. Waddill met several women but seems to have been smitten by only one. He had seen and spoken to her several times, and she seemed interested yet a bit aloof.

On April 22, 1837, Waddill dedicated himself to recreation and literary amusements. After attending declamation in the chapel, he decided to visit a fellow student, Mr. Vaughan, in his room. Known as a bacchant[38] who partied more than the rest of the students, Vaughan seemed to be focused when it came to painting and was quite artistic. Waddill felt that he might receive "inbounding inspirations" from Vaughan's paintings to give a rest to the amusements of the day.

Waddill walked in Vaughan's room and commenced examining the pictures with all the apparent gravity of a connoisseur of painting. One picture

---

37. Diary of John P. Waddill, page 14 Vol. 1 – Reflections April 21, 1837.

38. A reveler, usually drunk with spirits. A boisterous reveler.

set against the wall drew Waddill's attention. He felt that his very soul could not keep his eyes from turning in the direction of the picture. There were others drawn as well, yet that picture emitted such an indescribable charm that his eyes continuously directed toward its lovely features.

It was the portrait of a young lady in the glowing bloom of youth and health; her complexion was delicately fair, and in the language of an unknown author, "the snow of the lily was shaded with the blushing tints of the rose." Her eyes were lovely beams with all the splendor that intelligence transfers into the organ of sight. To the enraptured beholder, those eyes revealed the source of their kindling: love. And told to the enraptured beholder that they were partly kindled by feelings of love.

The background represented the western horizon immediately after sunset. Clouds of deep purple tinged with brilliant light around their edges floated in the lovely streams of light, which, in the distant horizon, the departed sun threw upward. The scene was charming, and if it had been drawn apart from the portrait, it would have been sufficient to fill the heart with feelings of rapture. But the picture of the lady threw the background so far in the shade, not one in ten who would look upon the painting would ever see the floating clouds.

Waddill realized the source of his attraction to the painting. He knew the female sitter. For that reason, with amazement, he looked closer. He knew from his acquaintance that the picture had not been overdrawn. It was the local woman with whom he was smitten. After staring at this painting for some time, and ignoring the rest of Vaughan's works, Waddill was tempted to ask how he got her to sit and pose for the wondrous portrait.

But he did not ask. He stared for a while longer and then left the room. Walking to his room, Waddill could not get her off of his mind. He was struck, as sharp as a bolt of lightning would strike him. He could do only one thing that would help him get through this night. He felt a passion for this woman who sorely tempted him.

He stayed up and wrote a poem:

The Portrait

Sweet portrait in thy features bright
I recognize that face of light
Which oft has filled with woe and joy
The heart of many a luckless boy!
One has poured from his glowing breast

A wish that thou wouldst make him blest
And save from death's cold hand a heart
"That claims you as its dearest part."
One has stood tranced in speechless awe
When bursting on his sight; he saw
So many charms, in radiance join
As made you seem to him divine.
He loved! But dared not to tell his love,
For fear that thou wouldst disapprove;
And thought that you, in truth, must be
Too fair, too pure, for such as he!
Others inspired by love, thy praise
Have sung, in sweet harmonies lays,
Filling each copse, each lawn, and grove
With plaintive warbling of their love.
But thou hast scorned the simpering throng
That made their love to thee in song,
And sent them with their wailing lays
"To sing some other maidens' praise,"
To others you have seemed to turn
And view their case with deep concern:
In gentle words you sought to pour
Relief; but only wounded more.
Still as they urged, you only said,
Deep in your heart their names were laid
Engemed by Friendship's treasures rare
"But love could never enter there!"
And I, condemn me not, must own
I think you're made for heaven alone![39]

He was wishful. If only he could give her this poem. Shy to the point of fear, he failed to approach her. She seemed aloof, yet it must be her persona as a lady not to show that she was too willing, he thought. The fact that she sat for a painting did show a bit of looseness that John had not noticed prior to this. Perhaps he would seek this further.

---

39. DJW, April 22, 1837, vol. 1, pgs. 15–16 . The word "Engemed" could only be poetic license taken by Waddill to mean, "Within gems" as though she was "gemed" with jewels.

Waddill continued to write. It was only 2:00 p.m., yet he was in his room waxing poetic. He began to think of his youth. As he was alone, he pondered his memories, and wrote "Memory—An Essayical Retrospection"[40]

He wondered if he was the pragmatic learned man that he thought himself or a hopeless romantic. Perhaps as he matured he was becoming a bit of both. Whichever, he would continue his studies but write as often as possible. On the same day, he wrote "The World"[41] about wisdom and folly. The following morning, before chapel and the morning worship, he wrote "Song,"[42] a poem of love.

He had to admit one thing: that the woman he felt this passion for was part of the reason he began to write so much. He hoped few days would pass before he saw her again.

Church at Augusta

The young students at Augusta were required to attend church. Faculty would preach most Sundays, but on many occasions, guest speakers and pastors would be invited from all over the United States. Many of them challenged and inspired Waddill, but several—those whose preaching degraded Christianity—were also a complete disappointment, Waddill listened to all of them. Of some, he was quite critical. His views would be considered open minded and receptive to ideas and concepts.

One such disappointment arrived on Sunday, May 21, 1837. This preacher proclaimed from the pulpit that he as a Christian was persecuted above all sects and religious denominations in the world. Perplexed, Waddill thought it may be for the commiseration of mankind in their favor, or it may be for the purpose of satirizing, or denouncing, those who believe not in the tenets that they profess. He was inclined to believe the latter to be the true reason. He had never, since he had the misfortune or happiness, or whatever appellation may be given it, to sit under the sound of a sermon and go away without having heard from the lips of the speaker the most dreadful denunciation upon deism, atheism, and indeed all other denominations that professed a belief contrary to that of Christianity.

Waddill felt that:

40. DJW, April 22, 1837, vol. 1, pg. 16.

41. Ibid.

42. Ibid.

If one let it be known that he was a deist, then those men professing the Christian faith, and upon whom that man had looked as the firmest friends; that he had professed as such that degree of horror and dismay that would urge their departure from the most contagious and deadly malady that ever tainted, and dissolved the organization of man. When this deist would be referred to by them, his name would be mentioned as the name of one who had been cut off from life in the very commission of some horrid crime. His name would scarcely be breathed above the breath; and when he would chance to meet one of them, they would greet him with a low bow, a monosyllable, and pass from him with the speed of desperation.

Now should this deist go to vindicate himself, and his principles, the meek and lowly followers of Jesus, grasp for the lightning of love and then attempt to send them blazing, at his head. They let loose all the hell hounds of damnation upon him, cursing him as an encumbrance of the earth, and one whom it would be doing God's service to have burned alive at the stake.[43]

Waddill wondered what caused him to be such a cynic. His life had highs and lows like any other. Belief in God was not the issue. It was the pettiness of those professing Christ to be so judgmental. He wrote another poem, "Written in Despondency."[44]

John Waddill was a few months from completing his college studies, and he wondered when the man that he was becoming was created.

---

43. DJW, May 21, 1837, vol. 1.

44. Ibid.

CHAPTER 11

End of Term

As John P. Waddill was ending his third term, he continued to read books to broaden his mind. During this time, a popular book was *Lander's Travels— The Travels of Richard Lander into the Interior of Africa* by Robert Huish.[45] As an English explorer, Richard Lander was fascinated by African life and traveled the continent while keeping voluminous notes. He made three expeditions, on the last of which African tribesmen murdered him, at age thirty, in 1834.

Waddill read *Lander's Travels* at the end of the semester, knowing he would not get credit for it. But he had committed to reading and to never cease learning. After reading the book, he noted:

> I have read Lander's travels in Africa this week, and with them was much pleased. These are by no means well written, but being so full of incident they could not fail to interest a person of my disposition. Many persons are much interested in the reading of novels, romances, and such writings: and indeed their passion for such works appears to be so powerful that it entirely destroys their taste for all other works. I must confess that I am entirely ignorant of the cause of such a propensity, unless it may be ascribed to a species of mental disarrangement, brought on by an overheated imagination fed and encouraged by forcing the mind to give up her claim to the reflective faculties and by making an idol of the organ of marvelousness—In my opinion we must bring ourselves to the belief that what we hear, is true, before we can be in any manner interested in it; This being the case it then follows that we must believe, when reading a novel,

---

45. Robert Huish (1777–1850) wrote of the three expeditions of Lander to West Africa in 1835.

if we are interested in it, that it is all true or at least the major part of it is, founded upon, and inwoven with facts in such a manner that it would be impossible to cast away any portion without rolling ourselves of some important fact."[46]

End of the Term and College

John Waddill finished his term and became eligible to leave Augusta. He had received a letter from Thomas J. Hickman asking if he was ready to come back to Louisiana to pursue the law. Hickman again offered help. But Waddill did not feel satiated. He wanted more. His desires to learn more in a formal setting outweighed his desire to leave. He spoke to George Waters about it early on Monday morning, September 4, 1837.

There was to be a funeral preached by the professor of languages at Augusta, Burr H. McCown. It promised to be interesting as Professor McCown was well respected and a brilliant man. Born in 1806 in Kentucky, McCown had converted to Methodism in 1826. The Kentucky Conference appointed him to preach under Hubbard H. Kavenaugh, and he became a professor at Augusta in 1831.[47]

Just one week prior, Joseph M. Trimble, a professor of mathematics at Augusta, preached a funeral. Although Professor Trimble was also very talented and respected, Waddill remained unenthusiastic about attending another funeral to hear a sermon. Professor Trimble was the son of the former Governor of Ohio from 1826–1830, Captain James Trimble.[48] Due to his interest in politics, Waddill found himself inclined to listen when Trimble spoke. John knew that Trimble had the potential to go far in life.

It was a foggy morning as Waddill looked out the window of their room and stated his thoughts to Waters:

> This preaching of funerals is a very ancient custom, and originated in the rights of the ancients. We are as a mass very superstitious with regards to funerals, and it is but rarely you will find a family of indi-

---

46. DJW, July 27, 1837, vol. 1, pg. 21.

47. Albert Henry Redford, *Western Cavaliers: Embracing the History of the Methodist Episcopal Church* (Southern Methodist Publishing House, 1876).

48. Joseph M. Trimble later wrote and published *Semi-Centennial address of Rev. Joseph M. Trimble* before the 1876 Ohio Conference of the Methodist Episcopal Church in Columbus, Ohio.

viduals so hardy, when they lose a member, as to pass him from the mansion to the grave without a funeral. The preachers of the protestant persuasion will tell you that it is not for the benefit of the dead, but for the living. How if the dead cannot be benefited why preach the funeral at all? Does it not all most invariably happen that if the person whose funeral is preached, is not a member of the church (that is a believer in Christianity) the innuendoes which the preacher throws out concerning his future destiny are calculated to harrow[49] up the bitterest feelings against the decrees of Providence that are said to have consigned him to an endless eternity of woe?

Waters questioned his cynicism. Waddill stared blankly and said:

No. I am questioning all that we do in the Name of God. Hypocrisy. If this is the most common result of funeral preaching, especially to an enlightened audience—I mean enlightened by science, and the inception of the noblest sciences in which the human faculties are capable to receiving and not duped by superstition, are rendered frenzied by fanaticism and bigotry—why preserve in the custom? Would it not be better to drop it altogether, and leave the survivors to another more persuasive course of theological instruction? Nothing appears more rational than it would. But if were are to always follow out the custom of selecting orators for the purpose of telling all the vices and frailties of our friends, without leaving the dark picture with one of his virtues, and finish the figure, end by telling us he is in hell; I can then in all the fullness of my soul exclaim with hope and say:

"Oh let me live unseen unknown
And unlamented let me die;
Steal from the world, and not a stone
Tell where I lie! ----"[50]

Waddill had turned back to stare out the window. George Waters stood there wondering what happened to his roommate. His cynicism seemed to be burning a hole in his heart. George could offer only his presence to soothe the pain that John appeared to be experiencing.

---

49. Harrow: to plow up, bring to the top.

50. DJW, September 4, 1837, vol. 1, pg. 23.

The next morning, John Waddill continued his discourse as he wrote more comments about church in his diary.

> I did not go to church yesterday, in consequence of being informed that the church was full; and there was but little room left, for the eleventh hour comers. But would I have gained anything materially by going? I am confident that I should have a heard a moral lecture and would have been exhorted to do unto all men as I would they should do unto me. But do I not know that proverb, or rule? Then why go to hear it again? If I am acquainted with the golden rule, and everything which it can teach, it then becomes me to follow out its principles.
>
> Now one of these principles is, that I wish no man to compel me to do anything against my will, nor do I wish anyone to act against his will to gratify me. If I have had gone to church today, it would have been against my will, and consequently the whole sermon would have appeared to me, as a discourse calculated to mar my happiness, and as a means by which the clergy intended to discompose the tranquility of my mind by forcing me to listen to a long prescription for the healing of my soul, when I was under the firm conviction that it was not at all sick.
>
> It is a truth beyond reputation; that if you wish to bring a man over to your opinions and proselyte him so completely that there is no possibility of his falling off from him you must do by humoring his caprices as much as is possible so to do; and every opportunity which presents its self for convincing him by argument lay hold of it for that purpose; but never urge too far, lest you should raise a suspicion in his breast that you intend bending him to your will, whether he is willing or not; Or by your manner you may induce him to believe that you think him so weak in judgment, that it is impossible for him to discover right from wrong, and by this means you will so wound his vanity that he will shun you ever after, as he would the presence of a demon.[51]

No one would tell John Waddill what to believe. He had enjoyed the free thought process of attending college and took full advantage of it. He would

---

51. DJW, September 4, 1837, vol. 1, pg. 23.

strive to educate himself by continually reading many points of view and not limit his curiosity to certain subjects. The political process attracted him greatly. Now that the term had ended, Waddill had to make a decision. He decided to go to the president to seek advice about his future.

CHAPTER 12

Beginning of Another Term at Augusta College

September 4, 1837

In September 1837, the preparatory department of Augusta College was in full force. Waddill had been at college for three sessions, and the toll of the bell at 9 a.m. had invariably been the signal for him to hasten to the chapel to hear prayers, and when that ceremony finished, to retire to his room to recite his lessons. This had been Waddill's life for eighteen months, but now, he wrote, "a change comes o'er the spirit of my dreams." The sensations of the day produced in John Waddill a vivid character, one that he would not soon forget.

Now came time for Waddill to move forward with the rest of his life. His college course was finished. He would leave his professors for the purpose of learning a profession and to practice those principles of science and knowledge that he had learned at Augusta. He did not want to leave. He cherished his time there and wanted more, not sure that he had learned enough or that it had satiated his desire for formal learning. He knew that he would never stop educating himself, but the formal learning process challenged him further.

He was alone in his thoughts that morning. It had been a long and hard struggle that he knew would continue through life and with the obstacles to advancement that he would soon face. The sole means for his development laid within his own energies.

Other students had means of support to aid in their transition beyond college. Waddill had neither father, mother, nor wealthy friend upon which to depend, except Hickman. When he thought of being alone in the world and that he must stand or fall by his own exertions, he felt a confidence in his abilities, a glorious independency of means that was at once the precursor and invincible leader to the fulfillment of his most sanguine wishes.

He wrote his final thoughts: "Hope in all my trials stands by my side to cheer me through the surrounding gloom, and bid me of firm nerve and bold heart. But I suffer myself not to be lead too far by the smiling nymph, and take care always to keep firm footing upon things terrestrial, so that at all times I may not be so far from the earth as to break my neck should I be so unfortunate as to fall...."[52]

Waddill felt both despair and hope. Despair from not knowing what the future held, and hope mainly because of Thomas J. Hickman of Louisiana. Hickman had helped him upon his move there and encouraged him greatly to seek his formal learning, even helping him financially through college. Waddill would not forget his generosity. As fate would have it, at 4:00 p.m. that same day, he received a letter from Hickman, dated August 4, 1837. It was a harbinger of pleasing intelligence, yet not quite as substantial as he wished. From the letter's contents, Waddill looked forward for a speedy remittance, which would be the account needed for his departure to the sunny South.

Waddill planned to travel with a light heart, for he felt like mixing again with the busy scenes of life. The uproar and turmoil of human existence suited him much better than the dry monotonous rounds of college labors and enjoyments. He gloried, at times, in the whirlwind toil of business, where Greek meets Greek in all their pride of strength. "It's there that my tongue feels loaded to overflowing what the thoughts of my brain, and my bosom heaves with impatience to give scope to my feelings,"[53] Waddill wrote as he thought of Rapides Parish and Marksville and how both places teemed with commerce and excitement.

September 5, 1837

That morning, Waddill answered Hickman's letter. After writing his response, Waddill sat down to read it, but he could not focus on the task. His thoughts were far away, visiting the theater of his future exertions. The vivid pictures he dreamed up sometimes made him forget where he was. Waddill felt that his life would be full of events and exciting trials, though the magnitude of which he had not the most remote conception. He told his classmate, Mr. Miley, who was staying with him while George Waters traveled east:

---

52. DJW, September 4, 1837, vol. 1, pg. 24.

53. Ibid.

Time! Time! Is all that I want! Time and me against any other two, and I fear nothing. It is consoling to my feelings when I cast my eyes over the history of the great ones of the earth, to see that they have, in the majority of instances, arisen from the middle class of human family. The penniless poor, have had but few opportunities to cultivate their intellectual powers sufficiently for those pasts in times of danger and emergency, which required acuteness of judgment, combined with a prompt decision of character. The rich are generally too much occupied with the enjoyment of their wealth to devote much of their time to the laborious task of acquiring a large fund of knowledge, drawn from rigid investigation, and long study. But the middle class society is the bone and sinew of every nation; from them a nation draws her generals, her lawgivers, and in most instances her civil officers. From Hildebrand the great Pope of Rome to Ben Franklin, yea to the present hour the greatest revolutions and reforms have been affected by men from this class.

Miley, who was about to travel east, tried to stop him. He had hoped to soon travel to Louisiana to visit Waddill. Unable to stop, Waddill finished his thoughts thus:

We find these men in the middle class in every age wielding the whole powers and energies of the contemporary fellow beings; and if they trample upon the rights of mankind it is only in those nations where the executive is superior to the law of the land; but in a Republic, they are the guardians of Liberty, and the uncompromising opponents, in most instances, to the law defying as a tyrant who aims at self-aggrandizement by the destruction of his country's freedom.

Waddill wondered whether he just cared more than others or was it just that he was expressive. As he noted in his journal:

Let me then take courage, and persevere in my undertaking; let nothing dismay me while health, is secured to me as an investment; for in health I have all things. Although I say this myself, I have surmounted obstacles, from the opposition, of which the nine tenths of the human race would have quailed with fear and trembling. I do not wish to boast of myself in saying what I have already said; for while I have done many things to my credit, I have left undone many others, with which a reasonable portion of fortitude, and sagacity I could have accomplished with ease. I have let them pass by at the moment of the contact and in a moment more blushed at my own timidity regretting in the bitterness of my soul the loss of the opportunity.[54]

Morning of September 7, 1837

Maxwell W. Bland was a student at Augusta College who finished at the same time as Waddill, though he was a bit younger than Waddill, born in 1816. Bland was from Yazoo County, Mississippi, and told Waddill that he thought he would go to Louisiana and see what it was like. Waddill did not know whether to believe Bland since he seemed to be a bit on the temporal side of life. He was the life of the party at most gatherings but at times a bit immature. Since Waddill knew that Bland might be going to Louisiana, he did not want to lose contact with him.

Waddill began to write a letter to Bland when W. Schoolfield and Joseph A. Soule showed up at his room. Soule was the son of Bishop Joshua Soule, a Methodist from Tennessee.[55] He had been a student and returned to study law. Waddill was a bit jealous since he could not afford the formal study of law and would have to study on his own to take the bar exam. Waddill liked Soule, whom he considered a young man of great promise. He had a mind of the first order, and he was tolerably well cultivated, being a graduate of Augusta College. Joseph Soule's principles were noble, his integrity indisputable, and on the whole, Soule was capable of eliciting confidence from all his acquaintances. Waddill hoped to maintain a lifelong relationship with him, but he knew that was not very likely.

Schoolfield also intended to study law, though Waddill did not know him as well. When they left, Waddill went with the two young men to the courthouse in Augusta to procure some law books. He stayed with them for about a half hour and then returned to his room to finish his letter to Bland and to begin reading.

---

54. Ibid., September 5, 1837

55. Bishop Soule was born in Rhode Island, but later moved to Tennessee. Joseph Allen was born in 1815 and after college lived in Nashville where he died in 1879. Horace M. DuBose, "Life Of Joshua Soule," *Methodist Founders Series* (Nashville: Tenn., House of the Methodist East Church, 1911).

Before he began, two more young gentlemen, both by the name of Keith and both studying medicine at Augusta, paid John a visit. It was entertaining, but John was ready to study. The bell for supper interrupted their meeting, and they returned to their homes as Waddill went to eat.

After dinner, Waddill went to the post office to mail a couple of letters, and as soon as he returned to his room, he began reading the law books. The book he chose to read that night was *Russell on Crimes*.[56]

Waddill's fascination with the law continued. Although he had begun working toward studying the law in 1828, he now had a different perspective. Russell laid down the law in a most equitable manner, he thought, and noted nothing at which a criminal could grumble, unless it be in their treatment of some cases where the criminal had been known to be insane before the committal of the alleged crime. He noted but one case where this had occurred, and the conviction of the culprit in that case may have arisen from the ignorance of the jury.

Waddill wanted to discuss this case further with Joseph Soule. He decided to walk to where Soule was staying even though it had rained all morning, but it seemed to be waning, and with hope, the sun would be shining when he left. Soule was excited to enter a discussion that would likely turn into a debate.

Waddill spoke to Soule:

> My first point is that it is too frequently the case, that jurymen selected to try the most important cases are totally ignorant of all law, and even the very nature of the law, besides they have not a comprehensive knowledge of what make acts criminal. In my opinion, no man should be given over to capital punishment who, in the act of committing the crime, was not in full possession of his mental faculties. And for this reason no man should be tried for his life, unless by an enlightened jury, a jury every way capable of judging of the culprit's criminality. For it is certain that at least one half of the human race would consider a man capable of regulating his conduct in perfect accordance with the standard of moral rectitude, if he be only capable of knowing when he is in want of nourishment, or able to converse with some degree of rationality upon a few topics.

---

56. Sir William Oldnall Russell's book was originally published in London. The first American edition appeared in 1824, and is a reference still used today.

Joseph A. Soule thought that Waddill should stay and study the law. He argued that it appeared that Waddill wanted only those with some level of study of the law to be able to serve on a jury. Soule also commented on Waddill's arguments for those not in full possession of their mental capacity. He agreed that they should not receive capital punishment, but that was not the issue. Under the Common Law, he argued, it was the jury's decision to decide the culpability. In both situations— that is, knowledge of the law and mental capacity—it was up to the attorney to inform and teach a jury after their selection.

Waddill was poised with argument and ready to continue the debate:

> While you make valid counterpoints on those issues, let me point out that as I proceed in reading, I find another part of the criminal code objectionable. It states that a child or servant is not excusable for the committal of the capital offense when induced to the committal of such offence by the command of coercion of his or her parent or master. Now we are convinced that love of life is the most powerful affection of which we are capable of feeling. And if a child, or servant, should be threatened with death by a parent or mentor; provided they did not comply with a certain demand, there are in the performance of such command, to all intents and purpose excusable in the eye of justice, and consequently should be in the eye of the law. It may be urged that the law excuses in a former clause, persons in certain cases when coerced by superior force to the commission of crime but why not have put proviso in the other clause, and have stopped all cavil on the subject instanter? It is a lamentable fact that our laws in many instances are so complex, that it is almost impossible for persons in acquired merits and opportunities for study, to understand them at all. They require the most laborious amelioration before they can be separated, and reduced, to a lucid state.[57]

The discussion for that time was finished, and Waddill felt flushed with exuberance. He had the desire to go back to read more and would do so. As he left, the rain began to lessen, which certainly did not dampen Waddill's spirit.

As Waddill walked back to his room, he thought about the many objections he had to certain laws. He wrote:

---

57. DJW, September 7, 1837, vol. 1, pg. 26.

But such is the craft of man, that if the laws were not of the most comprehensive kind, it would be almost impossible to visit a culprit with merit punishment. He would contrive to throw someone else in to the vortex for himself, and by this means escaped. But if the laws are just, and the jury enlightened, there is but little danger to be apprehended, from the misapplication of the law, or the extent of the guilt, where the features of the case have been set forth in their true light.[58]

Waddill read more of Russell's law book the next day, but it did not interest him nearly as much as the day before. The laws of counterfeiting of coin were not as poignant. He did learn that mere possession of any tool or instrument capable of making or imitating any of the impresses on the current coin of the country would be in the eye of the law criminal to a certain extent. That person could be proceeded against as for a misdemeanor or felony.

---

58. Ibid.

CHAPTER 13

Classmates Departed

John Waddill was fully aware that he had to decide on plans for his future. Many of his classmates were gone, finding their chosen career paths. Waddill did not yet have the means to begin this move, and he missed the students who had. W. J. McClintick wrote a letter that Waddill received on September 9, 1837. He appreciated its nostalgia for recent friends with whom they had studied. Waddill delighted in the past stories of those that had started at Augusta with him and whom McClintick mentioned in the letter.

Waddill thought about those he would likely never see again nor correspond with. There were others, such as George R. Waters, whose paths would probably intertwine with his own and from whom he also received a letter.

This letter from George Waters was different. Waters's view particularly interested Waddill. In Waters's affectatious manner, there was something that many believed to be mysterious. Waddill felt that he had as good a right to judge Waters as anyone else, and in his letters and most of his writings, he described nothing but sincerity and a mind capable of comprehending and grappling with the most abstruse subjects.

George's letters were tinged with melancholy. In all confidential conversation, this trait frequently exhibited the strongest colors of warmth and the vividness of his feelings. He is one who Waddill long wished to retain in friendship; for in Waters's thoughts, he had discovered a kindred nature. The manner in which Waters conceived the ideas expressed in the letter was just as Waddill would wish a friend to write to him; for when he wrote in that manner, Waddill believed him to be a friend.

This concept proved itself as he received another letter from George Waters merely nine days later. Waters was in Washington, D.C., where, it seemed, he narrowly watched the movement of dignitaries. From his letter, Waddill could tell that George was fascinated and disillusioned at the same time. Waddill hoped that George would move to Louisiana soon, as they had both discussed for their futures.

Manual Labor Movement

On September 18, 1837, Thomas H. Whetstone introduced Waddill to a young man by the name of Pastor Scott, a Cumberland Presbyterian preacher from Tennessee.[59] Whetstone was born in 1815 in Cincinnati, Ohio, and had become close to Waddill while the two were at Augusta.[60] Whetstone became the first President of the Union Literary Society at the college. This society brought together students for gatherings and debating current issues. Whetstone was impressed with Pastor Scott and knew that Waddill would be also.

Pastor William A. Scott was born January 31, 1813, at Rock Creek, Unicoi County, Tennessee. He attended Cumberland College in Kentucky and graduated with distinction in 1833. In 1833–34, he was a student in Princeton Theological Seminary. He had united with the Cumberland Presbyterian Church in 1828, and at the early age of seventeen, he was licensed to preach. For a year before entering college Scott labored as a home missionary in various parts of Tennessee. He was chaplain in the army during the Black Hawk War, and in that service encountered many hardships and dangers. After about two years of labor in this way, he was ordained on May 17, 1835, in Alexandria, Louisiana. Dr. Scott was also engaged in various lines of literary work. He was a voracious reader and had a large library.[61]

In the pulpit, Dr. Scott was impressive. He had a large frame, massive brow, and commanding presence. His face beamed with kindness, intelligence, and earnestness. He had a sweet and powerful voice that filled the largest building and a ready command of language. His mind held a storehouse of truth, fact, and illustration, and with convincing argument and impassioned eloquence, he preached the gospel of salvation. Dr. Scott exercised great influence as an educator. Soon after his ordination, he established a seminary for young ladies at Winchester, Tennessee. From there, he was called in 1833

---

59. Cumberland County was not formed until 1856 in mid to east Tennessee from parts of eight counties in the Cumberland region and plateau. The reference is to the Cumberland Ministry of the Presbyterian Church.

60. Walter H. Rankins, *Augusta College, Augusta, Kentucky "First Established Methodist College," 1822–1849* (1949; Frankfort, Ky.: Roberts Printing Company, 1957), 28. He later became a State Senator in Ohio and died in 1865.

61. Scott eventually moved to California and was well noted there. He died in 1885. James Curry, "History of the San Francisco Theological Seminary of the Presbyterian Church in the USA and its alumni," (1907), 45–50.

to become president of the Nashville Female Seminary, which had between three and four hundred students.[62]

After Waddill found out that Pastor Scott had ministered in Alexandria and other parts of Louisiana, he had many questions. Waddill told him of his plans to move to the Alexandria area. Scott had extensive information of the region, so far as Waddill's limited acquaintance could judge.

Scott supported the manual labor education system, a movement that began around 1825 and grew thereafter. It derived from a similar movement in Europe. Strengthening the body and learning mechanics and labor skills in the morning followed by more traditional education in the afternoon, the movement allowed for a learning scheme that would improve both body and mind. Proponents claimed that it built character in addition to improving the thought process.[63]

Scott spoke in favor of the manual labor education system and the many advantages it possessed, particularly its inestimable preservation of health. The manual labor system of education required students to do manual work and exercise as part of the total educational process. Some argued that this left less time for math and science—in some cases they were eliminated altogether—but others argued that this would be best for the overall health and welfare of the students.

Waddill liked Scott's description of the system. He believed it to be good, where it was conducted along principles of equality, i.e. where it required the majority of the students to labor—when this is the case, brotherly love and equality of social feeling must be the consequences for such a course. Waddill believed that if the manual labor system promoted habits of industry and improved the physical energies, then it was well worthy of implementation.

Waddill hoped to maintain a relationship with Scott and knew that the pastor would go far in his field. He admired his faith and thirst for knowledge.

---

62. Ibid. See also John Seely Hunt, *A Manual of American Literature: A Textbook for Schools and Colleges* (Philadelphia: Eldredge and Brother, 1872), 584. See also for reference C. M. Drury, *William Anderson Scott: "No Ordinary Man"* (Glendale: Arthur H. Clarke, 1967).

63. Much of this debate ended about 1845 as most manual labor schools closed. See Will S. Monroe, "Manual Labor Institutions and the Manual Labor Society," in *Cyclopedia of Education*, ed. Paul Monroe, vol. 4 (New York: Macmillan, 1911), 156–61. Herbert Galen Lull, "The Manual Labor Movement in the United States," *Bulletin of the University of Washington*, no. 8 (July 1914): 375–76, 182; and Charles A. Bennett, *History of Manual and Industrial Education up to 1870* (1926),102–207.

Continuing Studies

Waddill went to the home of Rev. Joseph S. Tomlinson, the president of Augusta College. Known as the B.F. Power Home, it was located on Elizabeth Street. Tomlinson didn't expect him, but Waddill had urgent business. College courses at Augusta would begin the next day, and he wanted permission to stay a bit longer to study more as he made his plans to go back to Louisiana.

Waddill sought Tomlinson's advice on whether to continue at Augusta due to his financial concerns and future plans. Tomlinson told him of a plan to allow payment of tuition fees in proportion to the time attended. Waddill chose this option, thinking it would be for only a month. He also chose to move into Echo Hall, one of the first dormitories at Augusta, located on Frankfort Street. The next day, Waddill went to chapel and noted there were but a few students. It was expected that the college would be full within a few weeks.

Soon Waddill was taking mathematics and Latin with Dr. Tomlinson. He began his recitations within days and was full of confidence. His work ethic elicited a near grin from Tomlinson.

Waddill went to the courthouse to see if he could observe any cases. As a hopeful attorney, he observed that man's cleanest ideas were mingled with the doubts of the most perplexing nature—and it was frequently the case that when one believed that he had arrived at incontrovertible conclusions upon a subject, that at the same moment he found some obstacle that overthrows the supposed infallibility of his positions.

Such observations made Waddill doubt the nature of the law. These reflections came after watching a lawyer establish principle after principle, by bringing in evidence and law, and interpreting them entirely to the favor of his own case. Then when he had finished, his antagonist arose, remodeled the law and evidence, and to all appearances, satisfactorily proved all that the other had said or done to be erroneous. Waddill knew then that debating skills were imperative should he become a lawyer skilled in the courtroom. He would continue to debate every chance he had.[64]

Waddill read the English translation of Hegel's *Science of Logic*. Still, he struggled as he recited his lessons to Tomlinson. Hegel stated a goal in *The Science of Logic*. It was to overcome what he perceived to be a common flaw running through all other former systems of logic, namely that they all presupposed a complete separation between the content of cognition (the world

---

64. DJW, September 20, 1837, vol. 1, pg. 37.

of objects, held to be entirely independent of thought for their existence), and the form of cognition (the thoughts about these objects, which by themselves are pliable, indeterminate, and entirely dependent upon their conformity to the world of objects to be thought of as in any way true). This unbridgeable gap found within the science of reason was, in his view, a carryover from everyday, phenomenal, philosophical consciousness.[65]

That was not the end of his recitations. Waddill also recited mathematics, not his favorite subject and he felt inadequate. He was also getting weary. The lanterns were burning low when he moved on to his recitations in Latin, the third book of Virgil's *Aenead,* the subject Polydorus

As Waddill recited Aeneas's escape from Troy, he began to tell the story of the spirit of the tree that bled until it soaked the ground and then claimed to be Polydorus. Waddill livened up. He liked the study of Latin and the history of the Trojan Wars. That King of Thrace sided with the Greeks only after Troy fell, appealed to the caustic side of Waddill. He wanted to fight. Waddill regarded Virgil as a man of uncommon political powers. Virgil had ideas that were sublimely poetical in some places and beautifully practical in others.

---

65. "Science of Logic," Wikipedia, https://en.wikipedia.org/wiki/Science_of_Logic#CITEREFHegel-1969. See also G. W. F. Hegel, *Hegel's Science of Logic* (Allen & Unwin, 1969), 35–41.

CHAPTER 14

The Return of George R. Waters and Thoughts on Politicians

On September 20, 1837, George Waters returned from his four-week journey east. He had been in Washington, D.C., for at least two weeks during this time and wrote to Waddill about his travels. "Waters gave an account of the great men of our nation to the few of us that had remained at Augusta College. After listening, Waddill came to the conclusion that there are not so many great men in the world as there are supposed to be by many. He did believe though, that America, according to her population possesses her full quota on nature's noblemen."

Waters believed Daniel Webster was by far the most noble-looking statesman that he observed. Francis Rives of Virginia was the best speaker and made use of the finest languages of any of the members of either house of Congress that Waters had the opportunity of hearing—and he heard all who were celebrated for speaking.

Congressman Francis Rives of the 2nd District of Virginia was a supporter of state banks. As Francis Blair wrote to President Andrew Jackson on February 11, 1838:

> You will have seen Rives' Bill with surprise, after what I have written you. He has been playing a deep, hypocritical game." He came into the sub treasury, or independent treasury, scheme, which Jackson called the "divorce bill" because it would divorce the government from the banks, came up first in the special session of 1837, where it failed. It was brought up again in the regular session, coming from the Senate committee on finance, of which Silas Wright was chairman. It provided for keeping the public money in the Treasury at Washington and in four sub treasuries in other cities. It was introduced in the Senate Jan. 16, 1838. On Feb. 2, 1838, Senator

Rives of Virginia introduced a substitute providing for the selection by Congress of twenty-five state banks in which the public money would be deposited. Rives's scheme was supported by the friends of the defunct Bank of the United States, seemingly on the ground that it would prolong the existing state of confusion and eventually make it easy to recharter the Bank. The substitute failed to pass the Senate on Mar. 31 by a vote of 29 to 20. After some amendment Wright's bill passed the Senate Mar. 24, 1838, by a vote of 27 to 25, but did not pass the House.[66]

Waters continued to speak of the many characters serving the country. He regarded Senator William Preston, from South Carolina, as quite an ordinary looking man: his head was beefy in appearance, and his hair was red—yet Preston was undoubtedly a great man naturally and had improved his natural abilities by close application to study. The biggest complaint about him was his rarity in session. He missed about one in four votes and often could not be found.

Waddill quoted Waters's statements as follows:

Congressman Henry A. Wise is an ordinary man, both in appearance and mentality; his chief endowment being vested in low scurrility, and a general tendency to engage in contention. Earlier this year, when the two congressmen, Jonathan Cilley of Maine and William Graves of Kentucky had a duel on February 24, 1838, Henry Wise served as one of the seconds that resulted in Cilley's death. The survivor and the two seconds were recommended for censure. That failed, but a bill was introduced to "prohibit the giving or accepting in the District of Columbia, of a challenge to fight a duel, and for the punishment thereof."[67]

Waters continued his discourse on those in both chambers of Congress.

---

66. Francis Preston Blair to Andrew Jackson, February 11, 1838, from *Correspondence of Andrew Jackson*, edited by John Spencer Bassett, Library of Congress, http://www.loc.gov/resource/maj.01100_0165_0171.

67. "A Fatal Duel Between Members in 1838," History, Art, & Archives, United States House of Representatives, http://history.house.gov/Historical-Highlights/1800–1850/A-fatal-duel-between-Members-in-1838/.

Senator Clement Comer Clay of Alabama is also quite an ordinary man, as to his mental capabilities. He was Governor of Alabama before his election to the Senate. I could go on and on, but only one more, Senator Thomas H. Benton from Missouri is a fine looking man, and as I myself think, one capable of high mental exertion. He served as an aide-de-camp to General Andrew Jackson as a Colonel of a regiment of Tennessee Volunteers.[68]

Then Waters began to tell of the party process in Washington:

That all parties carry on everything at the capital in intrigue; It appears that the anti-administration will run the former Whig Senator John Jordan Crittenden from Kentucky, for President and Senator Thomas Ewing from Ohio for Vice President. He lost his last election but is strongly opposed to Andrew Jackson. Daniel Webster held frequent conferences with Crittenden, and it was believed that they were laying their plans for the next presidential campaign. It was well known that Webster sent his private carriage for Crittenden. Such conduct savors much of intrigue.

Waddill desired to witness the people and events of Washington, D.C., himself, but with minute funds, he could only wish to visit.

The Elam Family
September 27, 1837

Not all of Waddill's correspondence was as friendly as his with Waters. John Pamplin Elam, another cousin of William J. Elam, wrote a discouraging letter to John Waddill in the late summer of 1837. He was greatly distressed when Waddill suddenly left Elam and his land in the spring of 1836. His tone in the letter left a bitter taste for Waddill. He noted that it "raised his dander." Waddill hoped that Elam would one day see the foolishness in his attitude. Yet the letter intimated that it would be the last John P. Elam would write. Waddill wrote: "But it is a part of my creed to let everyone enjoy their own opinion; and when that opinion runs counter from mine, I use no very

---

68. "Thomas Heart Benton," History, Art, & Archives, United States House of Representatives, http://history.house.gov/People/Detail/9291?ret=True.

persuasive, nor violent means to bring it to my standard."[69] Waddill waited a day to answer Elam. Besides being a friend, he was distantly related to Elam on his mother's side, and maintaining good relations was important.

John Pamplin Elam was born in 1798, the son of Edward Elam and Jane Pamplin, who had moved to Tennessee prior to 1823. After leaving Williamson County, Tennessee, Elam moved to an area on Little River in Catahoula Parish, Louisiana. He became a planter with $40,000.00 value in land by 1860.[70] In 1850, the slave schedule showed Elam as owning eight slaves.[71]

Research of the family history on Waddill's mother's side can trace the family back to their native England. Robert Pamplin, born in 1633 in Essex, England, moved to Virginia, where he had a son, John Pamplin. John Sr. married Elizabeth Blagrave in Caroline County, Virginia, in 1730. Together, they had four children: John Pamplin II, born 1730, in Caroline County; William Pamplin, born 1740; Elizabeth Pamplin, born 1742; and Henry Blagrave Pamplin, born 1744. Elizabeth Pamplin married Frederick Browder and gave birth to Elizabeth Blagrave Browder. The Browder family then moved from Virginia to Tennessee. There, she met and fell in love with Samuel Waddill in 1809.

John Pamplin Elam moved with his parents, Edward Elam and Jane Pamplin, to Tennessee shortly after other family members had moved. Elam knew John Waddill as a cousin on the Pamplin side. Eventually, John Elam ended up in Catahoula Parish and encouraged his cousin to later move to Louisiana for its rich soil and plentiful land. Elam wanted Waddill to enter into planting also and did not agree with his decision to go to college to become a lawyer. He was bitter about it from the day that Waddill left for Augusta. Elam wrote:

> I have given you opportunity to make a living and you are leaving. It is a poor choice to think that going to a college will improve your standing. It is expensive and time wasted. I have land and you can work for me as long as you want to work. This is the way to go.

69. DJW, September 25, 1837, vol. 1, pg. 38.

70. See 1860 Federal Census, Catahoula Parish, schedule 1–Free Inhabitants, pg. 11.

71. See 1850 Federal Census, Catahoula Parish, schedule 2–Slave Inhabitants, pg. 191.

Waddill responded briefly, "This has been my desire for years and I will not reject the opportunity."

"You will regret this," Elam said bluntly as he turned and walked away.

Others in the Elam family eventually moved to the wilderness of Tennessee, but some made the journey to the Ayish Bayou area, settling in both east Texas and Arkansas. William Jefferson Elam, a teacher and surveyor, moved his family to east Texas, outside San Augustine. The move took place prior to the birth of his son Joseph Barton, who was born in 1821. When Joseph was five years old, the family moved to Ft. Jesup, Louisiana, in Sabine Parish, where William tutored the officers' sons. In 1833, another son, John Waddill Elam, was born. In 1836, William J. Elam acquired a land grant from the United States and the State of Louisiana, property that he settled on.[72]

When Waddill moved to Louisiana, he was naturally desirous of being with family on the Waddill-Pamplin side. William J. Elam extended help and found him to be quite a character. On September 8, 1837, Waddill wrote in his diary an Arkansas fable he heard from William J. Elam.[73] The story seemed preposterous, but as storytellers go, Elam was the best. The story sounds like an early version of the legend of Bigfoot. By any means, it captured the imagination of young Waddill.

The relationship between Waddill and cousin William J. Elam not only helped to influence Waddill's decision to leave Tennessee the first time but also to return to Louisiana after college. Between Thomas Hickman and William J. Elam, John P. Waddill felt enough support to make the state of Louisiana his permanent residence.

---

72. "Louisiana Early Settlers," Sabine Parish, www.genealogytrails.com.

73. DJW, September 8, 1837, vol. 1, pgs. 27–29. Judge Harmon Drew Jr., Circuit Court of Appeal in Louisiana, is the great-great grandson of William J. Elam.

CHAPTER 15

Late Enrolling in Class

September 25, 1837

As expected, new and old students began to arrive on campus. An old acquaintance, Richard Kidder "R. K." Meade, returned that day. Born in Ohio in 1819, Meade came to Augusta to further his education. Waddill was close to Meade and there for him three months later when R. K.'s father, David Meade, died, on December 20, 1837, at the young age of forty-four. John Waddill told him that he would never forget the years he had with his father. As time passed after college, Waddill found out that Meade married Jane Brockenbrough Graves of Clark County, Virginia, and had two children of his own, David, born in 1840, and Edgar Snowden, in 1845.[74]

On the same day as R. K.'s return to Augusta, Waddill noted meeting new student George T. McDonald from Lancaster, Ohio. McDonald was born November 19, 1817, and held high aspirations of becoming a doctor. Waddill heard from him several years later telling him that he had realized this goal.[75]

Debates

The professors at Augusta never let up on debates as part of the learning process and encouraged extracurricular activities in debate as well. Waddill was a member of the Patrick Henry Junto Club, which met regularly to debate. He believed it sharpened his skills and broadened his mind. One of the main national topics of 1837 was the matter of Texas. On the evening of

---

74. Captain R. K. Meade was an engineer in the Confederate Army and died March 4, 1862.

75. George McDonald fought for the Union as a physician and died on July 23, 1900. He is buried at Oak Hill Cemetery in Wyandot County, Ohio.

September 28, 1837, Waddill, Meeks, Morris, Greg, and Young (who volunteered his services after the regular disputants had spoken) set up a debate at the Patrick Henry Junto. Their round was selected to debate the negative on the proposition that Texas be admitted into the Union provided that Texas maintained her independence. Joseph Soule was presenting as the proponent of the proposal. Soule, Sheppard, Miley (in the place of George R. Waters, who was absent), and Whetstone were the disputants in the affirmative. Professor Kemp headed the panel, which included President Tomlinson and one other professor. The upperclassmen were invited, and about fifteen of them showed up, a fairly large number for the small college.

Soule defended first:

> Why should Texas be willing to be subject to a central government if it is already a nation within itself. Those opposed simply state, they should be equal to other states. It is our position that if Texas is to be admitted the benefits gained by such size and resources our country gains should outweigh the arguments against their independence. This union of two nations would be two countries joining and existing together, which is different than the settlement of territories after giving away land to settlers who set out west to populate the uninviting land. Many of our citizens desired to go to Texas to become free and even fought for Texas to obtain its sovereign status.

Waddill stood up for his session, and noticed that the President almost had a look of pride for him, when he took a breath and argued:

> I considerably oppose such admission; and in support of my opposition, here give some of my reasons. In the first place, it is unconstitutional to extend the territory of the U.S. beyond its present boundary. Now, as we have by the consent of the states in their individual capacity, adopted certain rules and regulations which we call the constitution of the U.S. and by whose dictates we have agreed to be governed, it becomes an imperative duty on our parts, individually, and collectively to abide by them; and to use every means within our power to preserve them, unless they should prove to be dangerous to our Liberties.
>
> And as the admission of Texas into the Union could not in any manner add to our liberties; or give more efficacy to the laws of our land, it is impolitic to admit her into a membership with the other states.

> Besides, if a nation is in the habit of frequently breaking the laws, or any law which she may have adopted, such laws, or law soon become null and void to all intents and purposes, in the eyes of the people. If the nation as a body regarded not its injunctions, the individual members of the nation would consider its tyranny to be forced to obey them; for no regulation that is frequently broken by those who have made it can have any intrinsic value in the eyes of others, and in a Republic like ours where the laws bear equally upon the government, and governed, if the government can break a law with impunity, the governed can claim for themselves the same rights, and consequently all laws subjected to such use, are of non-effect, and are incapable of being administered.

Waddill then sat. He knew that Waters would give better rebuttals; all of the team members agreed to change the typical format, allowing Waddill to give the two openings consecutively. The negative team sought to throw the affirmative team off balance.

Soule's team partner argued the next segment. Sheppard stood at the podium and proposed:

> The argument of unconstitutionality is weak. To uphold this position would require "us to still be the original thirteen colonies. This state of Kentucky would not exist. Further, President Jefferson, who was a strict constitutionalist, would never have agreed to the Louisiana Purchase, which practically doubled the size of our nation, forming states from this land.
>
> We merely propose that another huge territory be added as a state, with those citizens maintaining her independence. There is no clear indication or case law from our Supreme Court prohibiting such an action. It must be approved by the Legislative branch of our country, approved by the Executive Branch and if there is a challenge interpreted by the Judiciary. That is precisely what our forefathers envisioned and it is precisely what our forefathers did upon application of Vermont as the 14th state of our Union. Can we truly argue that our President George Washington was precluded from signing said agreement?[76]

---

76. Actually, it was an act of Congress that was signed by Thomas Jefferson, as Secretary of State on February 18, 1791. See: http://www.freedomandunity.org/new_frontier/fourteen.html.

It was an impressive presentation, but Waddill and his team had planned this well. Waddill stood up, and there was a look of surprise on the face of the judges. Waddill spoke:

> We will examine whether we could aid the cause of humanity any, by the admission of Texas into the Union; as it has been frequently affirmed that we would by so doing. The proposition has this language, "Provided she maintained her independence."
>
> Now, the very language of the proposition precludes the idea that it would be an act of humanity; For if Texas can maintain her own independence; she can stand in the need of no other power whatever, and is possessed of the most potent requisite of an empire, (via) strength. It is also presumable that when a nation possesses wisdom and policy enough to conduct itself through a revolutionary war against a superior enemy, that it possesses every material to conduct itself, through every vicissitude in time of peace. Furthermore; the territory claimed by Texas possesses all the natural elements of a powerful nation, being capable according to the best computation in square miles, to sustain a population superior in numbers, to England, Wales, Scotland, and Ireland. It is also greater in extent to Hindustan,[77] which sustains a population of 101,000,000. Nor is its territory sterile, and unproductive, but fertile in the extreme, and possessing one of the most salubrious climates on the globe, though the greater part of its extent. It is watered by some of the noblest rivers of North America, upon whose waters the Texan produce may be carried to some of the finest marts in the U.S. The head branches of these rivers, together with many of their smaller tributary streams possess every advantage of propelling machinery by water power; thus throwing out inducements in all parts of the country, for the erection of the cheapest and most efficient manufactories in all the continent of America. Manufactories of cotton cloth, will be eminently advantageous; as it will be formed easy, and profitable to erect such manufactories immediately in the vicinity of the cotton growing region, where the manufacturer

---

77. Hindustan actually means "Urdu speaking areas of the Indian sub-continent." Most Indians who use the word to describe India are probably unaware that it excludes a substantial part of modern-day India. "Of Hindu, Hindustan, Hindi," Rediff News, http://www.rediff.com/news/column/of-hindu-hindustan-hindi/20140911.htm.

will have the advantage of buying the material the lowest price, at which it can be sold; and then without taxing himself the cost of carriage he can sell it manufactured into cloth, to the customer, living within a few miles of his own establishment. Her climate and soil are also finely adapted to the culture of the sugar cane, and almost every tropical fruit.

She also has extensive prairies, covered with the most luxuriant herbage in the world, upon which innumerable herds of cattle and horses may be reared without the least expense to the owners. Nor is the climate or soil in the least deleterious to the raising of sheep; for the mountains parts of the country are almost as fitly adept to the growth and fleece of that animal, as the kingdom of Spain. She also possesses a considerable seacoast, beautifully indented with capacious bays and safe harbors, into some of which can be admitted the largest vessels, which float the ocean.

Now, after viewing Texas in the light we had just exhibited her, which is as correct an account of that country, as at this time can be given, it would be as absurd, as ridiculous to say that it would in the least aid the cause of humanity to admit her into the union, after she had been found capable of defending herself.

After finishing and observing the judges' reactions, Waddill felt extremely confident and wondered what Soule could say. Soule's team member Miley was not at a loss for words when he rebutted:

It sounds as though, with all of the glowing remarks of my opponent, that he is perhaps an agent for Texas itself, sent to encourage settlers to move to the territory and Republic of Texas. Perhaps, he is moving there himself!

For all of the reasons stated by my opponent, support even more the cause of why we, as the United States, should accept Texas as a state with independence. For it is true, that Texas and the people within it and the many more moving there, can support itself as a nation and does not need the United States for its continued existence. Our United States would benefit greatly from all of the natural resources contained within the territory, as opposed to having these people as potential competitors or even enemy.

In effect, we should do everything possible, including granting independence, in our acceptance of the application of Texas, should its citizens propose it. Finally, the arguments of constitutionality is without merit, as this very year, Michigan was admitted as our newest state.[78]

Waddill's heart sank. Miley had effectively used his own argument against his team's position. This was persuasive in debate, and John could see it in the reactions of the judges. Waddill's team member Meeks was still confident. He rose for the first time and rebutted:

Although the argument of the proponents is convincing there are two major flaws. First, why should a territory, or for that matter a republic dictate to our nation the terms of their admittance. All states should be equal and that was the intent of our forefathers in establishing our Constitution.

Further, we should be keenly aware that although Texas' fight with Santa Anna, which we all remember through the Alamo, does not mean that Mexico will sit idly by as the United States accepts a territory, which Mexico is so desirous to claim. Is it worth the blood of our citizens to fight for this, just to accept a territory, as worthy as it is, into our country. The argument is that it is not worth the bloodshed that will surely bring. We oppose the proposition.[79]

Each team member argued except for Young. Ultimately, the debate ended with both teams receiving high marks and applause. The judges were divided, yet Waddill's team opposing the proposition ultimately won them over, as Chairman Kemp announced to the students attending. The judges voted 2–1 that the negative carried the day. Waddill described the debate as *exhilarating*. He felt even more excited about the realm of politics, which he thought he would one day enter.

---

78. On January 26, 1837, the State of Michigan was admitted as our twenty-sixth state. "Today in History–January 26," The Library of Congress Digital Collections, http://memory.loc.gov/ammem/today/jan26.html.

79. Texas was admitted into the Union on December 29, 1845, as the twenty-eighth state. Shortly after its admission, the war with Mexico began. "Mexican American War," History, http://www.history.com/topics/mexican-american-war.

President Tomlinson approached both teams afterward. He wanted more debates on various issues of the day. He requested their help in having other students participate. He was a proponent of declamation and recitations, which he believed helped students learn their lessons. Tomlinson also believed that debates would strengthen the resolve of students to prepare them for post-college life. All of them agreed.

As Waddill lay in bed, he thought more of Texas and the courageous fight for its independence. He and the others were well aware of the fall of the Alamo. He wrote:

> Among the events of the world, which have transpired within our own recollection, none are better calculated to draw from our eyes a sympathetic tear, or arouse in our bosoms a spirit of revenge, than the fall of the Alamo; for there died within whose breasts, heart of nature's noblest mold pulsated; Heroes who threw themselves between the destroying wrath of a numerous and merciless enemy and their bleeding country. They may be truly styled the Spartan bond of America; for them, earth has produced none braver, or more devoted to the cause of liberty and their Country! Their country had but recently been overrun by an invading army: they had assisted in the expulsion of that army; and felt their souls expand with the beatific feelings of patriots, at seeing their country free. But another invasion threatened, they were called forth to stand upon the champions of the rights of man, by regarding the progress of the enemy, upon the borders of their country! They obeyed the call; and with patriot pride threw themselves between their country and the hostile army! But soon: yea in the very day-spring of their march, they found that their numbers were too few to repel the opposing force; But with Roman patriotism they determined, if unaided, to form a bulwark with their slaughtered bodies, which should paralyze, almost, with Medusean magic, the hearts of the advancing enemy.[80]

---

80. DJW, September 29, 1837, vol. 1 pg. 40.

CHAPTER 16

Continuing Debates

Augusta College's professors and the student body were excited for the administration to schedule more debates. It appeared that the term would be more dedicated to this method of student participation and involvement than previous ones. The two debate topics were extorted oaths and who was responsible for the debt of the country.

The first topic, which dealt with the spiritual issue of oaths that threats of violence had extorted, and whether they were truly binding, caught Waddill off guard. He argued law and the Bible as it related to such oaths. He distinguished between those non-binding under the law and those oaths to God that were forever binding to the person taking such an oath. He began to wonder where all of his faith in the Word of God, as stated in the Bible, came from. He thought he was principled and believed in God, but this subject made him contemplate much more than the issue at hand. Integrity was one quality that Waddill strived to attain and keep. He thought about it for days and wrote extensively in preparation.[81] Ultimately, his passion for political debates overrode any meditations of spiritual issues.

The next debate question, "Is the present depreciated state of the currency owing to Jackson's Administration?" attracted many of the students and professors who were not even required to be there. President Tomlinson himself judged the debate. This debate would comprise three-member teams. Waddill, Soule, and Meeks argued the negative; Waters, Whetstone, and Miley the affirmative. Waddill studied the issue. He read every journal and newspaper available to the students and spoke to others, recording his thoughts in his diary as he prepared for the debate. He did not like to lose.

George Waters began the debate (his last as a student):

---

81. DJW, October 3, 1837, vol. 1, pg. 40–41.

We present the issue of the question. 'Is the present depreciated state of the currency owing to Jackson's Administration' in the affirmative. It is clear that the President of the United States has such a powerful position that his ideas and concepts are merely under his control in Congress. The current Congress is comprised of a majority in the same Party as the President. Although, for a short time in the Senate when the opposing party had more members, it is without question that for his eight years as President, his party controlled congress and bowed to the demands of President Jackson. Now a President, or his supporters, may say that only Congress makes laws and the President executes the will of the Congress, we are all aware that the Party of the President will control which issues will be heard.

It is also well known that if a President has problems or disagreements with any laws passed by Congress, he has the power of veto and that is the strongest weapon. Overriding a veto is rarely if ever successful. In 1832, when this President did not have full control over the Senate for that short time, he vetoed the Re-Charter of the Bank of the United States in 1832.[82]

By vetoing this act, he has hurt our economy. He compounded the issue when he withdrew all U.S. Funds from the bank in 1833. Since then, many local and state banks came up in place of the void left by no National Bank. This could be the biggest reason for the collapse of our economy. The expansion of credit and speculation by all this lending caused inflation. Most of these banks had only paper banknotes and were not backed by gold or silver. Thus our currency is now depressed.

Waddill had asked his team if he could go first again. He liked that. They had watched him before and knew his skills and passion for debate. The team agreed.

Is the present depreciated state of the currency owing to Jackson's Administration?

---

82. President Jackson believed that re-chartering the bank of the U.S. gave it extra ordinary monopolistic powers. "Veto Message of the Bill on the Bank of the United States," Andrew Jackson, July 10, 1832, http://teachingamericanhistory.org/library/document/veto-message-of-the-bill-on-the-bank-of-the-united-states/

This is a question, which I think can be plainly answered; and also, that satisfactory evidence can be adduced to prove the negative. It is urged by the affirmative that, by vetoing the charter of the Bank of the U.S. in 1833, Jackson ruined the currency. This we think is incorrect, for by the declarations of the president, cashiers, and directors of that bank, it was affirmed to be as able to do its moneyed business, as extensively, and honorably as it formerly had.

This is proof sufficient, to show; that by her own admission, she (the U.S. Bank) was not injured by the veto. But we will examine the currency in that manner in which we think the question demands, and will endeavor to show what we think has ruined the currency. There has been an inordinate spirit of speculation existing among the citizens of the U.S. ever since the war. When the soldiers who had been called into service during the war were paid off, a flooding circulation of money was exhibited throughout the Union. At the same time the southern Indians ceded a considerable region, of the most fertile soil to the U.S. These lands, coming into market at a time when money was plenty, sold at an enormous price, and as uncultivated lands, at treble their value. Men who were of an enterprising character, immediately commenced a speculation in the land, and not having sufficient available funds, to make their purchases as extensive as they wished, they borrowed funds from others, at a considerable interest; with the expectation of liquidating the debts by the profits rising from the sales of their land. But they soon found that their lands had cost them much more, than they would be losing at the present sale, and consequently by selling them they would be plunging themselves the deeper in debt. The monies which they had paid out for these lands, had into the public treasury, and from there to the creditors of the U.S. where it totally disappeared from circulation,

This being the case, to meet the emergencies at this crisis, it became necessary for the speculation, to procure that which might be deemed to be equivalent for the money itself; and to compass this design, enterprising individuals, many of them the land speculators, formed themselves into various associations, organized banks, applied, and procured from the State's Legislature, chartered for the same. All the specie, now, that was lying in the hands of persons who did not wish to engage in the land speculation, or in the banking system, was bought up at a stipulated price upon credit, for the compose of a metallic capital in the banks—manufactories, internal improvements, and commercial speculations in the north, had the same effect upon the moneyed matters, that the land business had in the south. Europe for years had been torn by the most desolating wars, and the grain-growing portions of that continent, had suffered much during these contests, and were entirely unable to supply their usual guarantor of grain. It was to America, then that the nations looked for a supply for the article."

Waddill was on a high pace; he spoke faster because of the time limits. He had the audience mesmerized. He continued:

Beef, pork, and many other necessary for life were also supplied from this country.

These things opened up a new field for speculation, and from the success which attended the exertions of those engaged in it; others, who had been employed in farming or the mechanical arts, were induced to enrich themselves in the same way. Thus in a short time the whole country, and every lake and sea, became overrun with speculation.

These armies, and fleets of individuals, who lived upon the fat of the land, and suck the very marrow from the bones of the laborer, called upon the Banks to give new and more extensive emissions of their bills, and extend the benefits of their institutions for them.

These calls were complied with, without the least hesitation, and the country was immediately flooded with a paper currency, in such quantities, that it was madness to deem that it could ever be redeemed with specie. In 1818 the banks began to break in every direction; farmers, mechanics, merchants, speculators and all were whelmed in one common ruin.

The debate continued. Even though most of those attending felt that, from a personal standpoint, President Jackson was the party at fault, those present believed that Waddill's team won the evening with their points.

Waddill wanted to display revelry that night. The two debate teams decided to have a little fun and found a small pub in the town. They talked of debates and their abilities. Waddill told them that he would soon be moving back to Louisiana, though both teams wanted him to stay, as he was a good debater. But college was over for him, and John P. Waddill decided it was time to go.

Shortly after, he began packing his belongings and preparing for the journey to Louisiana. He wrote to Thomas J. Hickman and told him that he was prepared to come to his new home—Louisiana. He awaited Hickman's response.

BOOK II

THE EARLY LEGAL CAREER AND ENTRY INTO POLITICS OF JOHN P. WADDILL
1838–1847

CHAPTER 17

Leaving Augusta College and John P. Waddill's Law Career, 1838

After attending college, John P. Waddill moved back to Louisiana, to Avoyelles near the Red River, right outside of Marksville. He eventually settled in a home in Marksville but kept his property on the Red River to plant crops. His brother William, when he reached age sixteen in 1844, moved in with John in Marksville. Waddill later found out that his oldest sister, Martha Jane, married William S. H. Sanders in 1841. John's brother Frederick finally left the Tennessee farm and moved to Texas in 1837, a destination for many migrating west in the United States.

On December 27, 1837, while he was still at Augusta College, Waddill received a letter from Thomas J. Hickman with nine-hundred dollars enclosed. Waddill was sure that he would never have been able to go on with his studies without the encouragement and financial help of Hickman. During the nearly four years that Hickman allowed Waddill to work on Flag Land Plantation, Waddill had access to Hickman's library and funds for the work he did on the plantation. Hickman encouraged Waddill to finish his studies and study law. He also suggested working in Marksville, a very active community with fewer lawyers than Rapides Parish.

On January 3, 1838, John P. Waddill left Augusta College for Louisiana. On January 12, he arrived at Thomas J. Hickman's plantation. Not wasting time, on January 17, Waddill spoke to George R. Waters[83] about getting a job

---

83. The 1840 Federal Census shows Waddill's former roommate, George R. Waters, as owning one slave. In 1850, after the government started to keep slave owner records, Waters is shown as age forty and owning thirty slaves. He is also listed as esq. and in the category of being a licensed professional, perhaps indicating that he was a lawyer. After 1850, the author could not find another reference to the George R. Waters born around 1810. Perhaps he died in the 1850s.

in the clerk's office of Rapides Parish. Surely, his old friend and roommate could help. Waters assured him that he would get him a position but never came through.

"I have great doubts and am fearful that I will not have a job that would allow me to learn about the law, of which I wish to study. All I want is a little time to study, to be no burden to my friends, and to pay whatever money I may owe. When I accomplish this, I will be satisfied," Waddill wrote.

John Waddill was indebted to Thomas Hickman, who offered Waddill any help he needed, even, if necessary, a job staying on at Flag Land. Though this provided Waddill with a safety net, it was not his primary plan. Luckily, there was no need for this, as Waddill eventually got a job as a clerk.

On January 18, 1838, Waddill began his serious study of the law, hoping it would take only a year. He was a civilian in training. Waddill wrote, "If I can only find means for my continuance, I will fill measurably contented. Good health, and one year's study is all I ask for the present; the future must then provide for itself."[84] His study of the law was tedious yet methodical. He began by reading the Civil Code of Louisiana, which is based upon Spanish and French Law, contrary to the Common Law in all other U.S. states. Waddill would write and recite the coda articles much like he did in the classes at Augusta. The recitations helped him to memorize the laws, and then he would study cases to understand the meanings behind them. The Civil Code of Louisiana seemed to be much more pure in law than the Common Law of English-speaking states and nations.

Waddill did extra work for the three Hickman brothers on their rather large plantations and spent a lot of time at Bellevue, which William Hickman ran. The Hickmans allowed Waddill his time to study. Often while studying, Waddill's mind would wander into the political realm. He had little respect for elected officials, whom many considered dishonest. He was a Democrat and would never support the Whig candidates.

While studying the law one evening, he began to talk to William Hickman, hoping to get into a bit of a debate. It was February 23, 1838, when he went into the study of Mr. Hickman and began a long discussion with the approval of his listener about what a Republican politician should be.

He began:

---

84. DJW, vol. 1, pg. 55

The first qualification which a politician of the U.S.A. should have is an unreserved love of country. I do not mean merely a love of country, which gave him birth, but also, a love for the well being, and well doing of every soul inhabiting the realm. His next qualification should be wisdom, to discern, and intelligence to communicate what he does know. The third, should be a total and absolute disconnection from all party, or prejudice views in legislation or administration; for it is morally impossible for an individual to attempt to act as his sense and reason would direct him, and at the same time unreservedly support every party measure. Give an individual the above-mentioned requisites, and he is then qualified to make, or administer the laws of a Republican government. In the first place his patriotism will continually stimulate him to make his laws for the general welfare of the whole community, without any local provisions, which might prejudice the interests of another portion of the country. He would present bills for legislative deliberation, not for the sake of attaching himself the name of the prime member of every legislative act, but for the especial benefit of the nation, though he as prime operator should remain unknown in the enactment. His votes would be given only when he had maturely investigated the subject, and had seen whatever of good or evil it might produce. His wisdom and intelligence should give him importance in the eyes of his country, and in the estimation of the legislative body with whom he may be connected; and would enable him to give full force to every argument that he might see proper to produce. Though he be free from party, and prejudice, he would never be without advocates to his cause; for the wise and patriotic so far as they justly agree with him, would assemble on his side, and it would be more than the party the stock to be as follows.[85]

Waddill spoke to Thomas Hickman about this and took Hickman's response that he was naïve gently and thought about it much. He was accustomed to high-held beliefs from the various debates and high-minded professors. Was Hickman giving him the view of the general populace? Perhaps Waddill would review this in his thoughts.

---

85. Ibid., February 23, 1838, vol. 1, pg. 58.

Admitted to the Bar

On the October 22, 1838, the Supreme Court of the State of Louisiana licensed John P. Waddill to practice law. He beat his goal by more than two months. On April 26, 1839, Waddill permanently settled in Marksville as a lawyer.

Day-to-Day Practice

Aged twenty-five, Waddill struggled at first, since no one knew him and he had been a lawyer for only six months. Thomas Hickman continued to help by offering business referrals. Edward King came in to visit Waddill and told him about a claim he had.

On June 21, 1839, in excitement, he filed the lawsuit for Edward King. For whatever reason, he signed his named "Waddill, attorney for Petitioner," while most attorneys signed their full names.[86] Waddill was nervous as this suit was complicated and for a large sum of money.

He filed his first suit in Avoyelles Parish on May 20, 1839, on behalf of John Lee for a debt owed by Daniel Clark.[87] The debt was for $100.00, and his judgment was for $95.00.

James Burroughs, of Hamburg, owed Thomas Hickman $1,800.00. He was a sign maker and executed a Bill of Exchange. Hickman purchased the bill. Now he wanted to file a petition to recover from him. Interested in the case, Waddill accepted, knowing that it would be his first large suit in Avoyelles Parish. He looked forward to it.

He obtained a default judgment on September 14, 1839, since Burroughs failed to file an answer. Waddill would receive $100.00 in fees collected. This was a huge fee for Waddill, or any lawyer for that matter.

William P. Hickman, one of the Hickman brothers, had formed a business partnership known as Hickman and Martin. The partnership also hired Waddill for collections on notes. On April 21, 1839, in what was one of his first legal transactions, Waddill gave Hickman and Martin a receipt for a note for collection in the amount of $74.00. This relationship continued as Waddill received notes from Hickman and Martin for collection to file against James Brewski on February 6, 1840; April 3, 1840, against Victor Gould; June 11, 1840, while he was a partner with Ralph Cushman; and March 2, 1841, to

---

86. See Records of Avoyelles Parish Clerk of Court Archives [hereafter cited as RAPCC], suit no. 1092, *Edward King v. James Burroughs*, filed June 21, 1839.

87. Ibid., suit no. 1085, *John Lee v. Daniel Clark*, filed May 20, 1839,.

file against J. Ransdell.[88] The last record of dealing with the Hickmans in the Hickman papers noted above was J.P. Waddill witnessing receipt of payment on a note on April 13, 1849, for A.G. Lewis's payment of the balance due.

Waddill was befriending many citizens of Marksville and Avoyelles. He took special note of those who were outstanding in one way or another. He was learning to be his own man but did not hesitate to learn from others. He wanted to meet François B. DeBellvue, a respected gentleman of the community. After DeBellvue's commission as colonel of the Twenty-Second Regiment, Louisiana Militia, Waddill went to him to introduce himself.[89] Colonel DeBellvue died only five years later, in 1844.

On June 29, 1839, Waddill filed a petition on behalf of *John Lee v. B.B. Simmes*.[90] Bennett Simmes would later run against Waddill for Senate in a hotly contested election. This petition was for $200.00, and Waddill's fee was $20.00. Interestingly, Ralph Cushman represented Simmes in this case. Later, he and Waddill would create the firm of Cushman and Waddill.

Marksville seemed to be on the move. The Red River was a major travel thoroughfare for steamboats. Some shipping occurred, and many passengers reached the river at Marksville. Captain Henry Shreve had done great work in clearing the massive log jam on the Red to make the river much more accessible for trade and travel. Shreve's design of snag boats and the famous *Heliopolis* cleared the Red River by 1839.[91] Marksville greatly benefited from this. It also coincided with John P. Waddill's new practice.

In 1839, François B. DeBellvue, a respected man of Marksville, was commissioned colonel of the Twenty-Second Regiment, Louisiana Militia. Later, Pierre Couvillion was commissioned brigadier-general of the Eleventh Brigade in 1841.[92]

88. See the Hickman-Bryan Papers, f. 191–210.

89. *Biographical and Historical Memoirs of Northwest Louisiana* (Nashville and Chicago: The Southern Publishing Company, 1890), 615.

90. RAPCC, suit no. 1095, *John Lee v. B. B. Simmes*, filed June 29, 1839.

91. "The Great Red River Raft," Red River Historian, http://www.redriverhistorian.com/greatraft.html.

92. *Biographical and Historical Memoirs*, 615. It was in September 1845 that General Pierre Couvillion called on the militia to be ready for service in Texas in preparation for war with Mexico.

This became John P. Waddill's world. The population of the United States in 1840 was a little over seventeen million. For every city dweller, more than five farmers lived in rural areas. Only five cities had over ninety thousand people living in them. This included New Orleans, Louisiana. The Irish potato famine in 1845 began emigration from Ireland to the United States. This continued in 1850. The 1850 census had the United States with over twenty-three million people. The Fugitive Slave Law, which Congress passed as part of the Compromise of 1850, dictated that all citizens must assist in the capture of runaway slaves. The law galvanized the North against slavery.[93]

In the 1840s and 1850s, public schools were rare. Wealthy men wore top hats, middle class men wore bowler hats, and lower class men wore cloth hats. Tight sleeves on ladies' dresses became fashionable in 1841. Reading newspapers, visiting family and friends, and going to church provided regular entertainment. Injured workers received no wages if they were hurt on the job. Women and children earned $1.25 per day or less. The effect of germs was not understood; therefore,, infection was not understood.[94]

During this time, John Waddill formed relationships with men and women that galvanized his future in the political arena. Day-to-day living as an attorney required one to be popular.

At this time, the members of the bar in Avoyelles Parish were Ralph Cushman, William Bishop, John P. Waddill, James S. Edelen, Henderson Taylor, and J. H. Cosden. Ralph Cushman was very well known and a good attorney. He represented a wide variety of clients. Judge Baillio served from 1840 until 1846, when the office of parish judge was abolished.[95] In the index of petitions of the Avoyelles Parish Clerk of Court, William Bishop and Henderson Taylor were very commonly listed as attorneys for plaintiffs and defendants.

In 1841, Alanson Pearce,[96] from Evergreen, paid a visit to John P. Waddill's spartan, candle-lit office for assistance. Pearce was a planter and managed Oakwold plantation. A petition had been filed against him for $362.00

---

93. "Timeline of United States history (1820–1859)," Wikipedia, https://en.wikipedia.org/wiki/Timeline_of_United_States_history_(1820–1859).

94. Ibid.

95. *Biographical and Historical Memoirs*, 612.

96. RAPCC, suit no. 1356, *Kirkman, Abernathy, and Harris v. Alanson Pearce*, March 8, 1841.

for a debt that he acknowledged he owed. He had told his creditors he would pay, but they seemed quick to file the petition.

After reviewing the petition, Waddill advised Pearce that the attorney for his creditors was Henderson Taylor, whom Waddill knew well. He felt he could avoid the appearance in court and defense. He would get it released for a total fee of only $15.00.

Thus began a relationship that would prove to be profitable in several ways to both Pearce and Waddill. They would become business, political, and, with their wives, personal friends. The lawsuit was settled immediately, along with a release and dismissal, by March 27, 1841, just nineteen days after the petition had been filed.

It is interesting that Alanson Pearce had come to Waddill for legal advice. In 1838, Pearce had retained Ralph Cushman in petition No. 1018. Cushman continued to represent Pearce even after Ralph Cushman and John P. Waddill formed a partnership.

The new firm Cushman and Waddill filed its first petition on January 23, 1840, on behalf of James Rey Jr.[97] Apparently, the partnership had just begun, because on the same day, John P. Waddill alone filed a petition on behalf of Aaron S. Nestor in suit number 1175.[98] On the same day, Ralph Cushman filed two separate suits under his name only. Apparently, these clients had retained each attorney prior to the partnership.

Just prior to this new business alliance, in January 1840, John P. Waddill began signing his full name rather than "Waddill, attorney for petitioner."[99] Waddill and Cushman had opposed each other several times in Waddill's first year of practice. For instance, Cushman had represented Garrett Edelen on a petition to enforce a note Waddill filed on June 27, 1839.[100] The Edelen family may have had a problem with Waddill since he also filed a petition against Zenon Bordelon Edelen on November 2, 1839.[101] In this case, F. B. DeBellvue represented Mr. Edelen.

The relationship with Asmaron Ledoux and his company continued with Waddill, even after his association with Ralph Cushman. Cushman and Wad-

---

97. Ibid., suit no. 1170, *James Rey Junior v. Victoria Bordelon*, January 23, 1840.

98. Ibid., suit no. 1175, *Aaron S. Nestor v. Gilbert E. Elmer*, January 23, 1840.

99. Ibid., suit no. 1164, *William Voorhies v. Patrick Glaze*, filed in January 1840.

100. Ibid., suit no. 1094, *John L. Lowery v. Garrett Edelen*, June 27, 1839.

101. Ibid., suit no. 1151, *A. Ledoux v. Zenon Bordelon Edelen*, November 2, 1839.

dill filed a petition for A. Ledoux and Co. against Zelian Mayeux on a past due account on April 4, 1840.[102]

It appears that the last time that Waddill and Cushman opposed each other was in Waddill's petition on behalf of Turner Woodruff on December 31, 1839. Apparently, the town of Marksville did little to celebrate New Year's Eve in 1839. This was on a past due note that John Morrow signed under the representation of Ralph Cushman. Waddill succeeded in obtaining a judgment for $220.57.[103]

Interestingly, the fact that Waddill served as an opposing attorney against Bennett B. Simmes did not affect the relationship Cushman had with Simmes. When Mechanic's Bank filed a petition against Simmes on a $600.00 note in March of 1841, the firm of Cushman and Waddill handled his defense.[104]

The very next day, Cushman and Waddill filed a petition on behalf of Samuel W. Henarie against Daniel Clark.[105] This was the second time Waddill sued Daniel Clark.

During their association, Cushman had a separate arrangement when Carrollton Bank was a party to a lawsuit. Apparently, the bank wanted Cushman, but did not Waddill's involvement. Cushman assured Waddill that it was not personal. This held true the entire time of the association. In Petition number 1344, filed in February 1841, Carrollton Bank filed a petition, and Cushman signed "Ralph Cushman." Waddill tried not to let it bother him.

William Bishop was one of the attorneys who began advertising when Marksville began to print newspapers. In a petition Cushman and Waddill filed on October 3, 1840, on behalf of John Sterling, Bishop filed an answer on behalf of James Rabalais.[106] Waddill noted that William Bishop was a worthy opponent. Waddill actually learned a bit from Bishop's style. Whenever he saw techniques of other attorneys, he observed it and filed it in the back of his mind to use in the future. Waddill was setting his style as an attorney. He wanted to be a gentleman, yet aggressive. He did not mind taking a controversial case.

102. Ibid., suit no. 1209, *A. Ledoux & Co. v. Zelian Mayeux*, April 4, 1840.

103. Ibid., suit no. 1160, *Turner Woodruff v. John Morrow*, December 31, 1839.

104. Ibid., suit no. 1368, *Mechanic's Bank v. Bennett B. Simmes*, March 10, 1841.

105. Ibid., suit no. 1371, *Samuel W. Henarie v. Daniel Clark*, March 11, 1841.

106. Ibid., suit no. 1290, *John Sterling v. James Rabalais*, October 3, 1840.

One such case was the petition Waddill filed on behalf of Mary Roberts against John Simmes.[107] Women's rights were not recognized very often in those days. This suit involved Mary Roberts's claim that her husband, John Simmes, whom she married in 1827, had "abandoned his affairs" and mismanaged her paraphernal money and property. It was a rare claim, one lawyers rarely argued successfully. Roberts renounced the community of acquets and gains all in an effort to avoid the debts her husband had created. The suit referred to her substantial separate assets that she brought into the marriage.

The appointed parish judge, Gervais Baillio, presided. The judge heard the case and shortly after ruled on the merits. He dismissed the claims of mismanagement in favor of John Simmes at plaintiff's cost. The decision weighed heavily on Waddill. The only redeeming outcome was that Mary Roberts was able to renounce the community. At least she would not lose more from Simmes's mismanagement. It was a bit late, however, as she had lost most of her assets.

The case of *Marguerite Marcotte v. Pierce Normand*, Marcotte's husband, brought another rare pleading. Waddill filed this petition, claiming that Mr. Normand neglected to educate his children despite being rich.[108] Samuel Briggs, a popular attorney at the time, represented Normand.

This lawsuit had an effect on Waddill. He had just married Julia Malvina Barlow on November 26, 1840.[109] Waddill knew that he wanted children and made an oath to himself to educate them, at whatever cost.

This marriage took place at the residence of the Widow Fountain Barlow on Red River in Avoyelles. Waddill's good friends Charles D. Brashear, William H. Duvall, and William Edwards served as witnesses to the marriage ceremony, which Judge Gervais Baillio—the same judge who ruled against Margueritte Marcottt—performed it. Waddill vowed to make sure his children would receive a proper education.

During this time, Waddill took note of Henderson Taylor, who quite often represented Union Bank in lawsuits. He was a true gentleman and an effective

---

107. Ibid., suit no. 1201, *Mary Roberts v. John Simmes*, March 6, 1840.

108. Ibid., suit no. 1318, *Margueritte Marcotte v. Pierce Normand*, December 11, 1840.

109. Ibid., Marriage license number 438. Included was a $200.00 bond required to be posted by John P. Waddill, to be paid upon any legal impediments to the marriage. John and Julia married on her seventeenth birthday, and Julia, as a minor, had to receive written permission from her father to allow the marriage.

attorney. Interestingly, in 1844, a great Whig meeting was held at Marksville, where the organization appointed a committee to attend the convention at New Orleans. Chosen to attend were Henderson Taylor, Samuel W. Briggs, Pierre Normand, and Charles D. Brashear.[110] Waddill was a loyal Democrat and would not stand for the principles of the Whig party. His election to the state Senate in 1847 after defeating the Whig candidate James E. Howard (and B.B. Simmes) gave Waddill new purpose. Howard, who came in second, had moved from Mississippi with his wife, Joyce Holmes, to Avoyelles Parish near Hamburg. Before his death in 1860, he became a prominent planter and popular figure in Avoyelles, serving as president of the police jury.[111]

---

110. *Biographical and Historical Memoirs*, 614.

111. Ibid., 637.

CHAPTER 18

THE COURTSHIP AND MARRIAGE OF JOHN P. WADDILL AND JULIA BARLOW

Marksville in August requires one to make sure that he or she dresses in a manner that allows the body to sweat without clothes sticking to the body. For attorneys, who generally dressed as gentlemen, this meant undergarments to absorb the sweat since most of them dressed with the suit coat, which caused more perspiration. August 15, 1840, was one of those sticky hot days that caused much sweat. The humidity was high, and as Waddill left his office at 11:00 a.m. on this Saturday to post two letters, he had put his suit coat on to walk the short distance to the postal office. James Rey Jr. had been appointed Postmaster in 1828[112] and had been opening on Saturdays for several years due to the tradition of most people in the parish coming to Marksville on Saturdays to do business with the local markets. Saturdays were very busy in the town of Marksville.

This particular day, carriages were coming into town. Waddill happened upon Mr. and Mrs. Barlow, who lived on Red River. As Waddill approached them, he said hello and tipped his hat. When he looked up, Mr. Barlow was assisting his young daughter from the carriage. As she stepped out of the carriage, he noted that she had a bonnet and a very pretty light blue dress. When she looked up to see who was saying hello, Waddill saw her face and stopped in his tracks. He knew the Barlows had a daughter, but he had not seen her in quite some time. As a gentleman in his late twenties, he was a bit embarrassed

---

112. The first post office in the parish was established in 1816 before the town of Marksville was officially named and was called Avoyelles Parish Post Office. It became Marksville Post Office in 1821. George Gorton was postmaster then. James Rey was postmaster till 1843 when A. Durand was appointed. The second post office was established in Borodino in 1837. Corinne L. Saucier, *History of Avoyelles Parish, Louisiana* (New Orleans: Pelican Publishing Company, 1943), 118.

that he was attracted to this young woman, who was only sixteen years old.

The courtship began with an invitation to the Barlow home on the Red River. Waddill's heart raced at the thought, and he decided he would cancel anything he had scheduled to go that evening.

After two months of courtship, Waddill asked Mr. Barlow for his daughter's hand in marriage. The response was simple: after she turned seventeen, he would consent to her marriage to Waddill and sign the documents necessary for relief from her minority. They would hold the ceremony on her birthday: November 26, 1840.

Waddill could not have been happier. He told his friends of his plans, and they eagerly awaited the day. Minority status required the father to give written consent and a bond that the husband must post. John P. Waddill posted a $200.00 matrimonial bond, and his father-in-law granted written permission with his signature, "E. Barlow."

Judge Gervais Baillio, who had just succeeded Judge Bordelon in July 1839, performed the ceremony. Life was looking up for John P. Waddill. He was a young lawyer with two years of experience and was now married to the beautiful Julia Barlow.

One of his witnesses was his friend and former sheriff, Charles D. Brashear, who served until 1839, then was replaced by F. Barlow. Another friend of Waddill, William Edwards, replaced Barlow as sheriff. Sheriff Edwards appointed Eugene Caillteau as his deputy.

CHAPTER 19

Physicians in Avoyelles

Julia Waddill was a sickly woman who did not have much stamina; but she always recovered from various illnesses, and eventually gave birth to five children. Waddill got to know Dr. Leroy K. Branch very well. Branch was born August 30, 1816, three years junior to John. He was born in Maury County, Tennessee. This county was immediately south of Williamson County, where Waddill was born. Dr. Branch had moved to Alabama as a young man, but he was educated in Greece County, Kentucky. He received his medical training at the Medical Institute of Louisville (now University of Louisville) from where he graduated in 1840. He moved to Avoyelles Parish in the Bordelonville area, shortly after graduating, and began his medical career. He also served on the Avoyelles Parish Police Jury. Waddill felt a common bond with Dr. Branch and would continue to seek him as his family doctor. [113]

Dr. G. E. Elmer lived near John P. Waddill in Marksville. He was born in 1813 and married Marie Angela Barbin on May 30, 1838.[114] They had five children, Edmond, Louisa, Guilbert, Edouard, and Mary. Dr. Elmer was known for innovative practices. The American *Journal of Medical Science* commended him for his treatment of dysentery with creosote.[115]

---

113. *Biographical and Historical Memoirs*, 621. Dr. Branch's oldest son, Dr. John S. Branch, was also educated at the University of Louisville and took some courses at Tulane. He also practiced in Avoyelles Parish, residing in Evergreen, Louisiana.

114. Dr. Gilbert Eli Elmer died in Marksville in 1883.

115. Dr. Elmer noted in the *New Orleans Medical News and Hospital Gazette* (January 1858), that epidemic dysentery of a very malignant and fatal type prevailed in a malarious section of Avoyelles Parish twelve years since, and resisted ordinary treatment. Creosote in doses of two drops in gum Arabic mucilage, given every two hours arrested the disease. See *The American Journal of the Medical Sciences*, vol. 35 (J.B. Lippincott, Company, 1858), 570.

Dr. Andrew R. Kilpatrick of Woodville, Mississippi, noted in the 1847 edition of the *New Orleans Medical and Surgical Journal*, volume 3, that he had treated a patient, Mr. J. S. of Avoyelles Parish, who labored under general dropsy in 1838. The man was thirty-six years old, and Kilpatrick pointed to the patient's heavy drinking, often to excess, and residing in the low marshy country, along with some hereditary taint, as the causes of this malady. The patient's mother had died from this same disease. He had had hydrothorax some years before that, according to Kilpatrick, "My friend Dr. G. E. Elmer, who was his medical attendant," had cured. He noted that Dr. Elmer had treated with general remedies till the dropsy was removed. Due to the patient's indulgence in ardent spirits, the disease recurred. Remedies used in the past were powerless. The patient became swollen to an immense size and moved only with the greatest pain. He could not lie down at all and "was obliged to sleep sitting in a large arm chair."

On July 2, 1839, Kilpatrick saw the patient in consultation with Dr. Elmer. They resorted to the operation of paracentesis abdominis. On July 3, Dr. Elmer tapped the patient in the presence of Dr. Kilpatrick and several neighbors. J. S. bore it well.

> The pulse varied but little, and he was sustained by the use of a brandy toddy while the fluid was passing off." After discovering that he could bear it, they drew off all of the water that they could, and upon measuring it, found they had eight gallons. It was of a pale straw color and coagulated when heated.

> The incision was dressed with an oiled rag and compress and the entire abdomen and thorax was firmly compressed by a roller. His extremities, head and neck were still distended with fluid, and when we visited him next day, we discovered that they were now shrunk, and the skin hung in huge loose folds and wrinkles, while the abdomen was again enlarged so much that he was obliged to relax the bandage to procure relief. I tapped him and drew two gallons more, making ten gallons in twenty-four hours. This is more than any on record, save one mentioned by Baron Stoerk, which yielded twelve gallons at one time.

> While conversing on the subject, Dr. Elmer proposed that as hydrocele could be cured by injecting a stimulating fluid into the sac, might not ascites be cured in the same way? The great size of the

peritoneal sac and the danger of inflammation in that membrane would seem to forbid a resort to this measure. But might not a part of the same fluid, after being exposed to the air, be injected back into the sac and produce the adhesive inflammation?

The patient at this time placed himself under my care. I found all remedies of no avail in the prevention of the disease. In two months the water had accumulated to the same amount and I drew off eight gallons. I continued to visit him and tap him whenever the fluid would distress him; sometimes twice a month, and sometimes once in six or seven weeks. He did not regard the tapping as much as some do a "cupping."

From the 3rd July, 1839, to the time of his death in October, 1842, he was tapped fifty-seven times and the fluid discharged amounted in all to about three hundred and sixty gallons, being more than eleven barrels. I regret very much that I was absent at the time of his death and there was, consequently, no post-mortem examination.[116]

Dr. Elmer was a caring and knowledgeable physician. The parish was fortunate to have him.

Doctor Benjamin Tasker Dulany

Dr. B. T. Dulany was born in Virginia in 1811. He eventually ended up in Avoyelles and set up a practice in Marksville. His father was also a doctor with the same name who died in 1833. His grandfather Benjamin T. Dulany (Sr.) knew George Washington personally. He married Josephine Coral Marsolla on December 27, 1842. They ended up raising four children.[117]

---

116. *The New Orleans Medical and Surgical Journal*, vol. 3 (L. Graham, 1847), 593–94.

117. It was noted in the *Times-Democrat*, a New Orleans newspaper, on July 9, 1898, that Dr. B. T Dulany died in Alexandria and was interred in the Rapides Cemetery in Pineville. The procession moved from the residence to the Catholic church and then the cemetery. Rev. L. Menard, priest of the church conducted the services. See pg. 10.

Doctor David M. Murdock

Dr. David M. Murdock was born in 1818 in South Carolina. He married Sara Jane Murdock, age nineteen, on October 23, 1843. They moved to Marksville, where he set up his medical practice. By 1855, they had three children, and his wife was twenty-four years old. Sara Jane was born in Wilkenson County, Mississippi.[118]

Doctor E. L. Briggs

Dr. E. L. Briggs was a planter and a physician who had land on Bayou des Glaises in the prairie. He had over forty slaves in the 1840 slave census. In August 1835, he had purchased 170 acres in Section 12, Township 2 North – Range 3 East. It was acquired via patent through the land office in Opelousas. The following year, in February 1836, he purchased 201 acres located in Section 1, Township 2 North – Range 3 East. He would drown in May 1846 after celebrating the recruitment of volunteers in Avoyelles Parish for the war against Mexico. He had too much to drink and tried to go home at night in an inebriated state.[119]

Doctor Joseph Moncla

Dr. Joseph Moncla came to Avoyelles about 1837. He was the nephew of Jean-Baptiste Moncla, who came to Avoyelles from Moncla, France, sometime before 1810. The first Jean-Baptiste died in 1818, leaving no progeny. His nephew Dr. Moncla was born in 1806. He came to Avoyelles about twenty years after his uncle died. Dr. Joseph Moncla died in 1883.[120]

---

118. *The Avoyelles Pelican* 20, no. 49 (April 19, 1862) noted that Dr. D. M. Murdock was appointed assistant surgeon and Dr. L. K Branch as the chief surgeon of the Avoyelles Regiment of the Louisiana Militia. They had the authority to exempt any male from military service. The notice was on page 1 and dated March 1862. By 1860, Dr. Murdock was listed on the 1860 census as having five children. By 1870, he moved to Desota Parish and had eight children.

119. *The Times Picayune*, June 3, 1846, pg. 2, noted his drowning death May 23, 1846.

120. "Origins of Some Early Family Names in Avoyelles," http://www.avoyelles.com/.

Doctor Donat MacEnery

One of Waddill's closest friends and confidantes was Dr. Donat MacEnery, whose name spelling was many times listed as "McEnery" as his younger brother Samuel Douglas spelled it. Samuel Douglas McEnery became governor of Louisiana in 1881 and was re-elected to a full term to remain governor until 1888. He later became a U.S. senator from 1896–1910 for the State of Louisiana.[121] Dr. McEnery was elected as alderman in 1852, at the same that James McEnery, another brother, was elected mayor of Marksville.[122] James McEnery was appointed postmaster in 1848 and was again elected mayor of Marksville in 1858.[123] Dr. MacEnery spelled his name with the "Mac" as his signature shows on the original will of Samuel Bass. He was married to Lucetta MacEnery and died in 1855, shortly after Waddill. Born in 1811 in Ireland, he was a heavy drinker (Waddill believed that he drank too much) who enjoyed life. He was also a good doctor who cared for the Waddill family on a regular basis.

---

121. "Samuel D. McEnery," Wikipedia, https://en.wikipedia.org/wiki/Samuel_D._McEnery.

122. *Biographical and Historical Memoirs*, 616.

123. Ibid., 617.

CHAPTER 20

Spring Creek Academy

Waddill found out pretty quickly that just because a person came from a family with wealth and good reputation did not necessarily make all of their children reputable. Through his career, Waddill represented families of Pearces and members of the Robert and Wright families. Some of these families had property in the Bayou Boeuf region in Rapides and Avoyelles. They were well respected and had been successful planters.

Joseph B. Robert was somewhat of a rebellious family member who would set off and disappear on occasion. He was born in 1799 and had married Mary A. Griffin Robert and had two children, Sarah Evolina Robert and Franklin Agrippa Robert. Sarah had a similar reputation as her father. Some described her as a "muchly married" lady.[124] Her first husband, Joseph Addison Cocke, was killed at Marksville.[125]

---

124. George Mason Graham Stafford, *Three Pioneer Rapides Families –A Genealogy* (Baton Rouge, La.: Claitor's Publishing Division, 1968), 97.

125. The killing of Joseph Addison Cocke was noted in an 1862 Marksville Newspaper, *The Avoyelles Pelican*, February 22, 1862, pg. 1. "Homicide—It is too often our painful duty to record bloody scenes that take place in our little village, and today we are adding a very melancholy one to the list already too long. On Saturday last, at about one o'clock in the evening, Joseph A Cocke, a well known planter of Bayou Jack, formerly of Red River in this Parish, and Augustin Deshautelle, a member of the Marksville District Militia Company, met in front of Paul Michel's Coffee House. They exchanged but a few harsh words when at a distance of about four paces they instantly resorted to their weapons. According to the general version of the affair, Cocke fired twice with his revolver, and Desheautelle replied by firing once with his double barreled gun, loaded with shot lodging all the deathly contents in the right breast of C., who one minute afterwards fell a corpse upon the coffee house's gallery. Desheautelle delivered himself up to the authorities, and on Tuesday last, Honorable E. N. Cullom after hearing the depositions of numerous witnesses

The son, Franklin Agrippa Robert, was born in Cheneyville in 1824 and later moved to Avoyelles Parish. He was educated at Spring Creek Academy in 1841. A well-respected educational institution in Rapides Parish, it was located in the beautiful pine hills southwest of Cheneyville, on Hurricane Creek, a tributary of Spring Creek.[126] The location provided higher and cooler pine-hills that were nice in the summer months.[127]

The school hired highly qualified teachers. One of them was Michael Ryan, a well-educated Irishman who came to the United States to teach the classics. He was a professor in ancient languages.[128] Ryan studied law and obtained his license after passing the bar. He was a respected attorney who later became a state senator. He and Waddill had political differences. Later, Ryan became a judge in Rapides Parish.

Another prominent professor, Dr. Jesse D. Wright, was one of the founders of Spring Creek Academy. He was a physician and a planter on Bayou Boeuf.[129] He graduated from Yale. He recruited highly respected teachers to help educate the youth.

On March 7, 1849, Waddill, representing the academy's administrator, J. D. Wright, obtained a judgment against Joseph B. Robert for a part of the debt sued on from several notes. One of them was dismissed.

In April 1849, Daniel R. Elred and Franklin A. Robert employed Waddill to have a curator ad hoc appointed to Joseph B. Robert, an absentee, and also to have an execution issued against him in their favor for which Waddill would receive fifty dollars. They also assumed to pay Waddill twenty-five dollars, which J. B. Robert owed Waddill as a fee in the case of *J. D. Wright administration vs. J. B. Robert*. Alanson G. Pearce also employed Waddill to have a tutor appointed to Sarah Evolina Robert, the minor daughter, to replace her tutor J. B. Robert, for which Waddill charged him twenty-five dollars. He filed the petition for tutorship on April 17, 1849. Sarah Evolina Robert, who lived with Pearce, was born in 1835.

---

of the fatal encounter, admitted Desheautelle to furnish bail in the sum of $2,500 for his appearance at the next Criminal Court."

126. Ibid., pg. 98.

127. The higher area was less likely to spread malaria from mosquitoes.

128. *The Avoyelles Pelican*, February 22, 1862, pg. 98.

129. Ibid., pg. 98.

Daniel R. Eldred became tutor and A. G. Pearce under-tutor. Eldred and Pearce were uncles of Sarah. Later, on November 30, 1849, Daniel R. Eldred wanted a partition of plantation on Bayou Clair, consisting of about two hundred acres, in the Parish of Avoyelles between himself and Sarah E. Robert, minor daughter of Joseph B. Robert and Mary A. Griffin. The nearest relatives—Septhinus M. Perkins, Edwin Epps, William Pearce, Wilson C. Robert, and Franklin Agrippa Robert, Sarah's older brother—held a family meeting. William F. Griffin, James B. Griffin, and William Clopton, although uncles on the maternal side, lived over thirty miles from the residence of the minor and were by law excused.

CHAPTER 21

The Reality of the Slave Trade

John P. Waddill purchased his first slave on February 8, 1842. He purchased this slave from William Lynch, as recorded in Book P page 457 of the records of Avoyelles Parish. Waddill had purchase eighty arpents[130] of land from William Edwards on May 6, 1841, as shows the sale of record number 5189 in Book P page 140 of the records of Avoyelles Parish.

As time went on and Waddill increased his holdings of property, much of it in woodland that needed to be cleared for planting, he thought that he might require more unfree workers. He felt ambivalent toward slavery. He saw it as a necessity and always promised to take care of his slaves. He purchased two more from the Estate of François DeBellevue in December of 1844 in record number 6143 recorded in Book R page 238.

Waddill purchased 480 acres from James Rey Jr. on Bayou du Lac in 1845, as recorded in record number 6319 in book S page 86 of the records of Avoyelles Parish. James Rey Jr. had been appointed postmaster in 1844[131] and had little use for the property. By the time Waddill purchased two tracts of forty arpents apiece in 1846 from the Estate of Elenzer G. Paxton in March 1846 via record number 6370 recorded in Book S page 173, he had quite a large holding of land. Unlike the stereotypical large plantations of the South, where property was contiguous and cleared, much of Waddill's nearly 540 acres was spread out and unimproved, with only portions of the property capable of growing crops.

With the labor of his slaves, Waddill continued to improve his property

---

130. An arpent was a measurement of length and, in some cases, area. It was based on the French tradition of about 180 feet in length. If a tract was described as a square arpent, that meant 180 feet by 180 feet. An arpent was smaller than an acre.

131. *Biographical and Historical Memoirs,* 617.

holdings; eventually, he owned nearly 1,600 acres in ten different areas of Avoyelles Parish. A considerable amount of acreage for the time, it was in different areas and not all improved. This made it difficult for Waddill to manage. He had to partner with various associates to plant and cultivate the crops.

CHAPTER 22

Joseph Barton Elam
Born June 12, 1821

Joseph Barton Elam was a cousin of John P. Waddill. His father, William Jefferson Elam, was a teacher and had a strong influence on Waddill. William Elam asked if he could send Joseph to begin reading law with him, in an effort to train him. Eventually, he proved successful in doing that.

Joseph was born in 1821 in Arkansas near San Augustine and present-day Hope, Hempstead County. William Elam moved to East Texas then to Fort Jesup in western Louisiana, Sabine Parish, in 1823. His brother, John Waddill Elam, named after John P. Waddill, was born at Fort Jesup in 1833. William and John P. Waddill remained close, visiting each other often over the years. Even though Waddill had practiced for only five years, he had developed a good reputation, and William knew that Waddill would help Joseph in his private study of the law. Elam also knew that Waddill had studied the law practically his entire adult life.

Joseph Elam moved to Marksville and lived with Waddill during the eight-month period that it took the understudy to learn the law and pass the bar. Elam received admittance to the bar to practice law in Louisiana in 1843. He began his practice in Alexandria and moved back to Sabine Parish toward the end of 1844. Joseph Barton Elam also helped to establish the court in Desoto Parish. He held his first court appearance in that parish on August 7, 1843. Although Elam started in Rapides Parish, he formed a partnership with Waddill in 1844 and worked in Marksville nearly the entire year.

Together, Waddill and Elam handled a case against Lewis Gorton on behalf of Rowland Robinson in suit number 1959, filed on March 30, 1844, in Avoyelles Parish. Rowland obtained a money judgment for $80.00 on April 3, 1844. They also filed a lawsuit on behalf of *A. Montanye v. William F. Griffin* on April 2, 1844, on a $1,520 promissory note. It might have made him feel a bit strange, but Waddill got used to filing against acquaintances and even friends.

While teaching and training Elam, Waddill was retained to represent Amanda Griffin against her husband, James E. Crawford, for mismanagement of her separate and parafernal estate. The suit took two years as it was filed in November 1842 in suit number 1658 and not finished until Waddill received a judgment in her favor on November 14, 1844. The judgment declared that Amanda Griffin would be separate in property within the marriage, allowing her to manage her own property. This was the last case Waddill and Elam handled as partners.

Elam aspired to be a politician. The law served as a tool for him to reach political goals. He was elected to the Sabine Parish police jury in 1845 and served as president of that body in 1846 and into 1847. He became district attorney in 1847. He later became the first mayor of Mansfield, after he prepared the articles of incorporation. He was elected to a second term in 1856.

Elam later served in the Louisiana legislature as a house member during the Civil War. From 1862–1864, he served as Speaker of the House. His brother, John Waddill Elam, was elected sheriff of Sabine Parish. The last step on the ladder of the political career of Joseph Elam was to serve in the U.S. Congress for two terms beginning in 1876.[132] He was widowed twice and had eight children with his third wife.

Not all went well in Marksville while he studied the law with Waddill. Although a quick learner, Elam seemed more passionate about politics than the practice. Waddill viewed the practice of law as primary, with politics a secondary interest. It seemed that Elam was the polar opposite. They agreed on most issues, as both were Democrats, though Waddill felt that Elam held his positions more for convenience rather than conviction.

Overall, Waddill enjoyed the time teaching his cousin and was excited for him to begin his nascent career. Eventually, Elam became a respected attorney known for his political acumen.

---

132. "Joseph Barton Elam," Wikipedia, https://en.wikipedia.org/wiki/Joseph_Barton_Elam

CHAPTER 23

Waddill Grows in Popularity

By 1843, John P. Waddill felt the effects of a successful practice. On June 5, he was appointed as the attorney for the police jury of Avoyelles. The *Expositor* newspaper noted the appointment in its story that listed the nine jurors elected to the police jury. Waddill's competition for the job was the well-respected William Bishop.

At this meeting, the police jury began to develop routes to improve bringing crops to market. William Pearce and A. G. Pearce of Oakwold were included in a group of men—namely Francis Cullom, George Keller, Louis Bonnett, and Baptiste Gaspard—appointed as commissioners to trace and lay out a public road, commencing from Gaspard and Bonnett's plantation, on Bayou Clair, and running so as to intersect the public road at the nearest and most convenient point, without prejudice to individuals. They were to make their report at the next regular session of the body.

This work brought Waddill closer to Alanson Pearce, who did much of the work. The two were nearly the same age and coming into their own in their respective lives.

A separate committee, including B. B. Simmes, Valerien Gremillion, pére, and August Moreau, laid out and traced a public road across the "cut-off" leading from Young Callihan's land to Dominique Coco's land, on Bayou des Glaises. This was all recorded in the minutes of that first police jury meeting.

The jury then appointed Simmes, John E. Frith, Monroe Havard, Thomas J. Spurlock, and Joseph W. Bell as commissioners to lay out a road from Dr. D. T. Orr's plantation, across the "Bend" to Samuel Jones's, and report back at the next meeting. Avoyelles Parish's transportation network would be progressing forward.

Another issue the jury brought up is to this day a touchy subject for citizens of Avoyelles. It dealt with driving deer with hounds to hunt them. In the September 1842 police jury meeting, the body voted to make it unlawful to drive deer with hounds or other dogs, on the north side of Red River, during high water. The Red River flooded frequently, and the police jury thought it was protecting the deer population. The north side of the river, which would be known as Ward One later, became a part of the parish with a solidly Anglo population, also called *cou rouge,* or rednecks, by their French neighbors. The area of Point Maigre also lay north of the river. The French part of the Parish thus also referred to those living north of the river derisively as "Pointe Megs."

In nearly every issue of the Marksville newspaper, the following lawyers advertised, something John P. Waddill did from the first newspaper ever published in town, on December 14, 1843, *The Expositor*: Edelen & Briggs (James and Samuel), Ralph Cushman, William Bishop, and Waddill. Cushman's ad had the most text. He advertised that he also worked in the surrounding parish for his practice, the United States District Court in Opelousas, and the Supreme Court in Alexandria.

Interestingly, according to the May 14, 1843, edition, F. B. DeBellevue, who had a good reputation, was being sued by the United States. A writ of *fieri facias* was issued to sell his land in the town of Marksville, which included his home and one "negro woman slave, named Roade, aged about fifty years." Waddill would eventually handle the administration of DeBellevue's Estate.

Incorporation of Marksville

The Villager or "*Le Villagois*" replaced it. Like its predecessor, it published in both French and English.

Le Villagois advertised that due to the act of the 1843 Legislature authorizing the "incorporation of the Town of Marksville, in the Parish of Avoyelles," an election would be called in the one square mile of the intended town on October 9, 1843. The advertisement started in the newspaper on September 21, 1843. Waddill decided that he would enter politics and run for one of the five seats as alderman. There would also be a mayor elected.

The election was postponed until October 20, 1843, and C. D. Brashear, a friend of Waddill, became the first mayor of Marksville. The five alderman elected were Waddill, William H. Duvall, James Rey Jr., Fielding Edwards, and G. A. Stevens. Inspired by this run, Waddill decided that he enjoyed electioneering and would continue to think about running for other positions.

The December 9, 1843, edition of *Le Villagois* noted a judgment entered on November 21, 1843, (shortly after election) in the suit of *Eliza Caroline Pearce Brashear v. Charles Duval Brashear* for $5,996.00 and a judgment of Separation of Property. (Apparently politics did not sit well with the couple.) They had married on February 5, 1829, and remained so for nearly fifteen years. Four of their ten children were born after this separation of property, including one of them on December 2, 1843.

Daniel T. Orr, esq. had been the state assemblyman for Avoyelles Parish when he died suddenly in October 1843. The November 4, 1843, edition of *The Villager* included the following:

> Died on Tuesday the 24th instant, at his plantation on the Bayou des Glaises, in this Parish after lingering illness, DR. DANIEL T. ORR, aged forty-eight years. His blameless life and the excellence of his character had won for him the esteem and affection of all who knew him. And the grief of friends, and tears of orphans deprived alas, too soon of doting parents can bear witness to the impendable [*sic*] loss which society and his family now sustained.
>
> The position which he occupied and the universal grief manifested at the announcement of his death regain at out hands men lengthened notice, which our limited space compels us to postpone for another number.

A special election was set for replacing him on December 12 and 13. The newspaper advertised the polling places as follows:

- In Point Maigre at the house of Laudrent Dupuy;
- On Bayou des Glaises at the store of Joseph Debouche;
- On Bayou Boeuf at the store of Ricord Co. in Holmesville; on Bayou Rouge at the house of Charles Cappell; and in Bayou Rouge Prairie at the house of John Botts.

In addition, the courthouse in Marksville would remain open for voting. The polls were open from 10 a.m. till 4 p.m. each day.

Lewis Gorton, who operated Gorton's Landing, had lived in Avoyelles Parish for twenty years and was a popular man in the Marksville area. He announced in the newspaper that he would run for the position. He placed an ad in the paper and seemed passionate as a candidate. The announcement ran on December 9, 1843:

> I have been induced, tho' the purest motives, and feeling a deep interest in the welfare of the Parish, to have my name inserted in the columns of the *Villager*, as a candidate for the State Legislature, to fill

the vacancy occasioned by the death of our lamented fellow citizen, Dr. D.T. Orr. I have not suffered my name to go out among you as a tool for others—I am no flea, to fly the tract—neither am I of the crab race, to back out. I belong to no clique or clan or party, calculated to deceive the good citizens of Avoyelles. No, fellow citizens, I am always ready and willing to stand by you, for my interest are identified with yours, and if I belonged to any such clique or club, that when your minds had been made up and you had come to the box to deposit your votes, I am not there, I have resigned in favor of some other person that you have never thought of. No—far be it from the independent feelings, which I hope I possess, to stoop to any thing so degrading; and if I had not principles, which soared above such contemptible acts, I think the good voters of the Parish of Avoyelles might well say, you are unworthy of our confidence.

Fellow citizens, I have no doubt there are more talented men, perhaps, you might select for your consideration—but for energy, industry and a warm feeling for the interests of the Parish, I will not admit of any.

I have resided in your Parish for the last twenty years; have married, and raised a family here, have been engaged in some public capacity, almost ever since I came to the country, as the records of our Courts show, and if I have not succeeded in gaining your confidence, in this time, I fear I never can. And as for my principles on the subject of Banking, I am in favor of a Bank on good, sound, solvent principles, but am opposed to a spurious paper money currency.

I am aware that when a man suffers his name to come before the public as a candidate for any office, he puts himself up as a target to be shot at, by every person disposed to take a pop and let them pop. I think that I am beyond their wounding me mortally with their shots; I only ask the free and voluntary voice of the people, through the ballot-box, to be taken without any interfering, and if I get but one vote, I will have the satisfaction of getting that honorably.

Gentleman, I remain your obedient and humble servant.

Lewis Gorton
Avoyelles, Dec. 8th, 1843[133]

---

133. *The Villager*, vol. 1, no. 12, December 9, 1843, pg. 2.

Another candidate, Evariste Rabalais had, to correct some rumors, apparently. He printed the following in the same edition of the newspaper:

> It is not my wish to come before the public by written communications, yet circumstances render a word necessary. It has been circulated by the enemies of Democracy that I intended, previous to my nomination, to be the Whig candidate, and that finding the Democrats strongest I turned to them; this I deny in toto—Should any of my friends want proof, they can have them by calling on me.
>
> E. Rabalais Avoyelles, December 8, 1843.

The next week, the paper printed the outcome. The election for the State Representative to replace Dr. Orr was held on the December 11, 12, and 13 of 1843. Evariste Rabalais, Democrat, won by a large majority.[134]

The Villager, December 23, 1843

The editors of the paper complained about the mail and its delivery of papers to them, which prevented timely distribution of their newspapers.

> The Mail from Alexandria, due last Monday, failed, which has left us entirely without news. Can any person inform us why the post office that was to be established at Gorton's Landing, is not in operation? We ask the question, because we would receive our papers a week sooner through that office than we now do for according to the present mail arrangement all letters and papers from below (New Orleans, Baton Rouge, etc.) have to pass thro' the Alexandria post office, which, by the mail route, is some seventy or eighty miles above this place, before they reach here.

This was a legitimate complaint. In Marksville, Gorton's Landing was south of Alexandria on the Red River. The editors wanted the mail to stop in Marksville and not have it go north to Alexandria, then south by land.

That same edition of *The Villager* noted that the Democratic party of Avoyelles had gathered for the 1844 presidential primary, which would meet in New Orleans with other parish delegates on January 8, 1844. Zenon

---

134. Ibid., vol. 1, no. 13, December 16, 1843.

Lemoine was called to the chair at the courthouse meeting. Waddill was appointed secretary, and Ralph Cushman was asked to make "a few but forcible remarks."[135] General Pierre Couvillion, E. Rabalais, John H. Harmanson, and F. Ricord were appointed as delegates to the New Orleans convention. The General Convention would be held in Baltimore, Maryland, on May 4, 1844. They adopted the resolution for John C. Calhoun to receive the nomination as the first, last, and only choice for president. They also voted against the establishment of the bank, declaring it unconstitutional, and ultimately destructive of the liberties of the people.

A week later, *The Villager* editors complained again about the failure of the mail:

> The mail due on Monday last again failed. We have not received a mail from Alexandria or Opelousas for the last three weeks, which has been, in part, owing to the high water. The contractor might, we understand, with very little expense continue the mail regularly to this place, by keeping a horse on this side of Bayou des Glaises swamp and bringing the mail across in a boat.[136]

In the same edition and on the same page, *The Villager* publicly thanked Lewis Gorton, of Gorton's Landing on the Red River, for a New Orleans *Picayune* that arrived dated December 19, 1843. Waddill was also pleased as a subscriber to receive any newspaper from another city within ten days of its publication.

High water affected mail delivery. In 1840, there was flooding. Avoyelles Parish had the Atchafalaya on its eastern boundary, which was fed by the Red River and the Mississippi River. The Red River dissected the northern portion of Avoyelles. If both rivers were high, the backwaters would flood huge portions of the northern and northeastern portions of the parish, greatly damaging thousands of acres of crops.

The newspaper noted that the Red River was higher than it had been in 1840. The banks overflowed in December 1843. "The water from the Red River was running through the prairie, between Red River and Hydropolis. The planters on the River and Bayous have been greatly damaged."[137]

---

135. Ibid., vol. 1, no 14, December 23, 1843.

136. Ibid., vol. 1, no. 15, December 30, 1843, pg. 2.

137. Ibid, pg. 2.

People called it the "prairie," this northeastern part of the parish, which the Red River bounded to the north, and bayous and swamps and the Atchafalya to the east.

CHAPTER 24

NEWS FROM *THE VILLAGER*
SEPTEMBER 23, 1843

Atrocious Murder —

One of the most painful duties we ever performed is now before us—in recording the melancholy and tragical murder in this county on the 11th inst., of Mrs. Mary Ann Chapman, wife of Mr. Joseph Chapman, and daughter of the late Col. Barnard Johnson. The circumstances attending this most unfortunate and heart rending occurrence, are thus detailed to us by a friend: During her husband's absence from home, she was by some means enticed by the negroes into a corn field about 150 or 200 yards from the house, and there murdered by one of them, by means of a rope thrown over her neck in a running noose. After being thus strangled, she was carried to the opposite side of the field, dragged over the fence, so violently as to leave some of her hair torn out upon the rails; and thence taken some 60 yards further into a thicket, and the body then concealed under the bark and rotten pieces of an old log. This occurred, it is supposed, between 10 and 11 o'clock in the morning. Mr. Chapman came home about usual dinnertime, and inquiring for Mrs. Chapman, was told that she had gone to visit some of the neighbors. He consequently experienced but little uneasiness about her absence, though thinking it a little strange, at the same time, that she should ride an animal of which she had usually been afraid. He awaited her return until dark, when, she not appearing he ordered his horse and thought he would ride over to Mrs. Newman's, her aunt, whom he had heard her say she intended visiting. Not finding her there or at any of the neighbor's houses where he went, he became alarmed, suspecting that all was not right. Procuring the assistance of some neighbors, he arrested three of his Negroes; search was made that night, and on the following day, when she was found in the situation above stated. The horse he was told she had rode was also found in a thicket about a half a mile from the house, with its brains knocked out by a large piece of timber.

Mrs. Chapman was in the 25 year of her age, and has left a husband, two brothers and three small children, the youngest, infant of 6 months to mourn her loss. In this irreparable loss a wide breach has been made in the bosom of her friends and relatives, which time cannot efface, or memory forget.

Much excitement, we understand, was produced by the circumstances and at a meeting of some 400 or 500 citizens the question was submitted whether the Negroes should be burnt upon the spot of the murder. Much to their credit, however, it was agreed that the law should be permitted to take its course, and the Negroes were accordingly committed to jail on Tuesday last. The principal in the tragedy says that he killed his former master in another State, and was run off to this state. — Selma(Ala.) Free Press.

This caused consternation to many citizens in Avoyelles, even though it occurred near Selma, Alabama. Many citizens showed special interest to this cast. When murders such as this occurred, most slaves were hung.[138]

Constitutional Convention Election, 1844

The State of Louisiana called for a constitutional convention to begin in 1845 in New Orleans. For Avoyelles Parish, Willis B. Prescott[139] and Pierre Couvillion were elected to serve. The convention began January 14, 1845.[140]

---

138. "Slavery in the United States–Slave Crimes," https://eh.net/encyclopedia/slavery-in-the-united-states/.

139. Willis B. Prescott died in the Spring of 1857.

140. "Proceedings and Debates of the Convention of Louisiana: Which Assembled at the City of New Orleans January 14, 1844," [i. E. 1845] Besancon, Ferguson & Company, printers to the Convention, 1845.

The outcome of this convention was not an improvement in Waddill's eyes. He actually thought about running as a delegate, but his fairly new practice and service as councilman on the Marksville Council was cause enough not to run. His wife of four years would not have been very happy either. Waddill knew he would be running for re-election to the town council at the end of 1845, so he decided not to run as a delegate.

Waddill thought that if the opportunity would arise in the future, he would serve in a constitutional convention. He believed that he could offer much wisdom as an attorney who saw many flaws in the Louisiana Constitution.

In December 1845, Waddill ran again for the position of alderman of Marksville. The new mayor to take office for 1846 through 1847 was A. C. Armstrong. Waddill returned to the council, where he sat as an alderman with Aristide Barbin, F. Ricord, Ed Generes, and J. H. Barbin.

Adophe Lafargue Moves to Avoyelles Parish, 1845

John P. Waddill believed that education of the youth of the parish was paramount. He never stopped educating himself. He subscribed to many quarterlies and newspapers and was always reading. He was very excited to hear about Adolphe Lafargue being appointed parish superintendent in 1851. He was paid $300 per year and had a solid background. Lafargue came to Avoyelles in 1845; he had taught at Natchitoches and at Jefferson College previous to his move. He was a native of France and taught at Cottonport and Marksville, and he took over *The Villager*.[141]

Waddill had heard of Lafargue when he began teaching in Marksville. He made a point of meeting him when he was appointed superintendent in 1851. Unfortunately, the legislature dissolved the position of superintendent and abolished the next year under the premise that the superintendent received too much in funds for education.[142]

Before the elimination of the position, Waddill visited Lafargue at his home. Little did Waddill know that Lafargue would eventually make Bell Tavern his home. C. D. Brashear built the Tavern in 1850. T. B. Tiller con-

---

141. The first newspaper in Avoyelles was *The Expositer*, which was first published December 14, 1842. John P. Waddill advertised as an attorney in this paper. It lasted for only nine months, and *The Villager* began in August 1843. A copy of the first newspaper hangs on the wall of this author's office.

142. Saucier, *History of Avoyelles Parish*, 71.

ducted it. Brashear, Waddill's friend stood in his wedding in 1840. In 1851, Adolphe Lafargue had not yet moved into this building.[143]

Legal Work

One of Waddill's more interesting legal cases was the petition he filed on behalf of *Rose Rabalais v. François Decuir* in suit number 2143 on November 1, 1845. The allegations were that Decuir used separate funds of his wife and that he mismanaged them. Waddill obtained a separation of property judgment and a money award of $884.06 due to Decuir's mismanagement.

In one of Waddill's boldest moves, he filed a suit on behalf of the illiterate Pierre Normand, as his mark "X" on the legal document demonstrates. He filed this suit personally against Judge Gervais Baillio. This was the same judge who performed the wedding ceremony for John P. Waddill and Julia.

The petition was in suit number 1884 and originally filed in November 1843. The allegations were that Judge Baillio took advantage of Pierre Normand on March 19, 1843, March 15, 1842, and March 16, 1842. Charges were imposed by the Judge for payment to Baillio "as charges on fees for official service by him (Baillio)." Waddill alleged that these payments were "illegal being for other higher and gratified than those allowed by law." Mr. Pierre Normand was granted a judgment for $7.00 as Judge H. Boyce rendered on April 29, 1845.

Friendship and acquaintance played little role in determining what cases lawyers accepted to handle. In suit number 1930, which Ralph Cushman filed in early 1844 on behalf of New Orleans & Carrollton R. R. and Carrollton Bank filed against E. L. Briggs, John P. Waddill, and Nelson Durand. The defendants had co-signed a note for $1,500.00 that Daniel T. Orr, who died in November 1843, executed. Judgment was rendered in favor of the plaintiffs.

During the time that J. B. Elam worked with Waddill, they filed a joint suit on March 30, 1844. Suit number 1962 was on behalf of Joel Hadspeth against Lewis Gorton and Samuel W. Hadspetth for default on the sale of

---

143. Adolph Lafargue continued to lead Avoyelles Parish in education. He later began and founded Marksville High School in 1856. Adolph was born in 1818 and died in 1869. His son A. D. Lafargue held the position of parish superintendent and sponsored the first Avoyelles Parish institute, held in April 1897. Speakers were E. L. Stephens and E. L. Hines of the State Normal School in Natchitoches, La. A. D. Lafargue eventually married Waddill's daughter Mary Florence Waddill, and later became State Superintendent of Education. Ibid., 79.

slaves. It was alleged that the defendants were in default of payment on the sale that occurred on January 11, 1841, totaling $1,500.00. Judge Henry Boyce granted the plaintiffs judgment in their favor.

On April 2, 1843, in suit number 2037, New Orleans & Carrollton Rail Road Co. sued C. D. Brashear, Fielding Edwards, and J. P. Waddill. The defendants confessed judgment for $380.00 on April 30, 1845.

In suit number 2030, Auguste Voinche sued Pam Boifsielle and Gaudoir & Boifsielle. Waddill represented Pam Boifsielle. Judgment was rendered for $80.00 against the defendants.

The firm of Labadie and Jacqueline was a hardware store located at 59 Old Levee Street, New Orleans, Louisiana. This store was founded in the 1820s by John Labadie, then later taken over by Jean Labadie and his partner, Pierre Jacquelin. They operated as Labadie and Jacquelin.[144] Waddill served as their local attorney in Avoyelles. He handled several lawsuits for them for debts that customers left unpaid. Labadie and Jacquelin were of French descent and advertised frequently in the *Picayune*. In the March 15, 1837, *Picayune* on page four, the firm advertised fifteen boxes of brass locks from Marseilles with two keys each, especially made for armoirs. The partnership terminated as of April 3, 1847. On the front page of its April 18, 1847, edition the *Picayune* advertised the dissolution of the partnership between Labadie and Jacquelin. L. Sperier Hardware purchased their entire stock. The new firm remained at the same location.

---

144. Lot 1406: Rare Labadie and Jacquelin, New Orleans, New Orleans Auction Galleries, May 23, 2010, http://www.invaluable.com/auction-lot/rare-labadie-and-jacquelin,-new-orleans,-1406-c-6c7fd90982; See also 1842 City Directory - Orleans Parish, LA, available at http://files.usgwarchives.net/la/orleans/history/directory/1842cdgl.txt.

CHAPTER 25

THE MEXICAN WAR, 1846

Working as an alderman took its toll on Waddill's practice. He did not have as much time to balance his family, his legal career, and his farming. Many people in the community expected him to be available at their beck and call since he was one of their representatives to government. Marksville's charter was not really complicated, but organizing the growing town was not an easy task. Many traveled to Marksville because of its location, and new people were moving to the area to seek their fortune in the fertile soils of the Avoyelles Parish. On weekends, many from the outlying areas came in to do business that they would be able to do only on Saturdays.

Waddill served two terms as alderman, and it affected him financially in a bad way. He enjoyed serving the public and grew in popularity, however, and his wife, Julia, encouraged him despite the stress it placed on him. She knew that he thrived on politics even on this small scale. Julia also understood John's passion for serving people and knew that he could go far in the political realm.

Their first child, Thomas Hickman Waddill, was born in 1842. John wanted to name him after Thomas J. Hickman due to his debt of gratitude, and he lived up to that promise. Hickman and his brothers had helped him tremendously. He had no idea if he ever could have gone to college without the financial help of Thomas J. Hickman. His son would be a constant reminder of that.

John's brother, William Waddill, moved in 1844 to Marksville, which pleased both John and Julia. William was closer in age to Julia, and he helped with the chores and other duties. W. W., as John called him, helped at the office also.

News of Fighting in Texas with Mexico

John P. Waddill was a patriot who loved his country so much that he probably overestimated its ability to fight in wars. As Mexico continued to have problems with Texas in the 1840s, its government threatened the United

States with war if it annexed Texas as a state. This caused many disturbances. In April 1846, the fighting escalated. News of the conflicts arrived in Marksville, at which time Waddill recorded his fiery thoughts.

> The Mexicans had some days previous crossed the Rio Bravo--or Grand[e], and had intercepted the communication line between Taylor before Matamoras, and Point Isabel at which latter place all of his stores for the troops were deposited. Taylor left on the 3rd with a considerable detachment of his troops; say 1800, to open the communication, leaving not over 700 before Matamoras. The Mexicans thinking it a fine opportunity to cut to pieces the troops that were left, made an attack on the entrenched camp of the general and were repulsed as before stated with immense loss. The news was carried by Captain Walker[145] of the Texas Rangers on the 5th to General Taylor at Isabel. He left on the 6th for the camp opposite Matamoras determined to cut his way through or fall in the attempt. A heavy command was heard, when the vessel which brought the news to New Orleans sailed, and it was supposed, that another attack have been and was then being made by the Mexicans in over troops. The Mexicans, have about 10,000 troops in and about the vicinity, and their numbers are daily increasing. War now has fairly commenced between the U.S. and Mexico. Where it is to end no one can tell. Thus far our prospects are good. Our army has proved itself worthy of our confidence and it will be sustained by the nation. Volunteers are already flocking to the support of Taylor and ere this he must have received a reinforcement of 5,000 men: Our government as yet, has no knowledge of the events taking place in Texas.[146]

---

145. Captain Samuel Hamiton Walker, of the Texas Rangers, was somewhat of a legend in Texas. A fighter who had fought in earlier Indian Wars, he never passed up a chance to fight. During time away from the Mexican War, he convinced Samuel Colt, who had gone bankrupt, to change the style of his pistols. He came up with the Walker Colt, a six-shooter, .44 caliber that was extremely popular into the next century. He was later killed in the war on October 9, 1847, at Huamantla, Tlaxcala, Mexico. He is in the Texas Ranger Hall of Fame. See http://www.texas-ranger.org/halloffame/Walker_Samuel.htm. See also http://www.geni.com/people/Captain-Samuel-Walker/6000000018172804011

146. DJW, May 1846, vol. 2, pg. 1.

May 14, 1846

Waddill continued to try to make a living with his law practice and farming, but the weather was not cooperative for the latter. Unrelenting rain endangered his corn crop. At his law office, he worked on the estate of F. B. DeBellvue Sr., who had suffered some economic hardships before his death. James Rey Jr., a man Waddill knew well, and from whom he had purchased land, claimed that DeBellvue's estate owed money to the estate of George Guillot, for whom DeBellvue had been administrator. Now John Stirling, who administered DeBellvue's estate, was being called upon to make those debts good. The chirographic debts[147] were thought to have been paid by the estate administrators. Waddill sent his brother-in-law, H. C. Barlow, to see Rey about these unsecured debts.

Meanwhile, Waddill continued to worry about the weather. With the Red River already high, rain continued to fall. The water in the coulee between Marksville and Hydropolis was full.

Then there was the impending war with Mexico. Word had not arrived yet that the U.S. declared war on May 13, 1846. Waddill believed that General Taylor's army was under siege before Matamoras and that another battle had been fought. Waddill felt confident, in fact, overconfident. He wrote:

> if an engagement has taken place, I feel sure that our army has triumphed. The Mexicans cannot whip us and give us one man to their three. The American soldier is equal to any on the globe. So is the American sailor. Should England go to war with us, she will rue the day. She may beat us for a few months; but so soon as she gets the war spirit properly aroused in the United States she in turn will be beaten; and she will besides lose Canada and the whole of Oregon. We have offered her a compromise for Oregon, over the 49th degree to the ocean; she has thus far refused. If she still persists war is inevitable: we will then grapple with these conquerors of the second, of the sikks, of the Afghans, and of the whole of India and part of China.

---

147. A chirograph is a medieval document that has been written in duplicate, triplicate, or very occasionally, quadruplicate on a single piece of parchment, where the Latin word "chirographum" (or equivalent) has been written across the middle and then cut through. By this means, both parties to an agreement could possess a copy of its written record, and each copy could be verified as genuine through introduction to, and comparison with, the other. "Chirograph," Wikipedia, https://en.wikipedia.org/wiki/Chirograph.

> We fear not the contest. We can bring into the field annually for 50 years 500,000 soldiers. We can cover the oceans with our fleets and we can enlighten the world with our politics and system of government. We fight for liberty and justice and not for conquest but should conquest follow the success of our arms, we receive the subdued states into our great confederacy, not as slaves, but as freemen like ourselves."[148]

The sun, in all its glory and splendor, came out the next day. John thought that even with the damage to his crops that it was almost compensated by the beauty of the wild, luxurious southern verdure. He thought back to his days as a boy in Tennessee, how he roved through the forest, with no object before him, to be canopied over by glorious foliage. He continued his thought process with the following:

> I have often sat me down upon the ancient mounts of young America, and wondered, what had destroyed the race, that made them; what had obliterated the intelligence that destroyed them; and whether or not they had a written language which had also been destroyed, and thus forever barred our entrance to their decayed forest trees and aged vines and have thought that perhaps the red man of our forests, the roving hunters of the wilds had torn down their redoubts, their places of defense, and as is his would have destroyed every soul that inhabited there. We must believe, that in ancient times, a race greatly superior to the red man, or Indian inhabited this continent. That a race highly civilized, and intelligent, built the great city now in ruins in Central America, cannot be doubted.[149]

With the dry weather came further particulars about the army on the Rio Grande. The Mexicans, it appeared, continued their attack on the American entrenched camp on May 5 but were repulsed. It appeared that they made their attack only by a cannonade.

General Pierre Couvillion had called upon the Louisiana state militia in 1845. There had been an order for a draft of the militia, but it was countermanded as volunteers had already turned out in sufficient numbers to repulse the Mexicans. Judge L. Saunders was supposed to be coming to recruit

148. DJW, May 14, 1846, vol 2, pg. 2.

149. Ibid.

cavalry. Saunders had been commissioned as a colonel to raise one thousand mounted gunmen. They would be used against the Mexicans but also to attack the Comanche, should they begin raids on the Texas frontier.

Waddill wrote a call upon the citizens for Avoyelles, and a service commenced printing it. The pamphlets were handed out and posted. J. Redmond carried it as a rallying flag to arouse the spirit of the citizens. A meeting was to be held on Tuesday, and Waddill and others were to give speeches in favor of the war. He was excited.

The parish ordered a drum and purchased material for a flag. The parish appeared very patriotic. Waddill felt that the country was safe since citizens would volunteer to fight. In Marksville alone, F. P. Hitchborn, J. Redmond, Victor Rebouché, H. W. Edgar, John Pluncket, and John Robinson had volunteered. The sheriff of Rapides Parish, Leroy Stafford, resigned his office and volunteered also.[150]

The ladies of Marksville finished the flag. It was made from common materials but looked quite good. During this time, Julia had been visiting her mother on the river. She arrived at Foulk's Landing on May 16, 1846, where John met her. By then, no further news of merit had come to Marksville about the war. Julia's mother had remarried W. Duke after the death of Julia's father. Waddill had gotten to know Mr. Duke and sent him all of the newspapers he had relative to the military operations on the Rio Grande. Waddill knew that he would enjoy reading them. His stepfather-in-law's patriotic passion matched John's.

May 17, 1846

Reports began to trickle in from New Orleans. The most recent news was that New Orleans had deported about four thousand volunteers to fight with Zachary Taylor. Many of the best families in Rapides had sent some of their members to the relief of General Taylor. Ralph Cushman had returned from New Orleans and spoke of the great patriotism in the city. He stated that some were going for glory, some for money, and some without any object at all.

Cushman also brought bad news about the mercantile trade in New Orleans. A. Rivarde & Co. had failed, causing a possible loss for Waddill. From

---

150. He was later killed in the Battle of the Wilderness in 1864, fighting for the Confederate Army. His son, David Stafford, later became sheriff. "Leroy Augustus Stafford," Wikipedia, https://en.wikipedia.org/wiki/Leroy_Augustus_Stafford.

them, he had obtained a draft on W. Edwards, and the draft was eventually accepted. He was thankful.

Some were concerned that the affairs of the army on the Rio Grande were worse than had been reported. Waddill could not verify the truthfulness of those rumors.

May 19, 1846

This was a big night in Marksville, and for all of Avoyelles, for the purpose of raising volunteers to send to rescue General Taylor's army in Matamoras, rumored to be surrounded by ten thousand Mexicans. The meeting was scheduled at half past 11:00. More than one hundred persons, many of them ladies, attended. Sheriff Fabius Ricord presided over the meeting; A. Servius helped as secretary. Ricord spoke a few appropriate words, addressing the meeting and explaining its object.

Ralph Cushman then stood to address the crowd. It hushed. His address had considerable effect. Waddill was called upon next. His was rather short, maybe 10–15 minutes.

> When the mention of war comes up, many men flinch. Yet there are times that our great nation must face the opposing forces to prove to the world that we will not be taken advantage of by anyone! This is the first time we are fighting on foreign soil and must do so to protect our own states and its citizens. If we fail to enlist what can we say about our great country? It is necessary to fight the evil of war to protect ourselves. We must save General Taylor and those fighting to preserve what was fought for only seven decades prior! Are you ready to join?

The crowd hurrahed and clapped and slapped each other on the back. Waddill could feel that he was able to influence others by his speaking ability. Henderson Taylor then was called on and continued with a short speech. Victor Rebouché, a recent immigrant though a volunteer already, made a great speech in French, which excited the Creoles present.

After the speeches, Hitchborn and Redmond, previous volunteers, went forward for the purpose of receiving more. Nineteen more joined and were to leave on Saturday, just four days from then, May 23, 1846. The group present raised $200 to purchase horses and saddles for those who had none. Most of the volunteers did have them, so the money would be used for supplies and the five or six with no horses.

That afternoon, Dr. E. L. Briggs, a friend who Waddill enjoyed to have around for conversation, came to Waddill and Julia's home to dine. After eating, they had coffee and talked for an hour or two about many subjects, including religion and the propriety of raising a company of gentleman volunteers and disciplining them.

At ten minutes before three o'clock, the doctor and Waddill went down into town, he having subscribed five dollars to filling out the Horse Company. Waddill paid the same for him to A. Marge, who had the subscription with Daniel McCall at Madam Maillet's Corner. He and McCall informed Waddill that they were then going home. Waddill went off to another place and entered a small room with three other gentlemen, where they amused themselves at whist[151] for the balance of the day. During the evening Waddill heard Dr. Briggs speaking very loudly in an adjoining bar room as though he was becoming intoxicated. After some time, Waddill heard no more of him and concluded he had gone home. About sundown, Waddill started home and saw the doctor sitting on the courthouse fence, conversing with James H. Barbin. Waddill saw no more of him, but when he went to his office, Waddill found McCall sitting on the gallery before W. M. Bishop's door, holding his own and Dr. Briggs's horses; he said he was waiting for Briggs. Waddill went home, and about a half hour afterward, Waddill heard the doctor discharge a pistol. He went to bed at J. B. Devers. At nine o'clock in the night, James Tyrell persuaded Briggs to get up and go home, and he would accompany him. His friends attempted to persuade him to stay, but he started for home. Waddill was very worried about his friend and Dr. Briggs.

The nineteen volunteers who were going to fight for the U.S. army in Texas and Mexico were Freeman P. Hitchborn, Lewis S. Taylor, David J. Redmond, John Robinson, Thomas Jackson, Julien Desheautelle Jr., John Pluncket, Alexander Kimball, James Tyrell, Hugh W. Edgar, John G. Hollenback, Victor Rebouché, Joshua Starnes, William Milligan, C. N. Robincott, Stephen H. Milligan, William Gollighar, John M. Phillips, and Clemment Mills.

---

151. Whist was a popular card game in the 1800s requiring partners, each being dealt thirteen cards. It is based on one suit being the trump, and winning each played hand of four cards, till all cards are played. Each winning hand is a trick. The most tricks score the highest.

May 20, 1846, The Drowning of Dr. E. L. Briggs

This morning, Waddill started for Bayou des Glaises. When he arrived at Mansura, six miles off, he learned that Dr. Briggs had drowned in the night crossing the Bayou Boutte, which had overflowed its banks. He and Tyrell arrived at the woods near Mansura where the roads forked. Tyrell took the public road, but Briggs took the one most usually traveled. When Tyrell arrived at the bayou bridge, he called loudly for the doctor but could not hear him though a short time previously, he had answered his call. He went to the doctor's residence, and after waiting about an hour, he took the doctor's lady servant and went in search of him. They crossed the Bayou Boutte and swamp, and after they had ascended the hill and proceeded about three hundred yards, they found where the horse appeared to have thrown and dragged the doctor a short distance. A few yards from this, they discovered where the doctor had passed on foot toward home. They tracked him to the edge of the overflow; the water having covered the land there, they could not follow his traces farther. The water was shallow until it reached the bridge, and there, a deep and rapid stream flowed toward the swamp of Red River. By this stream Briggs must have fallen.

Waddill was distressed over his friend. He was intelligent, but he did drink a bit too much. Since he often drank with him, John felt somewhat responsible. Waddill was traveling this area of the parish in an effort to collect the various clients and persons owed him. He stayed the night with William Clopton, another friend from the Big Bend.

May 21, 1846

Waddill dined at the house of E. L. Briggs. He saw Richard L. Slaughter there, and the doctor's "girl," Rachael Smith, a black woman. The doctor had not been found. The bayou and swamp had been searched for the body, but to no purpose. Waddill returned home, but whilst in the prairie, some four or five miles from Marksville, a heavy shower of rain overtook him. When he arrived, soaked, news of the war reached him.

More Battles in the War with Mexico

Waddill learned that two battles had been fought on the Rio Grande between the U.S. troops and the Mexicans. General Zachary Taylor commanded the American troops in person and General Mariano Arista those of the

Mexican Army. Taylor, hearing a continual cannonade for several days at or in the direction of Matamoras, left Point Isabel (where he had gone for provisions) with two thousand men to assist the Americans in the fort opposite Matamoras. At 11:00 a.m. on May 8, about twelve miles from the fort, he came into contact with about six thousand Mexicans under Arista. Taylor immediately commenced the battle, which continued until sundown. On the next morning, May 9, he carefully examined the position of the Mexicans and, at about 3 o'clock, boldly attacked them. The battle continued terribly until sundown when the Mexicans gave back; Taylor's dragoons boldly charged upon them and took eight of their cannons. They were completely routed. The Mexican Army fled toward the river and Matamoras, came in range of the American fort, and received its fire. They crossed the river, but many drowned in the crossing. Both sides suffered severe losses. One-hundred fifty of the Americans were either killed or wounded. The Mexicans lost over two thousand, either killed, wounded, or missing. General Rómulo Díaz de la Vega with other officers of rank became a prisoner. La Vega was brought to New Orleans and was now with General James. The U.S. forces took all the baggage and camp equipage of the Mexicans, plus ammunition and enough small arms to last a campaign for two years. The Mexicans reinforced their provisions and numbers previous to the battle, with eight thousand troops in Matamoras. Waddill also leaned that Mexican General Mariano Perades was marching to the seat of war with fifteen thousand men. Waddill felt that he also would meet the same welcome that Santa Anna did in Texas in 1836. Unless some accident prevented it, certain capture awaited him and his men. Louisiana had turned out five thousand volunteers for the service.

Waddill was supremely confident about the U.S. Army. He wrote:

May 22, 1846

There is nothing new today. The body of Doctor E L Briggs has not yet been found. A spirit of war is abroad in the land and from appearances we are able to raise a volunteer army 500,000 strong. We cannot be beaten by an enemy. All Europe might be arrayed against us and we would prove victorious. Our country is rich and contains more natural resources for defense or aggression than any other nation of the earth. The great valley of the Mississippi contains nitrous, Sulphur, lead, iron, copper, and coal enough to supply the world. In war we will use them.

May 23, 1846

On this day a meeting of the volunteers of the Parish of Avoyelles took place at Marksville. Since the last meeting they had heard glorious news, the Army on the Rio Grande had been victorious in two battles. They have proven to ourselves, and the world, that in contests of skill or strength, we are equal to any of the nations of the earth. No foe can attack the U.S. with impunity, the charge of the famed lancers of Mexico, had been met, and terribly repulsed by the U.S. infantry. They have slaughtered their soldiers, routed their army and captured some of their generals and artillery. It is true that the U.S. tactics did much for us in the engagement but the mighty impulse which freemen feel when fighting for themselves and their country's glory, did more.

Waddill further wrote:

As a nation, the policy and practice is peace and where we go to war not infrequently, do we bear the taunts and insults of the aggression until forbearance ceases to be a virtue. But when we do commence the combat, we do so with a determination to triumph. The principles upon which our government is founded are, that all men are free and equal, and that governments were framed to correct evils, not to extend them; to protect life, liberty and property, and not to destroy them. Then with the success of our arms we receive the subjugated nations into our great confederacy as sister states, and invest them with all the blessings we ourselves enjoy.

We had a meeting today of the volunteers, who exercised on horseback for many hours.

Waddill also heard that the body of E. L. Briggs had been found. It was in a state of putrefaction some forty or fifty yards below the bridge on the Bayou Boutte in the branches of a tree that had fallen in the bayou.

Sunday May 24, 1846

It had been a tiring week for Waddill. He could not wait to relax and go to church. He wrote:

Today I have read a great deal. At 15 minutes before 11 o'clock I attended church and heard M Davies preach. He gave us an excellent sermon. He appears to be a man of fair talents with a good English education. He is poetical, quiet, in his discourse. I would be glad to hear a sermon from him, or such as him, twice a week; but that pleasure is denied me; as they are preaching but once in 3 weeks. I read the greater part of Scott's 'Rob Roy' today." (Sir Walter Scott's popular Scottish story)

CHAPTER 26

THE MEXICAN WAR CONTINUES

John Waddill went through some trying times over the next few months. Business kept him from much pleasure, and the loss of Dr. Briggs affected him greatly. When he began his diary again, he wrote:

August 7, 1846

I have left a wide gap in my diary, a multiplicity of business having caused me to neglect it. Many things have transpired worthy of note since the 25th of May, which cannot now be registered. Since that date the Americans have taken Matamoras, and Camargo from the Mexicans, without firing a gun. The independent Treasury bill, and a tariffs Bill on ad valorum principle, have passed our congress and became laws of the land. They were great Democratic measures. The bill for improving rivers and harbors, and a bill to reintegrate certain citizens for French spoliations have passed congress, and each of them have been vetoed by the President, which veto killed them as their friends, could not carry them over the veto. Congress adjourned on the 10th August. The Louisiana volunteers to the number of six thousand have been disbanded by order of the Secretary of War, after service of three months. They were offered the privilege of remaining twelve months but they would not do it. It is now rumored that Santa Anna is in Vera Cruz, in consequence of a revolution, in his favor extending all over Mexico, and that General Peredes is in prison. We have also rumors that California has declared its independence, and placed itself under the protection of the United States. The English Ministry have been changed. Sir Robert Peel having resigned, and Lord John Russell, having taken his place. Previous to the resignation of Peel, the court of England received the treaty of Washington settling our rights to that territory of Oregon on the 49th degree of

North Latitude. We have at this time, in the Gulf of Mexico, a larger fleet than ever we had a float on the ocean before.

It is rumored that the President has proposed peace with Mexico.

I did not do much today. I wrote some on my brief in the case of Frels Benoist, in the case of Blauchard versus Frels. I read some, and I conversed some.

I have come to the conclusion not to patronize the groceries so much as I have done; especially in the way of dram drinking and billiard playing. I lose thereby my time, my money, and my reputation. It has rained considerable today. I fear that we will have a wet spell.

Waddill stuck to his word about the drinking. The death of his friend Dr. Briggs affected him greatly. He made a mental note: he had not felt the respect of the others who watched him that May afternoon and evening when he drank and played cards. That was not the life he wanted.

September 9, 1846

Waddill continued to study and prepare cases for argument. He had the Fels case coming up that would be complex and sought help. It was to be in Alexandria, so he requested George R. Waters and John K. Elgee for assistance. Waddill needed to relax and was entertained when his neighbor William Edwards brought him three Saturday *Courier* newspapers to read. Each of his friends knew how much John craved reading the newspapers.

There was one that Waddill specifically appreciated.

In the one of the 15 of August 1846, there is an interesting lecture by George Lippard,[152] on Thomas Paine and his services in our Revolution. It is thought that Paine by his pen did as much to establish our independence, as did Washington by his sword. After the conclusion of peace, the thanks of the citizens of the United States, was, through congress, tendered to Paine. Paine was a man of great intellect; he

---

152. George Lippard was a famous author and journalist who gave a lecture that ran in many newspapers of the time about Thomas Paine. See, in particular, *The Carolina Watchman*, March 13, 1846, pg. 1. http://pabook2.libraries.psu.edu/palitmap/bios/Lippard__George.html

was the friend of mankind, and his writings have done more to ameliorate our condition, than have the writings of all the fathers, and saints of Christianity, put together. I speak not of his "age of reason"; for that is a work as yet, I have not fully read. But I speak of his political, and other writings. His Rights of Man and Common Sense have sown the seeds of rain in the foundations of every throne in Europe. As for his religions opinions, they rest with himself and his god. But who is there, that will dare, swear that he was wrong. Does he not teach a sublime doctrine, does he not give us a more exalted idea of the deity and his great attributes of wisdom, omnipotence, love, mercy,… than do all the writers, of Judaism, Christianity, Mohammadism, etc. does not he show God to be a wiser and better being than any of these? Every noble feeling of our souls answer that he does.

As Waddill continued his practice, he made note of his debts. He had to repair his carriage to be able to travel to Alexandria on the Fels case. It cost him $4.85 to have Joseph Guillot repair it. He further wrote that he bought twenty-six barrels of corn from the slave of Dr. Leroy K. Branch at sixty cents per barrel, totaling $15.60. L. Chabert had sent a ream of printing paper the size of the New Orleans *Bee*, a popular newspaper of the time, on behalf of a client, the editor of *The Villager*, George A. Stevens.

September 11, 1846

As Waddill continued to work on the Fels case, he leaned more on his associates, especially John K. Elgee, who, in Waddill's eyes, was a remarkable man. Irish by birth and education, he married a beautiful but poor Irish girl, which drew the displeasure of Elgee's mother, who was allied to the aristocracy of the country. Elgee had been educated in the Protestant faith, but when his mother discarded him, he left his native land with his wife, who had been the innocent cause of his troubles. In the year 1830, or thereabouts, he landed in America. He settled in the state of Louisiana and, for some time, taught school, for subsistence. Sometime in the year 1832, his devoted wife died after bearing him a daughter. This daughter he sent to Ireland to be raised and educated by his mother. She received the little stranger, as a relative should. Elgee, being a man of good talents and indomitable energy of character, studied law whilst teaching school and, in 1833, received admittance to practice as an attorney and counselor at law. In 1835 or thereabouts, he married the widow of Judge Thomas L. Scott, of Rapides Parish. For three or four years, he made but little noise in the profession, but from 1839 on, he began to take a stand as a lawyer, which soon put him at the head of his profession. By the mid-1840s, he became known as one of the ablest lawyers of western Louisiana.

To Waddill's disappointment and dismay, the Supreme Court continued Fels's case. There were too many other cases to be handled for that term.

CHAPTER 27

The Browder Family Cousins

While in Alexandria, Waddill saw his cousin Bartlett Milton Browder of Lake Providence. He was not very well. Waddill wrote that he was a reformed man—temperate, not drinking anything stronger than lemonade. Bartlett Milton Browder was born in Tennessee in 1811. His family, John Waddill's mother's family, had also moved from Virginia to Tennessee. Browder's father, Frederick Avery Browder, originally moved to St. Francisville, Louisiana, and had a plantation there near the Mississippi River. Bartlett also had a brother, J. J. Browder. Both attended Norwich University, a military school in Vermont founded in 1819. Bartlett became a well-respected attorney in East Carroll Parish, settling in Lake Providence. He married Narcissa J. Hewelette in 1835.

He began to tell Waddill a rather sad story about other relatives. He informed Waddill of those in New Orleans, such as the respectably rich Mr. Ladoux. Waddill thought that he was from thirty-five to forty years of age and his wife about nineteen. Browder said that Mrs. Ladoux's father, William Brand, was now at Louisville. Her father, being a widower, some fifty-five or sixty years of age, married an Irish girl some twenty years of age, whom he had employed to instruct John's cousins, Jane and Anna. They had been married only a short time before she persuaded the old man to sell his estate, which amounted to $300,000, and turn it into money. He did so at a great sacrifice, and his young wife got possession of $80,000 to $100,000 of the money, and the old man paid his debts with the balance. His whole fortune then lay in the hands of his young wife, and she persuaded him to go with her to Ireland for the purpose of educating Waddill's cousin (now Mrs. Ladoux). Once in Ireland, she invested the funds for her own benefit in some manner or other and persuaded the old man to then go with her to Italy. He did so and took Anna with him. When they arrived there, his wife defied all of his claims to the money she had invested, and he and Anna fell at her mercy. The old man and his daughter were badly treated by the woman who had robbed them. Anna wrote the facts to her brother, Frederick who was in the U.S. Navy as a midshipman. Frederick immediately set out from the United States for Italy and brought away his father and sister to the United States. The old man, William Brand, was brought back and left at Louisville, with Frederick supporting him.

John Waddill gloried in the act of his cousin Frederick Brand. He and his two sisters, Jane and Anna, were children of Waddill's mother's sister, Anne G. Browder, deceased wife of William Brand. Waddill found the story of such greed heartbreaking, though he found salvation in the story of his cousin Frederick's actions.

Christmas 1846

Continuing the tradition of celebrating Christmas on Christmas Eve and for three days after, John Waddill referred to his desire on December 28, 1846, to return to work. He was ready.

> Well! Christmas is over with me. I must now leave off pleasures and go to work, but labor is pleasure. He who does not count it so must want energy. Where is there a man with noble aspiration who does not love to labor, if there be any such, he can never succeed. Wealth, fame, and all that make life desirable is gained only by work, by energetic application. This Christmas has been remarkably warm and the weather continues so. We have had some rain, but as yet not a great deal. At this time, the Mississippi River is very high. It is now almost even with its banks and has backed Red River up to Gorton's landing. This year has been, to the South, a disastrous one. The corn crops were bad. The entire cotton crop, or three fourths at least, thereof, was destroyed by the caterpillar in Louisiana. The sugar crop of the state will not be more than half what it was last year in comparison with the land in cultivation. This year Avoyelles has been raising sugar and our yield has been greater than in any other parish. Though but three planters in our parish have grown cane this year. They are Evariste Rabalais,[153] Francis Cullom, and Lodowick

---

153. Evariste Rabalais owned property on Bayou des Glaises. He was one of three landowners appointed by the police jury in 1834 to inspect the levees raised above the 1828 high waters along the south side of Bayou des Glaises, from the mouth of Bayou Rouge to the line of Leon Gauthier's. The levees were made by owners of the

Tanner.[154] Many are planting cane for next year and, I expect that a considerable crop of sugar will be made in Avoyelles next year.[155]

Lodowick Tanner had been sued by Thomas J. Hickman on a note that was signed January 1, 1843, for failure to pay. A judgment was finally rendered on December 18, 1847 for $550.00 plus $4.00 cost.[156]

The New Year 1847

Waddill never celebrated much. He remembered his thoughts and promises to himself since the death of Dr. Briggs. He also was very reflective about the events of 1846.

January the 1, 1847

This is New Year's Day. A day to be spent by many in feasting, and all other amusements that can be thoughtful of the old year has some never to return again.

Vast principles developed themselves in 1846, events of mighty import transpired within that year. Our war with Mexico commenced in 1846. Since its commencement three terrible battles have been fought and won by the U.S. troops, to wit one at Pali Alto, one at Resaca, de la Palma and one at Monterey. In every engagement our troops have been successful. We have taken many of their cities among which are Matamoras, Courargo, Monterey, Tampico, Saltillo, Monclova, Santa Fe, Monterey on the Pacific, and many others of less note. Our armies are now marching upon Victoria in Tamaulipas and the

---

land along the route. See Saucier, *History of Avoyelles Parish, Louisiana*, 154.

154. Lodowick Tanner was the son of Joseph Tanner and his first wife Elizabeth Lanier and was born in South Carolina. On October 11, 1819, he married Ann Martha Eldred, who was born to Esther Susannah Robert, the ninth child of Captain Peter Robert and Anne Grimball. Esther had married Randal Eldred Jr. Lodowck Tanner died at his home, Tiger Bend Planatation, on Bayou Boeuf, Rapides Parish on October 5, 1849. Tiger Bend was near the boundary line between Rapides and Avoyelles Parish, but fell in Avoyelles. Stafford, *Three Pioneer Rapides Families*, 152.

155. DJW, December 28, 1846, vol. 2, pg. 8.

156. Hickman-Bryan Papers, f. 96–114; C.45 1841–1843

city of San's Louis, Potosi. Santa Anna is at San Louis Potosi with some 20,000 Mexicans. He declares that Mexico will never make peace with us until the territory of the Mexicans is free from our soldiers. General Scott has gone to the seat of war in Mexico, and we hope that ere long through the vigorous operations of our armies and their officers that an end will be put to the war. Some of the members of congress have presented restitutions to the House of Representatives, instituting an inquiry with regard to our military officers establishing provisional governments in Mexico, where they have taken possession of departments and paces.

On the 30th of December 1846 August Marye died.[157] He was agent of the branch of the New Orleans and Carrollton Railroad Company, in Avoyelles. He was much of a gentleman, and died regretted by all who knew him. I attended his funeral yesterday, which was attended by a large concourse of the citizens of the parish. The funeral service was performed by the Reverend Mr. Calo of the Roman Catholic Church. It was long, and as I thought unnecessary and absurd in some particulars. The deceased left a wife and a large family of whom will inherit the acquets and gains. I charged only five dollars for the same, what was five dollars too little.

I played euchre[158] tonight at my residence with my wife, David Dever, and my brother-in-law. [159]

In December 1846, Waddill had begun discussions with Henderson Taylor, the attorney for the syndic of the succession of Samuel W. and E. L. Briggs, the doctor who had drowned, to purchase part of the property belonging to them. It was on Bayou des Glaises in the western half and northeastern quarter of Section 35 TINR4E, a total of eighty acres.

Waddill wanted the land, and his closeness to Dr. Briggs made it personal for him. On February 5, 1847, he purchased the property on credit as file number 6554 recorded in Book T page 64 in the records of Avoyelles Parish,

---

157. "Louis Victor Marye, Rapides Parish Louisiana," *Biographical and Historical Memoirs*, available at http://files.usgwarchives.net/la/rapides/bios/maryelv.txt. He also was a banker near Marksville in an area now known as Cocoville.

158. "Euchre," Bicycle, http://www.bicyclecards.com/how-to-play/euchre/.

159. DJW, January 1, 1847, vol. 2, pg. 9.

Louisiana, shows. In 1849, he paid off the debt in full. The estate of Samuel W. Briggs, a well-respected attorney, and the estate of Dr. E. L. Briggs sold the eighty acres, leaving much more land in their estates. The brothers had all done well.

Waddill's estate was growing. He had also purchased 133 acres from Michael Fogelman and filed this deed on January 5, 1847, file number 6531 in Book number T page 42 in the records of the Avoyelles Parish clerk of court.

CHAPTER 28

CHALLENGING DECISIONS IN THE PRACTICE OF LAW

Many times as a lawyer Waddill noticed that he had to take an opposing position to a casual acquaintance. He often wondered how that person felt when he would file a petition against his or her interest. Did they understand it was business and not personal? Probably not, Waddill thought.

On January 11, 1847, Waddill witnessed a bizarre series of events that led to tragic circumstances. A public account of what happened made it into the local paper, *The Villager*, on January 14, 1847. The story also ran in several national papers, including the *Picayune* in New Orleans. It ran as a front page story.

The story told of the killing of Lewis Gorton, the well-known and respected owner of Gorton's Landing, which happened on Monday, January 11, 1847. To summarize the newspaper account: Gorton came to Marksville to fetch his carriage that had been seized by T. B. Tiller, a merchant in the town. Tiller claimed that Gorton owed him money, so he had taken the carriage. Gorton did not appreciate the manner in which this happened, so he rode into town on his horse, entered Tiller's premises, took the bridles and harnesses, attached them to his horses, and departed for his home.

Monroe Phillips, partner and brother-in-law of Tiller, witnessed all this but did not stop Gorton. He did tell Tiller about it immediately, however, and Tiller and Phillips armed themselves and made threats against the life of Gorton. They came into town at full speed in pursuit of Gorton. Five minutes passed when a report of a firearm "announced plainly" some act of violence.

The parties had met up at Mrs. P. Normand's plantation not far from Marksville. According to Tiller, who was arrested, Gorton, upon being overtaken, alighted immediately and ordered his servant to hold his horse. He turned to Phillips and was in the act of aiming his gun at him when the latter drew a pistol and, running under the muzzle of the gun, shot Gorton dead. The ball struck the fore part of the left shoulder and passed entirely through the breast, lodged beneath the skin near the nipple of the right breast, causing immediate death.

Phillips then exchanged horses with Tiller and fled, taking with him Gorton's gun, which he grabbed from the victim. Tiller went home with the disputed carriage. Tiller was arrested for "accessory to the murder of Lewis Gorton," and the magistrate decided that the case was not bailable. The trial would be held before Judge Cushman, Waddill's former partner.

Waddill knew both men well. He was a witness to most of the events that passed on the January 11.

> On today about 12 o'clock John L. Generis, William H., and myself (John P. Waddill) were standing talking together outside of the fence at the southern end of the recorder's office in Marksville. Lewis Gorton of the parish came up near us and called me to him. I went to him and he informed me that he had come to demand of Tiller, or Phillips a carriage belonging to him while said Thomas B. Tiller forcibly detained from him. He likewise stated that he had come to take the carriage and that he would have it before he left and exhibited to me, a shot gun (I think a single barrel one) which he held in his hand. He wanted me to go with him and see him demand it. I told him that I would have nothing to do with the affair. I turned off and joined my companions telling them that I thought there would be a desperate difficulty in the village in a short time.
>
> Gorton went up to R. Robinson's, found the family at dinner and dines. He and Robinson went to J. B. Tiller's store immediately afterwards, took the carriage, broke the fence, and took the carriage jeering and started off with the carriage Tiller not being present. Tiller came up immediately, and he and his brother-in-law, J. M. Phillips pursued Gorton, overtook him about half a mile from the courthouse, and Phillips shot and killed Gorton. It is said that Gorton was in the act of shooting at Phillips, when Phillips shot him. It is likewise stated that Gorton was getting out of the carriage, with the gun in his hand when he was shot by Phillips. Phillips has made his escape Tiller has been found over as a witness against Phillips in a bond of $1,000. W. Edwards, Fielding Edwards and myself went to post his security.[160]

---

160. DJW, January 11, 1847, vol. 2, pg. 9.

This is where Waddill entered into a predicament. Gorton was popular with the French and Creole population. Waddill knew both families. He believed that Philips should be prosecuted. Waddill decided to defend Tiller, despite the outcry. The French and Creole groups expressed great sympathy for Gorton. On January 12, T. B. Tiller was arrested, and he underwent preliminary examination at 11:00 a.m. on the thirteenth. Waddill and W. Edwards went to Sheriff Ricord to deliver Tiller to him so they could post the bond. Tiller's release seemed to anger the community even more. Gorton had been a client of Waddill and actually still owed him money. Waddill decided that he would never make Gorton's family pay the debt.

Due to the popularity of Gorton, it could have hurt Waddill to continue in his representation of Tiller. Waddill thought of Tiller's family. Mrs. Tiller was a true lady in Waddill's eyes, and they had a son only nine months old. His wife was young and amiable. Waddill wanted to help more but could help only as a lawyer. Waddill wrote, "Alas, poor human beings, this is truly some of the trials which we are heir to."

The hearing came, and Waddill began his argument for Tiller as to whether charges should continue.

> My client is before you on a charge of aiding and abetting J. Monroe Phillips in the murder of Lewis Gorton, which happened on the 11th of January 1847 in this parish. The circumstances which led to the death of Gorton are these. Tiller had in his possession a carriage, which he claimed as his own. Gorton, upon the day on which he was killed, came into Marksville armed and determined to take the carriage by force, should he not be able to do it otherwise. A witness who saw him advised him not to do it and told him that he was a married man, that he had a large family of young children, and that he should have respect for his wife and children and not run himself heedlessly into danger, where he might lose his life. Gorton persisted in his intuition of taking the carriage, and when the witness saw his determination, he begged him to leave his gun in witness's office. Gorton told him no that he would want it; for he had been shot once and if there was any hostilities, that he would like a hand in them. He then left witness and proceeded with one Rouland Robinson to move the carriage from where Tiller placed it by his store, broke fence of Tiller, went into his enclosures, and into and out house took the gearing or harness which he there found, put them upon his horse hitched the horse to the carriage, and started off with it. Whilst Gor-

ton was harnessing the horse, Phillips who had charge of the store for Tiller, and who had the carriage and other property in charge, came from his dinner and asked Gorton what he was doing. Gorton observed that he was taking away the carriage. J L Generis a witness saw Phillips immediately afterwards and told him that Gorton was taking off his carriage. Phillips observed that he reckoned Gorton had fixed it with Tiller.

Tiller came up immediately afterwards, found the carriage had been forcibly taken off by Gorton and that Gorton armed and determined to carry off the property at all hazards, he sought for a gun, got an old piece that would not shoot, and he and Phillips went in pursuit of Gorton overtook him some half a mile off, and in a contest in endeavoring to retake the carriage from Gorton, Phillips shot him. In all this it does not appear that Tiller was doing anything more than in endeavoring to wrestle property for a man, who had in a violent manner and armed, taken away from him.

After hearing the district attorney and further arguments, the judge decided that Phillips would have to answer to the charge of murder. The judge also decided that no charges would have grounds against Tiller.

When Waddill left the courtroom, Gorton's family glared at him, and he felt it. He did not want to be congratulated. This was his hardest day ever in the practice of law.

Later that summer, in June 1847, a company of militia, including the volunteers from Avoyelles, under Captain C. Moreau, and Lieutenants H. C. Barlow and F. B. Barbin, paraded in Marksville in response to the request of a lieutenant of the 17th U.S. Infantry. It was a glorious parade and finally brought some joy to the souls of Marksville.

BOOK III

THE LATER LEGAL CAREER AND ENTRY INTO STATE POLITICS BY JOHN P. WADDILL
1847–1852

CHAPTER 29

Election to State Senate
September 22, 1847

On August 7, 1847, John Waddill won nomination as a Democratic Party candidate for the State Senate. As a loyal Democrat, had Waddill not received the nomination, he would not have run without the party support. His opponent for the official nomination was Bennett Barton Simmes.

A mass convention was held in Mansura, Avoyelles Parish. After a nomination speech by William Bishop, one of the oldest members of the bar, who began by extolling the virtues of the young attorney, John P. Waddill, the crowd became excited. The political process was important to the people in Avoyelles, but it was also entertainment. Simmes was the candidate of choice by the Creole population. He electioneered for the nomination for weeks before the assemblage of the Democrats. Waddill was at a disadvantage because he could not speak fluent French, especially Creole French, and Simmes could and did.

"Je parle français. I am one of you and I speak French. I want to represent you in the State Senate because I understand you better than anyone else. Yet, I will abide by the wishes of the party vote," B. B. Simmes shouted after receiving his nomination from George Barron, who opposed Waddill greatly.

Barron, along with Gilbert Bordelon and Leandre Roy and other influential Creoles, opposed Waddill mostly because of his being a Protestant. Simmes lived in the eastern part of Avoyelles and would later have the town of Simmesport, on the Western bank of the Atchafalaya River, named in his honor. This area marked the confluence of the Mississippi River, which veered in a 'u' shape at the mouth of the Red River, together comprising the headwaters of the Atchafalaya River before the Mississippi veered back to continue its path to New Orleans and the Gulf of Mexico. The Atchafalaya, much wider and deeper than the Red River, continued south to Morgan City.

B. B. Simmes had a reputation for his ability to persuade people. Two stories circulated about this reputation. The first involved two creditors to whom Simmes owed money. Waddill was familiar with Simmes's debts as he had represented a creditor whom Simmes owed money and defended him during his association with Ralph Cushman. The two creditors were said to have visited Simmes to collect their debt. They were entertained so much by his conversation that they left without even talking about the debt he owed them. The second story was one where his wife witnessed him kissing another woman. She flew into a rage. Of course, he denied it and said very calmly, "Well my dear, are you going to believe me or your own eyes?" "You, of course, darling," his wife replied.[161]

Waddill detested the fact that one's faith would have an effect on an election, but he accepted it. Since he was a Mason, he received their loyal support, so that was all part of the process. The Catholic Creole support was important to Simmes. Despite Simmes's pledge to abide by the party nomination, he ran as an independent. Joseph Joffrion, G. Barron, L. Roy, G. Bordelon, and other Creoles demanded another convention after Waddill received 157 of the 289 votes cast. Simmes received 132. With the vote difference of 25, those challenging the tally had some support.

This issue bothered Waddill greatly. He shared his heart with William Bishop, the older and respected attorney, who had passionately nominated Waddill.

Bishop spoke with passion. He talked about Waddill's character and reputation and what a fine man he was. Bishop nearly wept with emotion.

Later, as the days passed, Waddill asked Bishop why the others opposed him. He wondered if it was due to his being a Protestant rather than a Catholic.

Bishop comforted him. He explained that since Waddill did not speak French, many distrusted him. In addition, Waddill was not born in Avoyelles.

Waddill greatly respected William Bishop, not just as an attorney but also as a statesman. He helped Waddill in his start as a young attorney. He also fought hard against him when they opposed each other as lawyers. Bishop always shook his hand after a legal fight. He was a classic gentleman.

His friend, Charles Brashear, who stood in his wedding in 1840 and continued to comfort him, encouraged Waddill. Despite the fact that Joffrion, Barron, L. Roy, and G. Bordelon stated that they would not support Waddill if another convention were not held, Waddill continued the fight and electioneered with passion. They lived up to their pledge to support Simmes on

---

161. *Biograraphical and Historical Memoirs.*

an independent ticket rather than support James Elihu Howard as the Whig candidate. Brashear, who had been active as a Whig, remained quiet in this race due to his friendship with Waddill.

Of course, Waddill's spirit was crushed. He had supported J. Joffrion when he was the candidate of the Democratic Party. Waddill had worked hard for Joffrion's election. The old and true Democrats stuck by him also. Joffrion had won by a small majority, by thirty-five votes, despite the other candidates receiving a combined majority. The Democrats all then supported Joffrion.

Now that Joffrion was arrayed against him, Waddill was not certain he liked politics and electioneering. He felt that Joffrion had forsaken him at the commencement of his political struggle. Joffrion was getting neutrals and other Democrats to join the political opposition. Joffrion, who had in the past espoused how he never swerved from the principles of Democracy, had a motto: "The voice of the majority should rule the Republic." He was not living up to the majority in this case, and his ethics were now in question. Waddill thought Joffrion had forsaken the sacred creed that had elevated his own career. He left his friends, who had sacrificed their time and money for his aggrandizement, in the hands of the enemy. He now stood aloof, coldly looking on at the death struggle of his friends, or he threw his aid and support in the scab of the enemy. Waddill wondered why.

Waddill thought long about this late at night. What reason could he assign for this? Joffrion said that he asked Waddill to become a candidate for the Senate, and that Waddill refused him, and afterward accepted the solicitations of General Pierre Couvillion and others. Waddill was a reluctant candidate, not sure that he should run. Many friends asked him to become a candidate, and at first, he refused them because he was relatively poor. He also did not like the process of electioneering. Yet when the Democratic Party, Waddill's party, through many friends, told him that his services were absolutely wanted, Waddill was convinced that their reasons were just, and he granted their request to become a candidate for nomination for the sake of unity and peace.

Waddill thought:

The above is my offense. I feel that I have committed no error, and I am determined to brave all opposition, and if I am beaten, I fall with the firm old Democrats by my side boldly opposing those principles which we believe ruinous to the cause of freedom. I have an abiding confidence in the firmness of the Democracy of this parish. The charge of inconsistency, which many have alleged against the Creole population, cannot be brought against them now. They are as firm as the Americans and go in as strong for principles. I think that with industry we can beat the Whigs and the disaffected by a 100-vote majority. If we do, it will be a great triumph, a mighty agreement in favor of the firm and unwavering character of our Creole population.

Waddill felt that because it was in his heart, the Creoles would sense it. Despite the fact that citizens in certain areas of the parish attacked him by calling him, in a pejorative way, "Americain," he was able to overcome the disadvantage of not being a Creole. With the combined support of some Creoles, Masons, and old Democrats, Waddill won the election. The final vote in November 1847 was as follows:

John P. Waddill – Democrat, 277 votes
James E. Howard – Whig, 209 votes
Bennett B. Simmes – Independent, 191 votes

It was not the 100-vote margin Waddill had hoped for, but he was pleased. He was especially pleased that Simmes came out third. James E. Howard was a prominent planter who had moved his family from Mississippi in 1838, purchasing a plantation near Hamburg. He had served on the police jury, including as president. He was married to Joyce Holmes Howard, also born in Mississippi.[162]

The House of Representatives vote was as follows:

---

162. Their son David C. Howard became a prominent citizen of Avoyelles Parish, as a planter in Moreauville. He was born of the union between James E. and Joyce (Holmes) Howard in Adams County, Mississippi in 1837. His mother was a member of the Methodist Church, and died near Natchez in 1858. David C. Howard attained years of instruction in Avoyelles Parish as he prepared for college. He attended Shelbyville University in Bedford County, Tennessee, and lacked only one year to graduate when he was obliged to leave school. He was married to Miss A. M. Gray, a native of Mississippi, but a resident of Louisiana, and they moved to their plantation, which was a part of the Gray estate in 1863. In the beginning of 1863, Mr. Howard enlisted in Company B. Eighth Louisiana Regiment Infantry, and served during the remainder of the war. His command was disbanded at Natchitoches. See *Biographical and Historical Memoirs*.

Julien Deshautelle – Whig, 361
Aurelien B. (Dominique) Coco – Democrat, 360
William F. Griffin – Democrat, 312 votes

This race was much closer and surprised Waddill. Had one of the Democrats not run, the Whigs would not have won. Because two of them ran, a one-vote majority changed the nature of Avoyelles representation by adding a Whig to the mix.

John P. Waddill would not soon forget those who he felt had betrayed him. It stung to have Democrats oppose him, but he would work hard to be a good senator. On January 13, 1848, John P. Waddill would arrive in New Orleans to take his seat in the Senate.

CHAPTER 30

Politics 1848, Senator Waddill

John Waddill thought holding a seat in the State Senate would likely help his law practice. He also felt he knew plenty about politics and history and would have something to give back to the people. Electioneering was not something that he thought he would enjoy, but he went at it as though it was his passion.

The Senate was set to meet and organize on January 17, 1848, and Waddill would have to leave his practice and his land in the hands of others. He wondered if it was worth it.

Many other issues of the day faced Waddill as he remained concerned about national events. On January 2, 1848, he wrote:

> Another year has passed away, and again our wheeling planet has commenced its annual circle round the sun. Old forty-seven has gone, with all of his events, anxieties to the tomb of time. Let us look upon the pictures, which He has daguerreotyped[163] upon the memories of men. At the thought, past events spread their mighty shadows before us, as acts worthy of the golden age illumine the canvas. Foremost in the great panorama, loom up the vast deeds of our own country.
>
> Whilst yet the year was in its infancy, our army under General Z. Taylor gained over Santa Anna, one of the most splendid victories ever recorded in history. At Buena Vista in the Republic of Mexico, this battle was fought six thousand Americans, contended against twenty

---

163. The daguerreotype was the first commercially successful photographic process (1839–1860) in the history of photography. Named after the inventor, Louis Jacques Mandé Daguerre, each daguerreotype is a unique image on a silvered copper plate. See http://www.daguerreobase.org/en/knowledge-base/what-is-a-daguerreotype.

five thousand Mexicans, and conquered. Great was the slaughter of the enemy. Immediately thereafter, General Scott took the city of Veracruz, and the castle of San Juan De Uloa. In this capture, our army took from the Mexicans near six hundred cannons, and an innumerous amount of other arms and ammunition besides some 6,000 prisoners. But look towards the city of Jalapa! What mountain do we see vomiting fire, thunder and smoke, with volcanic terrors? It is the hill of Cerro Gordo! It was there that General Scott again met the armies of Mexico, to conquer, to crush them.

A vast army of Mexico, was again on that day overthrown, and Santa Anna driven from the field in, inglorious flight whilst many of his braver officers were killed or captured by our army. Scott pursues his march, directed to the City of Mexico. On his way, Jalapa and Perote surrendered, and were occupied. The great city of Puebla surrendered to our army, with all of its munitions of war and fortresses. Scott again takes the road to Mexico, with a force of some 10,000 men of all characters, teamsters included. He was too weak to leave force sufficient to keep open communication with Jalapa and Veracruz. Weeks passed by and heard nothing of him, save rumors, and those frequently of a disastrous import to our little army. Anxiety was intense during this time, and often was the administration severely censured for leaving Scott with so small a force to overcome such powerful opposition in the heart of the country of the enemy.

At length vague rumors come through paper of the enemy of bloody battles fought under the walls of the city of Mexico, and that our army was at the mercy of the Mexicans, and that Scott had prayed for a suspension of hostilities. Hereby this glorious gloom was swept away, and two of the most brilliant victories burst upon us, that had crowned our arms during the war. The victories of Contreras and Churubusco. The countenance of every friend of this republic was lighted up with a smile, joy thrilled through every bosom, and every eye flashed with patriotic fire. Santa Anna with Valencia together commanding some thirty thousand Mexicans was again beaten, conquered and driven from the field. The city of Mexico was at the mercy of our gallant army. It trembled at its peril, it sued for an armistice. This armistice was granted by Scott for the purpose of entering into negotiations for peace.

N.P. Trist of the state department, was on the spot with our army ready at all times to extend the olive branch to Mexico, and put an end to the war. Commissioners were appointed by Mexico, to meet with Trist and confer; yet nothing was done. In their days the Mexicans treacherously broke the armistice, and General Scott gave orders to attack the city. Three terrible battles were fought. Three bloody victories were gained by our gallant little army. One of which resulted in the capture of the Molino Del Rey, another in the storming and taking of Chapultepec, and the other in taking the city itself. The army is now occupying the city of Mexico and the Mexican government is at Querétaro.

Waddill again showed his unwavering patriotism, despite the controversy within the government surrounding the war with Mexico. He then focused on how he would handle his personal life, legal career, and properties all the while serving Avoyelles in the Senate. It would not be an easy task.

Waddill's first year as a legislator was a learning experience. On January 13, he landed in New Orleans. On January 17, the Senate met and organized. The House did not. The cause of the House not organizing on that day owed to the political maneuvering of the Whigs. Some five of their party had not arrived, and without them, they could not elect a speaker. Waddill thought that they chose to violate the constitution and laws of their state rather than lose the chance of electing a Whig speaker. On Tuesday, the St. Landry delegation, numbering five Whigs, arrived. The House organized and elected P. W. Farrar,[164] a Whig, speaker. The Monday thereafter, the legislature in joint session elected Pierre Soulé[165] (Democrat) as U.S. Senator for six years, although the Whigs had two on joint ballot. The Democrats likewise elected

---

164. Preston W. Farrar from New Orleans presided over the last legislature to meet in New Orleans. The next session in 1850 would be in Baton Rouge. See his comments in Alcée Fortier, *The History of Louisiana*, vol. III, *1808–1861* (1904; repr., Cornerstone Book Publishers, 2012) 248–49.

165. Pierre Soulé was a French-born citizen who was exiled for revolutionary ideas. He moved to Great Britain then settled in New Orleans and became an attorney and politician. He later became the Minister to Spain. Famous for writing the *Ostend Manifesto*, which was an attempt to admit Cuba into the Union, he later opposed secession for Louisiana. He did support the Confederacy, but was captured by the Union. "Pierre Soulé," Wikipedia, https://en.wikipedia.org/wiki/Pierre_Soul%C3%A9.

Joseph Walker state treasurer with several Whigs voting for him. A Democrat was elected state printer. These unexpected triumphs of the Democratic Party owed their consummation to united action and to the reckless conduct of the Whigs in showing such a desire for office as to refuse to obey the mandates of the constitution on the first day.

Pierre Soulé would later assist Solomon Northup's effort for freedom while Soulé was still in Washington D.C. in 1852. As Solomon Northup noted:

> Senator Soule especially interested himself in the matter, insisting, in forcible language, that it was the duty and interest of every planter in his State to aid in restoring me to freedom, and trusted the sentiments of honor and justice in the bosom of every citizen of the commonwealth would enlist him at once in my behalf.[166]

The legislature met until, March 16, 1848, when both houses adjourned.

January 17, 1848

On this day, the Senate of the state organized by electing Horatio Davis its secretary and H. Colombe Davis his assistant. The Senate then proceeded to the election of sergeant at arms; Le Martre received the unanimous support of that body and was duly elected. Grass was elected door keeper, and Robert J. Ker was unanimously elected reporter. Four reporting clerks were then elected.

In the House of Representatives, all the Whigs but two refused to answer to their names. Thus a quorum could not be formed, and consequently the House had to adjourn. Waddill wrote in his diary:

> The reason of this unprecedented conduct of the Whigs was that all of the members of their party were not present in the city, and they chose rather to infract the constitution of their country, than to render doubtful their election of a Whig speaker and other officers. Their conduct deserves the condemnation of every honorable man in the Nation. If the absolute provisions of the fundamental law of the land is to be disregarded and trampled upon, for the purpose of security to a political party a paltry triumph, in the election of

---

166. Solomon Northup, *Twelve Years a Slave*, edited by Sue Eakin and Joseph Logsdon (1868; repr. Baton Rouge: Louisiana State University Press, 1983), 227.

officers. Think it time for the patriots of the country to crush the dangerous leaders of that political band, and with them the seeds of anarchy and misrule- I hope that the Democrats will never be guilty of such a breach of Law as the Whigs have perpetrated – above written.[167]

New Orleans, January 18, 1848 (written for the 17)

On January 18, the Senate met at noon. Duncan F. Kenner made a successful motion for the body to meet the house in joint session at 5:00 in the evening for the purpose of counting votes for auditor of public accounts. Maunsel White submitted a resolution approving the war and sustaining the president in his course toward Mexico, which, he moved, should lay upon the table for the consideration of the Senate, subject to their call. The Senate, after minor motions, adjourned business, until half past 4:00.

The House had met at 10:00, the St. Landry Whigs having arrived, and proceeded to organize, which they did by electing Preston W. Farrar of New Orleans their speaker and Alexander Guviller their chief clerk. Henry Phillips of Desoto was the Democratic candidate for speaker and obtained forty-six votes to Farrar's forty-eight. At the time of the vote, Phillips had a majority, forty-seven votes to Farrar's forty-six. But Representative De Jean of St. Landry, who had voted for Phillips, begged to correct his vote, which permitted him to vote for Farrar. While De Jean was correcting his vote, Representative Stewart, a Whig from Point Coupee, came in, and, though the voting had closed, was permitted to vote for Farrar.

At 5:00 the two houses met in joint session, and the count of the votes cast by the people of the state for auditor of public accounts, it was found that Louis Bordelon of St. Landry had a majority and was declared duly elected. Both houses then adjourned until 10:00 on the eighteenth.

Waddill was acquainted with Bordelon, the new auditor of public accounts. He had been Parish Judge of Avoyelles for several years. A noble-looking man, Bordelon was about thirty-eight or forty years of age, roughly six-feet tall, weighed nearly two hundred pounds, and had black eyes and hair. He had fine features and was quite intelligent. Bordelon also was a compassionate and clever fellow but a considerable office seeker. Waddill could not blame him; he was poor, and an office was necessary to his well-being. He was tolerably well-qualified.

---

167. DJW, January 17, 1848, vol. 3, pg.1.

New Orleans, January 19, 1848

The Senate met agreeably until adjournment. Its members gave several notices of bills and resolutions, among them one by Waddill that gave notice that he would shortly bring the following: "A bill for the relief of A. Derivas," "A bill for the relief of Valaire Dauzat and Raphael Dauzat of the Parish of Avoyelles," and "A bill to authorize Magistrates to appoint Constables in certain cases."

Resolutions the day before were offered to exclude John M. Bell from his seat in the Senate by W. Brashear. On the nineteenth, on motion of Colonel Porter of Caddo, they were referred, after considerable debate, to a special committee, to be reported on as early as practicable. The president of the Senate, Frasimond Landry, Lieutenant Governor of Louisiana, appointed M. M. Reynolds, L. G. Bryce, Col. Porter, D. F. Kenner, and Parham to serve on said committee. The message of the governor had been laid before both houses the day before. On the nineteenth, the Senate passed a resolution for both houses to meet in the House of Representatives and elect a state printer on Saturday, January 22.

New Orleans, January 20, 1848

Waddill wrote:

Today the Senate met agreeably to adjournment. During the morning hours, I gave notice that I would shortly introduce a resolution relative to the improvement of the navigation of Bayou des Glaises and Lake Pearl. Today in the Senate Resolutions Committee approval of the course on the administration were passed. Also declaring the Mexican War was brought on by Mexico. It also requested to instructing our Senators and requesting our Representatives to sustain the President in vigorous prosecution of said War to an honorable and satisfactory peace. That the acquisition of Territory as indemnity for the expenses and other damages against Mexico was proper and just. Further, that the President throughout had acted constitutionally. There were also resolutions offered expressing our gratitude to our army for its meritorious services in Mexico.

Waddill also gave notice that he would shortly introduce a bill to appoint another day than the one the constitution designated for the meeting of the legislature.

One aspect of serving in the legislature in New Orleans that pleased Waddill greatly was the quickness that news traveled. He made notes of several events in his diary.

On the twenty third of January, John Quincy Adams, a representative in congress and ex-president of the United States died. He was aged eighty years. He has served his country for years and was one of the great men of the age. His devotion to his country, to the principles of civil liberty, cannot be questioned yet I believe, many of his views were emotions, and some impracticable. But his intentions were correct. He was a scholar of the rarest kind. He was a poet, a statesman, and a philanthropist. His countrymen without distinction of parties will forever cherish his memory. He is the only man in the United States, there is for, who has served as a representative in congress, after having been President of the republic.

Whilst this great man in America, was rendering up his soul to God, the principles, which he had so long advocated, were overthrowing the Monarchies of Europe. France amongst, the most enlightened nations of the Earth, was pouring out her blood for civil liberty, and dethroning one of the richest Kings known in modern times. On the 23rd of February 1848, the people of Paris commenced a revolution. They sought freedom. They asked it of Louis Phillip, their citizen king, but their prayer was unheeded. They on that day sought not to depose him, but they wished him to dismiss Guizot, his minister of state and other ministries and they demanded their impeachment. This was denied. In three days Louis Phillip was deposed, himself and his minister Guizot, exiles in England, and in France a republic established. This lost some five hundred lives, but freedom at such price is cheaply bought. Our own revolution lasted seven years, and thousands of our noble ancestors laid down their lives in their country's cause ere we forced from Great Britain a reluctant assent to our independence. We thought this cheap for the blessings it brought. The whole United States sympathizes with France. We cheer her on her glorious career, and feel confident of her success. Two of the sons of the late king accede to the late revolutionary measures and say that they abide the orders and decrees of the provisional government now established. They are in Algeria, Africa. The Democratic influence of France is flashing like lightening through all Europe, Russia, and Ireland in a blaze. Already several attempts at revolution have taken place in England and Scotland. Sicily has thrown off the yoke of Monarchy and proclaims herself free. The noble Roman Pontiff, is given his people liberty as fast as they can bear it.

Waddill wrote that the German states were in a political ferment, and Austria was on the eve of revolution.

N. P. Trist, although recalled to the United States, appeared to have received a proposition of a treaty of peace from the government of Mexico. He signed the same, and an armistice was entered into between the American general in chief and the Mexican authorities.

The President of the United States submitted Trist's treaty to the U.S. Senate, and the Senate, with some alterations and amendments, confirmed it and sent it back to Mexico for its confirmation. The president appointed Ambrose Hundley Sevier[168] of Arkansas, a U.S. senator whom the Senate confirmed, as minister, with plenary powers to Mexico.

January 23, 1848

A great balloon, with a lady in the car, ascended from the west side of the Mississippi River in the town of Algiers. It shot up into the air a mile or higher and descended in New Orleans near Canal Street. The woman was uninjured.

Waddill attended the Methodist Church on Poydras Street and heard a sermon from the Reverend W. Winaris of Mississippi. He was disappointed. He had heard that he was an orator, but he found it to be a mistake. Winaris preached a good, sensible sermon, but he was not eloquent.

Waddill had commenced boarding with Mrs. Procter on Royal Street at twelve dollars per month. Board was not included.

January 24, 1848

On this day, an important election for a U.S. Senator took place in the state legislature. Duncan F. Kenner was the Whig candidate and John Slidell the Democratic. The Whigs, on a joint ballot, had a nominal majority of two.

---

168. Senator Sevier resigned as Senator to attend to this duty and never returned to the Senate. He ended up dying in Arkansas from complications of health issues he incurred in Mexico. "Ambrose Hundley Sevier (1801–1848)," The Encyclopedia of Arkansas History and Culture, http://www.encyclopediaofarkansas.net/encyclopedia/entry-detail.aspx?entryID=1760

When they came to vote, one Whig was absent, and another, Baldwin from Sabine Parish, voted for Slidell. A tie resulted. A second ballot finished with the same result. One of the Whigs made a motion, to be discussed in the Senate chamber, which turned out to be a sham to gain time. When the Senate left the house and went to its own chamber, a Whig moved to adjourn. It met a negative vote.

Eventually, the Senate again repaired to the House of Representatives, and the Democrats elected Pierre Soulé over D. F. Kenner by a majority of seven. The election of state printer then commenced, and the Whigs ran the editor of the *Bee* as their candidate while the Democrats ran Peter K. Wagner. Wagner was elected by a majority of two. So the Democrats succeeded in both elections. Waddill was well-pleased.

The legislature elected Joseph Walker, Democratic treasurer, over George C. McWhorter Whig, by a nine-vote majority.

The session went on until March 1848. By then, Waddill was anxious to go home to see his family. He did not know whether he liked being away so much, but it sure was exhilarating to serve.

Coming Home

When Waddill came home in March, he found his family very ill. They had not complained to him so as not to worry him. He regretted not being home to help. Waddill now had three children. Besides Thomas Hickman Waddill, born in 1842, he had a daughter, Laura Elizabeth, born in 1844, and another daughter, Ida Amelia, born in 1847. When he returned, Thomas had just recovered. Laura took sick, and then Ida, and next Waddill's wife, Julia. Ida and Julia both lay in a torpid state for three to four days. Ida was threatened with a congestion of the brain, and Julia vomited severely for three days, laying with fever and a total loss of appetite. On the fourth day, Julia broke out with the measles and continued to do so for two or three days. The doctor thought it could be scarlet fever as she had a sore throat. Ida remained sick as well, but after a few more days, both were better yet still weak. Waddill felt he had better start staying home more for his family.

In April 1848, Waddill began meeting with other local Democrats to form a Democratic Association for the Parish of Avoyelles. General Pierre Couvillion, a man Waddill respected greatly, served on this committee. The Democrats dined together at the Couvillion's and then drew up some rules.

The next day, as the diary puts it, Waddill "ground his wife's scissors." He joked with Julia, "I consider this scissor grinding a sharp subject, and any man who wishes to clip off the sprouts of domestic difficulties should always keep his wife's scissors sharp."

Julia laughed even when Waddill's joking around was not that funny. Waddill thought it was worthy of print.

April 17, 1848

On this day, Waddill had a visit from Julien Deshautelle, who served in the Louisiana house while Waddill was in the Senate. Deshautelle stated the purpose of the visit as legal in nature.

He needed an order of seizure and sale in favor of himself as the administrator of John Bon Garcon estate against Eugene Egan. He also needed a confession of judgment on R. W. Kay.

Waddill accepted the request to handle these legal matters. A week earlier, an articled signed only by "Truth" had appeared in *The Villager*. It lauded Deshautelle's actions in the House and took weak cuts at Waddill in the Senate.

Waddill suspected that Deshautelle, his client, colleague, and supposed friend, but a member of the Whig Party, had written the anonymous letter to the editor. Deshautelle had won office by one vote over Aurelien B. (Dominique) Coco, the Democratic leader, in 1847. The vote was 361 to 360 with William F. Griffin, also a Democrat, coming out third with 312 votes.

> Of course, Deshautelle felt it was not what he thought should be printed. He said he would tell Derivas, the editor, that he did not like his tone and not to use his name in his paper any more.

With a slight grin of sarcasm, Waddill thought that politics may be a beautiful study for some men but for others the practice thereof may be pleasant. For Waddill, it was a continual drawback on his happiness. He was a Democrat and gloried in the great progress of democracy throughout the world. He felt willing to sustain it and his government to the end of his days and with all of his energies, but in doing so, he did not wish to keep up with a continual frenzy on the subject but rather wanted to enjoy its blessing in soberness.

Julien Deshautelle left Waddill's office, wondering whether John suspected him of writing the letter. He would have to approach Derivas to keep up the pretense.

Mail and newspaper delivery continued to vex Waddill. He wanted news as fast as he could get it, and he complained about the delays to his fellow

Avoyellean, Congressman John H. Harmanson, a U.S. Representative from Louisiana. Born in Norfolk, Virginia, Harmanson pursued classical studies and graduated from Jefferson College in Washington, Mississippi. He moved to Avoyelles Parish in 1830 and engaged in agricultural pursuits. He also studied law and was admitted to the bar and practiced. He served as member of the state Senate in 1844.[169] Waddill wrote to Harmanson:

Dear Congressman Harmanson,

Today, I received many of the newspapers that I read. From some cause or other the New Orleans *Weekly Delta*[170] did not come with the mail today. It is strange that we are so treated about our papers. When the *Delta* comes regularly, it is ten days old. But now it will be 17. That will be carrying news on the old Paddy-go easy style, not in accordance with the age of Railroads, and lightning telegraphs. Why, the news is carried across the Altantic faster. The Cunard line is not over 13 days from Liverpool to Boston, but we poor devils in the South, wait seventeen days for the new from New Orleans to Marksville, a distance of 300 miles, not quite. I suppose though that we must bear it, and be glad that we get any papers at all. I receive the *Washington Union* in ten days. Today I received one. If the Post Master general does not look into this for us, we will be truly a benighted set. No one of us will know when the war ends with Mexico, until a year after its close. We could have the mail from New Orleans here in thirty-eight hours, if we had our rights. A Mississippi packet could throw it out at Roth's Point,[171] which is a Red River landing. From there the mail carrier could have it in Marksville in five hours.

---

169. Harmanson (January 15, 1803–October 24, 1850) was elected as a Democrat to the twenty-ninth, thirtieth, and thirty-first Congresses and served from March 4, 1845, until his death in New Orleans October 24, 1850. He served as chairman of the Committee on Expenditures in the Post Office Department (twenty-ninth Congress). He was interred in Moreau Plantation Cemetery, Pointe Coupe Parish, Louisiana. "John H. Harmanson," Wikipedia, https://en.wikipedia.org/wiki/John_H._Harmanson.

170. *The Weekly Delta* was a New Orleans newspaper begun in January 1848.

171. See "Routh's Point," in Captain A. A. Humphreys and Lieut H. l. Abbot, *Report Upon The Physics And Hydraulics Of The Mississippi River* (J. B. Lippincott & Co., 1861), 151

We must sue to the matter and get the arrangement made.

Harmanson was a friend and served on the Committee on Expenditures of the Post Office Department. Waddill did not expect any change, but he felt better writing and complaining than doing nothing. He had a thirst for knowledge, and the slow pace of the postal service irked him as a result.

On April 19, 1848, Waddill wrote that his wife was sick again. He worried about her frailty. She was sick often. She had gone out to her mother's. Thomas, their son, followed her on his pony, for the first time riding by himself. John could not help but worry that he would fall and be injured.

Waddill's day-to-day life continued as he had a concern for his crops and cultivation. Louisiana was becoming well-known for it sugar cane, and more farmers were planting cane in Avoyelles. On April 27, 1848, he wrote that the crops on Bayou des Glaises were looking well. Corn was as promising as he had seen, and cotton looked good. Some planters had hilled their cotton. Sugar cane was excellent. N. R. Selser has a field of the best cane that Waddill had ever seen at this season of the year. He thought that Selser would make two hogsheads per acre. He noted that W. F. Griffin's cane did not look so well but would end up good.

Waddill's complaint was with his workers. They had nearly plowed his crops over. They were throwing dirt to it but left much of his corn covered with clods, which he knew would injure it. He did not know how much he would raise but figured it would be enough for his purposes. Waddill cropped with William Edwards on the bayou. They had each one hand apiece and cultivated thirty-five to forty acres.

Levi W. Williams, who was imprisoned eighteen months by judgment of the District Court, broke out of jail. The sheriff was offering a reward of five cents for him.

April 30, 1848 – Temperance Society

A temperance society had long been in existence here—and some three months since took the name of the Avoyelles Temperance society. "Yesterday the society had an address from F. P. Hitchborn Esq., one of the members. His address was very creditable. The greatest defeat was that he did not deliver it in the best style—owing to his being unaccustomed to public speaking."

On the last Saturday of the month of May, Waddill would deliver the next address before the society. He did know not how to begin, but he would try and see what he could say on the occasion. Waddill gave it a lot of thought. When he began, he felt prepared.

Ladies and Gentlemen. It is not idle curiosity that brings us together on this occasion. It is in obedience to a law made and adopted by ourselves. That on the last Saturday in each month, we are found assembled here for the purpose of combining action with theory in carrying out a reform, which is to embrace and benefit the whole human race. We were born and we live in an age of science and reform. Old and venerated rites and customs, encrusted with the sanction of thirty centuries have been divested of their mysterious raiment by the philosophers of the present age and shown to be incompatible with laws divine and happiness of man. The investigating spirit of the nineteenth century confirms itself to no particular branch of science or reform in the habits or institutions of man. Yet, like the sun of our solar system it pervades with its rays all things visible or that can be found, by a process of analogist reasoning in creation. Whilst at that point a philosophical reformer is leading the mind of the blind, the deaf, and the dumb, through the intricacies of science and literature at this co-laborer is chaining down the lightnings and teaching them to talk. Whilst here we find our demonstrating the age of the world by the success in layers of rocks, earth and other superficial formation. There another is exhibiting the beings which is inhabited it previous, to the introduction of man.

From the above and various other facts we are convinced that the enlightened nations of the earth are filled with investigating minds, searchers into the progress and decay of empires and their inhabitants—reformers of the morals and minds of mankind.

In this investigation, the habits and customs of man—and their influences upon his health and happiness have necessarily received a large share of the time and application of the man of science and reformer. Physiology with mathematical precision has laid upon to our views the mysterious machinery of our physical system, and experimental chemistry has proven the manner in which it is nourished, and the principles that assist to its health and existence.

The love of life, or self-preservation, has induced man to search most diligently for the, principles and compounds which destroy animal organization and produce death if taken into the system. The whole family of the gasses are formed to produce death in all animal organizations, in their simple state.

Hydrogen; nitrogen; oxygen; carbon, etc. As the animal and vegetable kingdoms are now organized it is shown that the creator found it necessarily to introduce into the atmosphere, carbon in the proportion of one part to every two thousand and. Its destructive action upon animal organization, was, no doubt the cause, why omniscience, combined so small a portion with the oxygen and nitrogen, which make up that element—we respire. It exists in large-quantities in charcoal, and is disengaged then from, and by ignition. Experience proves that if a man should ignite a grate full of charcoal in a close room, and remain therein for an hour or perhaps a less time, he would expire from the effects of the carbon evolved from the burning coal.

It is likewise true, that in organized beings whether animate or inanimate, vessels—tubes and ducts are formed by the workmanship of God—so as to take up and assimilate with their several systems. Whatever may be taken or presented as food. In the animal kingdom, this nourishment is received into the system by eating in the vegetable part of creation nourishment enters the plant by absorption. In the animal kingdom a portion of whatever is eaten is likewise absorbed—nor does it become a part of the system in any other manner than by absorption. The whole animal kingdom is filled with delicate absorbing vessels—which and by chemical process forms it into flesh and blood. If it be possible for nature to combine it into such materials, but as before stated there are some things that produce disorganization in animals and of that member carbon is one. It has been shown that an atmosphere highly impregnated with carbon, is unfit for respiration, and if inhaled will produce death. The absorbents of the stomach, duodena's, and alimentary canal take up, as would a sponge, whatsoever may come in contact with them, capable of absorption. Poisons taken into the stomach are like food, absorbed by these vessels, disseminated through the whole system in the same manner as nutrient, the effect which they produce being contrary to the healthy action of the physical action of the animal functions must necessary tend to disorganization, and if the deleterious matter be continually supplied, death will result there from. It is true that the process is so slow in some instances, that death's approach is unobserved and perhaps unacknowledged to have resulted from the cause of poisons swallowed years before, yet by post mortem examinations, the effects of the poison has been deleted and it's destroying footsteps traced from its first introduction, to the tomb.

The composition of spirituous liquors is more than one half carbon, the most destructive of gasses to animal existence.[172]

Waddill was more resolved than ever to promote temperance. This began with his personal commitment to abstinence.

---

172. DJW, April 30, 1852, vol. 3, pgs. 4–7.

CHAPTER 31

FAITH CHALLENGE, MAY 1848

Waddill was a voracious reader. He enjoyed new ideas and loved to debate them. He never forgot the lessons learned at Augusta and continued that tradition. He began to read *Vestiges of the Natural History of Creation*.[173] At the time, Waddill was unsure of who wrote the book. It was not until 1884 that the author was confirmed to be Robert Chambers. The book connected, for the first time, natural science to creation. Chambers was affiliated with George Combe, who was the leading writer and believer in phrenology, a subject that was also controversial and which Waddill had studied at Augusta College.

Waddill had serious thoughts about the book and the theology of this subject. He wrote:

> It is a curious work. It gives a geological history of the creation for the Earth and its inhabitants, which is diametrically opposed to the account given by Moses, of the creation. The author has treated his subject ably, and so far as I am able to judge, he is right. He has entered a field, forbidden by Orthodox Christianity. He shows that the deity works by fixed, and unalterable laws, and not by personal exertion and application in the creation of a planet or zoophyte. He shows likewise that creation is progressive, that the laws made and fixed by Almighty wisdom, are still producing new worlds, new beings, and perfecting the old. The earth is progressing to greater perfection, daily. Those mighty changes have taken place in its surface, and productive capacities since its creation. He shows that the earth was incapable of sustaining organized life when first formed into a

---

173. Robert Chambers, *Vestiges of the Natural History of Creation* (London: John Churchill, 1844).

globe and that countless centuries must have rolled away before it was filled for the habitation of man. All of this I believe, Chemistry, that critic, which picks to pieces the mysterious webs surrounding all natural objects, demonstrates the truth that in nature there are some fifty or sixty simples which by various combinations have formed all things of which we have accessible knowledge. These simples under one combination will produce a stone, under another a man. Trees, shrubs, water, air, Earth, and flesh, are all reducible to the simplest substances alluded to above. The gasses when combined in certain proportions produce the flesh of animals, but when death destroys the living principle which keeps those gasses in that particular combination, they soon disengage themselves, spread abroad in the waters, earth, and air, and portions of them are again united in new beings and thus continually keep fulfilling their destiny pointed out by creative wisdom.

The old notorious of the Christian fathers concerning the Deity are fast giving way, and a nobler conception of his being and attributes is taking possession of the minds of men. We look upon him now as a mighty being, an incomprehensible principle, working by laws established, and unchangeable, though established by himself.

I am still reading the "Vestiges of Creation". I put but little faith in the author's theory of the animal creation. It is my opinion that the Creator, by fixed laws, brought forth the animal creation at such times as the conditions of the earth and atmosphere permitted.

F. P. Hitchborn

John Waddill respected certain men, especially those who stood for what they believed in no matter the circumstances. One of those men, F. P. Hitchborn,[174] had been one of the Marksville Volunteers in the Mexican War. He taught school in Avoyelles Parish for nearly three years, being disabled in one of his feet so as to prevent him from pursuing his trade as a means of support. In March 1843, Sheriff F. Ricord appointed him deputy sheriff, and he remained in that office until May 1846 and made an excellent officer. At the latter end of May (the United States being at war with

---

174. F. P. Hitchborn became mayor of Marksville in 1850. *Biographical and Historical Memoirs*, 616.

Mexico), Hitchborn volunteered and went to Mexico. He was in several skirmishes and fought valiantly in the siege and storming of the city of Monterey as a member of the Texas Rangers. After they were disbanded, he remained with the army under General Zachary Taylor until March 1847, principally, if not entirely, operating with the spy companies. After he returned, he was sick with rheumatism, and fever to some extent. His health improved, and for a time, he was very healthy, save for an occasional fever. He acted as deputy sherriff after his return from Mexico and performed the duties of deputy collector of taxes past due payments. He was interested in going to the seat of government and thence to the state of Maine to visit his relatives. He expended a great deal of money in his Mexican expedition and afterward for a man of his limited means.

More Newspapers

John Waddill never gave up on learning the news of the world. He utilized his friendship with Congressman Harmanson to obtain six subscriptions to the New York weekly *True Sun*.[175] He would send one copy to James R. Waddill, Perkins Mill, Missouri; one to Seth Q. Waddill (John's older brother), Jackson, Tennessee; one to Lemuel Miles, Avoyelles; one to F. P. Hitchborn, Marksville; one to himself; and one to James Ferguson, Holmesville, Louisiana.

Then, finally, the United States and Mexico declared and ratified peace. The Republic of Mexico ceded to the United States all of New Mexico and upper California, containing an area of 676,000 square miles or more, and the United States paid to Mexico twenty million dollars. The United States also quieted in its title to Texas, the boundary being defined as the Rio Grande up to Paso del Nort. Waddill wanted to write more on this subject, but as the treaty had not been published at Washington yet, he held back. There was no notice whether General Butler would, or had accepted yet, as he was commander in chief of the U.S. Army in Mexico.

Waddill also noted, "The Baltimore National Democratic convention on the 25th of May last, nominated as their candidate for President of the United States Lewis Cass of Michigan and for Vice President William O. Butler of Kentucky. General Cass has accepted, and in consequence resigned his seat in the United States Senate."

---

175. It ceased publication in 1848. "About The true sun. (New York [N.Y.]) 1843–18??,"Chronicling America: Historic American Newspapers, Library of Congress Digital Collection, http://chroniclingamerica.loc.gov/lccn/sn83030464/.

Waddill respected Zachary Taylor but could not support a Whig. "The Whigs have nominated as their candidate, General Zachary Taylor of Louisiana, and Millard Fillmore of New York, as Vice President." Waddill thought that the Democrats would beat the Whigs this election. He wrote:

> They had abandoned all of their principles and have taken a man as their candidate for the chief Magistracy, who openly avows that he knows nothing of the policy, good or bad, of his government. He says that he is entirely ignorant of the political questions that divide the citizens of our republic into two parties. But the Whigs have nominated him because as a general he was successful in Mexico. This is his sole qualification. They deserve to be, and will be most stingily beaten he hoped in November.
>
> They abandoned Henry Clay. His friends run him in convention against Taylor, but he could not be nominated. He is the embodiment of their principles, but the poor ole statesman, was abandoned for a man of straw in politics, on the score of availability. I esteemed General Taylor as a commander, and an honest man. But as a President he had no capacity. He cannot have, for he never mingled in politics or the scenes of civil life. He is no civilian. Cass and Butler are both civilians, both statesmen. Old Henry Clay was a gallant leader, and he is a great statesman. Never in his life have his friends been obliged to ask, what side he would take on any of the great questions which divide the two parties. Old Heal was always in the lead on the Whig side, ready and willing to show his hand. Though often beaten, his enemies had not much of which they could boast in intellectual combat; for Henry is a giant in intellect. Were I a Whig instead of a Democrat, I would support Clay for President against any man in the nation. But adieu gallant Harry, although Clay and I differ in their political opinions, yet I esteemed him as one of the greatest of our great men, and a patriot. The mighty principles, which Clay have so long supported by your daring genius, have been tamely surrendered, unconditionally, by those who should have died by his side.

From his earliest infancy, Waddill had been taught to look upon Clay as one of the brightest stars of the country, and should Clay go down to his grave while yet Waddill lived, he, with others of his political opponents, would drop a tear for his nation's loss in Clay's final departure for the tomb.

Newspapers in Marksville continued to be published.[176] E. J. Poster issued the *Prairie Star* at Marksville as a Whig journal, in August 1848. It was true that in the late 1840s and 1850s, Marksville and Avoyelles were ahead of their time in education and the publication of newspapers for such a small population.

Waddill Vents His Opinion
July 9, 1848

Apparently, in the local paper someone wrote an editorial and signed it "Avoyelles." In answer to the editorial, another anonymous writer wrote a response that riled Waddill. At issue was pay for legislators, and the auditor of public accounts was taking issue with paying salaries of teachers and others as appropriated. Waddill was incensed and knew that he had to write a defense of the pay and be critical of the auditor of public accounts with a well-reasoned letter. He wrote the following:

> Precedent is not law, unless persevered in for a time beyond which the memory of which ruineth not to the contrary. The opinions of Judge Woodruff are entitled to respect. Yet the constitution has given neither him nor his successor judicial powers. Therefor his decisions are but opinions and binding on no one but himself. Men of inferior abilities, to whom nature has been sparing of her gifts, may be permitted to use them as authority, for, unable to reason from cause to effect, they are broken, crushed, annihilated without a precedent. Some men are so dazzled by the glare of office that they never suffer themselves to examine into the specific extent of their duties but are continually assuming powers belongings to others, and rarely if ever are willing to surrender to the proper authorities the balance of powers belonging to others, and rarely if ever are

---

176. *Biographical and Historical Memoirs* writes of several as follows: "Le Pelican was issued May 28, 1855), by P. D'Artlys as the successor of the *Villager*, retaining the volume and issue number; D. A. Bland was editor. L'Organie Central was issued June 14, 1855, at Marksville, by Fenelon Cannon and S. Lewis Taylor. It was printed in French and English, and espoused the platform of the Know-nothings. F. Barclay was connected with this paper. On June 13, 1857, the editors announced the termination of their engagement with the Know-nothing party, and Adolphe P. Marcotte became editor. In May, 1858, A. L. Gusman, succeeded Marcotte and carried on this journal to its end before the war."

willing to surrender to the proper authorities the balance of powers not belonging to them.

The present Auditor of Public accounts may not be one of these, but should the writer of the article in answer to "Avoyelles" be elevated to that office, I would expect—unless he should find a precedent—an indiscriminate use of the powers belonging to the Legislator, Judge, and comptroller. Some men mistake abuse for wit, and impudence for reason, and they are alike unable to appreciate the one or receive benefit from the other. Such men are objects of compassion, unsuited of reprehension, for their malady is a misfortune and not of a fault.

The fact that the Legislature made a specific appropriation, for their purpose of enabling the members to draw their pay is not an argument in favor of the position assumed by the answer to "Avoyelles." Was no money paid to the members of that body, on the warrant of the Auditor of Public accounts previous to the enactment of that Law? An investigation will perhaps show that there was. If so, then why withhold the pay of the Teacher? Is he less worthy of his salary than the Lawgiver? Answer these questions. I will ask a few more. Did the members of the general assembly ask, or obtain an increase of pay? Did they consider themselves, contracting with their constituents, to perform the duties of Senate or Representative at four dollars per day and their mileage, when soliciting their suffrage? Did the Auditor of Public accounts do the same?

Was the salary of said officer fixed at $3,000 per annum? Did the first Auditor serve the public for that sum? Has the present Auditor been content therewith, or has he asked and obtained, since his intention, and additional salary of $1000.00?[177]

Waddill's argument was well-reasoned and appropriate. The fact that the auditor asked for a raise was by chance but helped the argument. The *Picayune* of New Orleans, in its December 5, 1848, edition, reported that the Louisiana Legislature met in an extra session. "A communication was received from the Auditor of Public Accounts announcing that he had settled the accounts of certain creditor agreeable to instructions. Also that he had procured

---

177. DJW, July 9, 1848, vol. 3, pgs. 12–13.

a loan of $9,000.00 from the Bank of Louisiana for public school purposes and asking for an appropriation to meet the same."[178]

On December 6, 1848, during the special session, Waddill filed a bill for the relief of teachers of the public schools for the years 1847 and 1848, and it was referred to the Committee on Education.[179] Waddill would not let the auditor of public accounts decide how much and when the teachers would be paid, when the Legislature already had appropriated the money. The whole issue disturbed Waddill since he felt that he had a close relationship with the auditor, Louis Bordelon, who hailed from St. Landry and was an Avoyellean. Bordelon maintained property in Avoyelles and visited often.

Bordelon remained the statewide elected auditor for several years. In October 1851, during his reelection efforts, he stayed in his family home at Bayou des Glaises, Avoyelles Parish, due to a severe attack of inflammatory rheumatism. He suspended his canvas for reelection due to the illness.[180]

---

178. *New Orleans Times Picayune*, December 5, 1848, pg. 1.

179. Ibid., December 6, 1848, pg. 4.

180. Ibid., October 24, 1851, pg. 1.

CHAPTER 32

Politics, Business, and Temperance
August 10, 1848

William H. Duvall depended on John Waddill for many of his financial needs and transactions. Waddill would hold money for him and order goods when they were large orders, such as for pork and flour. Duvall was aware that Waddill would always use safe steamboats and trusted him with his finances. He ordered on this day two barrels of mess pork[181] and one barrel of new flour.

Waddill had frequent business dealings with H. Frellsen & Co., a reputable business in New Orleans. In the same transaction, Waddill sent $70.00 that he owed on his account with them. His friend Fielding Edwards usually found a safe steamboat for Waddill to care for these transactions.

September 23, 1848

Waddill remained steadfast in his belief in the Democratic Party. He attended a barbeque given by the Democrats on Bayou Rouge in Avoyelles Parish. The Whigs were allowed to speak first; W. Frost made the initial speech. Frost, a lawyer from New Orleans, made a credible speech in his allotted hour, although he mainly filled it with a rant about the Democratic platforms and the military glory and exploits of General Taylor. He also mentioned many old Greeks and Romans and, with a grand endeavor, tried to prove that Millard Fillmore was not an abolitionist.

Peter Tanner, a planter from Rapides Parish, made a short, unostentatious Democratic speech. He, too, had an hour but took only half that time. Tanner was very active in public affairs and served in the state legislature for Rapides

---

181. Mess pork is barreled salt pork made from sides and shoulders of lightweight hogs, usually cut in portions of about four pounds each.

Parish. He owned about 3,400 acres of land on Bayou Boeuf, near the Avoyelles Parish line.[182] Later, Judge J. Y. Bryce of Rapides, a sterling Democrat, gave a speech, as Waddill wrote, with "irrefragable evidence sustaining the Democratic creed." Judge Bryce had served as chairman *pro tem* to organize the Democratic Convention held at Baltimore in May 1848.[183] The convention met at the Universalist Church at the corner of North Calvert and Pleasant Street.

The speaking stopped at one, adjourning for an hour to allow the crowd to eat. They did not start up again until three, at which time the attorney from Alexandria, John K. Elgee, who was very close to Waddill, spoke. Although Elgee was a Whig, Waddill thought that his speech was rousing.

H. Frellsen & Co.

Waddill continued to do business with H. Frellsen & Co. This well-known merchant company out of New Orleans had many connections with steamboats and their trade partners. On March 2, 1849, Waddill wrote a letter to Frellsen & Co., enclosing a draft drawn on Hugh M. Keary by his brother W. V. Keary in favor of Waddill for the sum of $2,587.56. A letter, to the care of Juan Y. de Egana, accompanied the draft to H. M. Keary in New Orleans.[184] A New Orleans importer of goods, de Egana, born in 1816, served as a director for New Orleans Canal and Banking. He had a large estate in Ascension Parish and many business ties to Hugh M. Keary. Waddill gave the letters with the draft to Fielding Edwards to be forwarded by the first safe steamboat to H. Frellsen at New Orleans.

W. V. Keary owned Catalpa Grove Plantation in northern Avoyelles and southern Rapides, just south of Cheneyville.[185] He and his brother,

---

182. Tanner sold his property to James Lemuel Pearce for $77,400.00 in 1859 and moved to Evergreen in Avoyelles Parish. He married Eunice Rebecca Bettison and they had ten children. Stafford, *Three Pioneer Rapides Families*, 306.

183. *The Daily Crescent*, May 30, 1848, http://chroniclingamerica.loc.gov/lccn/sn82015378/1848-05-30/ed-1/seq-2/ The paper's office was located at 95 St. Charles Street in New Orleans.

184. Juan Y. de Egana's portrait painting is in the Louisiana State Museum. He died in April, 1860.

185. Hugh M. Keary and W. V. Keary are mentioned by Solomon Northup as "Carey," which sounded phonetically like Keary. Eakin refers to W. V. as W. E., but Waddill clearly writes that his name is W. V. Keary. Northup, *Twelve Years A Slave*, 113.

Hugh M. Keary, owned the large plantation together, but Hugh spent much of his time in New Orleans doing business and participating in various business enterprises.

Division No. 44 of the Sons of Temperance

Waddill and his brother, W. W., had sworn off alcohol and supported others in Marksville in their efforts with the Sons of Temperance.[186] On March 2, 1849, the organization received its regalia, which Mrs. Fielding Edwards, Miss Henrietta Edwards, Misses Mary Jane and Margarette Robinson, Mrs. Julia Malvina Waddill, and Mrs. George A. Stevens made for it. This meant a lot to Waddill, since he still remembered events of the day his friend, Dr. E. L. Briggs, drowned after both of them caroused quite a bit.

The next day, Julia's mother sold 172 acres of land to Mrs. Eliza C. Brashear, the wife of C. D. Brashear, who now had a separate property regime. She received ten dollars per acre in a sale that was part cash with the balance to be paid by October 1850.

Waddill woke on March 5, 1849, excited about the opening of court that day. Ralph Cushman, his former partner, was now judge and would preside. The District Attorney, Patrick Barry, was in California and would not be present. In his stead, the court of appeal appointed Henderson Taylor, a respected attorney, to appeal on behalf of the state in criminal cases. He also agreed to prosecute and draw up bills of indictment.

Waddill finally had to pay J. K. Elgee for the legal work he had done in the estate of Mills, which took much longer than anticipated. Elgee was a good lawyer with a great reputation for public speaking and debating.

March 10, 1849

Stephen Franklin Milligan came to Waddill's office to ask Waddill to represent him. He wanted to head west in search of gold in California. He was not of age, but the legislature this year, thanks to Waddill, has emancipated him. He needed to collect some money from his father's succession.

---

186. The Sons of Temperance was organized September 29, 1842 in New York City. Its purpose was to help members with total abstinence from alcohol consumption. See Samuel Ellis, *The History of the Order of the Sons of temperance, from its organization on the 29th September, 1842, to the commencement of the year 1848; also, an account of its formation and introduction into the several states of the Union,"* (Boston: Stacy, Richardson & Co., 1848).

It did not take long for Waddill to review the situation, and he was happy to help. He did not agree that the young man should head for the gold rush, but that was his decision to make.

Waddill wanted to help. They would have to file against the former sheriff, F. Ricord, as the syndic[187] of his father's estate. Waddill knew that Ricord was not home, as he was on Bayou Boeuf, but he would continue to collect for the benefit of young Milligan.

Waddill could not help but wonder why this young man with potential wanted to head so far west. It was a dream of many in this country to strike it rich by quick means.

On March 12, Waddill collected $87.75 and a saddle from Ricord on behalf of Stephen F. Milligan. Stephen left for Alexandria after receiving this portion of the estate. He also proudly received the pistol holsters of F. P. Hitchborn, which the owner presented to him. These were the same Hitchborn used in his campaign in Mexico. Waddill's fee was $21.00.

On this same day, Richard, one of Waddill's slaves, went with two work horses to the Red River to make a crop of corn for his mother-in-law, Mrs. Bailey C. Duke. Waddill was somewhat apprehensive about planting on his property on Bayou des Glaises because of possible overflow. He was also concerned that his crops could be destroyed with transpiration water.[188] He wanted only to raise a good crop of corn.

March 11, 1849

Waddill was giddy with excitement that, for once, the newspapers arrived in a timely manner. With the papers arrived President Taylor's inaugural address. Waddill read the papers carefully and opined:

> Today, in this parish, we received the President's inaugural address which was delivered in the City of Washington District of Colombia on the 5th of March at 2 o'clock. It was reported by the western line of telegraph to New Orleans for the Crescent. No message of a President of the United States ever came so fast or quick before. Pres-

---

187. "Syndic" is the French word for "trustee," commonly referred to in estate law in Louisiana in the 1800s. The more common use today would be "executor" if there is a will probated, or "administrator" in those estates that are intestate.

188. Transpiration is the process by which excess water escapes from plants.

ident Taylor's inaugural is very short, not filling one column of the Picayune. It is a message without principle in it. He does not declare any particular policy. He says though that he will look to congress for advice, and intimates that he will sign all the acts of that body.

He has appointed a cabinet of rabid Whigs. John M Clayton is Secretary of State. Thomas H. Ewing of Ohio is Secretary of the Home (Interior) Department. Reverdy Johnson of Maryland is Attorney General. William Meridith of Pennsylvania Secretary of the Treasury. George H. Crawford of Georgia is Secretary of War. Jacob Collamer of Vermont is Post Master General and William B. Preston of Virginia is Secretary of the Navy.

General Taylor was elected, it is true, President of the United States in November last, but not by a majority of the votes cast for President. He is a minority President by 157,000 votes. Cass, the Democratic candidate, and Van Buren, the candidate of the Free Soil Party, receiving in the aggregate, that number more than Taylor. We venture the prediction that Taylor's administration will be far inferior to that of James K Polk, which has just terminated.

Since the organization of our government no administration had been more brilliant, more successful, nor more glorious to our republic, than that of James K. Polk. He being an experienced statesman himself, he surrounded himself with a cabinet of experienced and talented men. James Buchanan Secretary of State had only stood high in the counsels of the nation and so had W. L. Marcy Secretary of War. Robert L. Walker, secretary of the Treasury has proved himself one of the ablest and most enlightened statesmen, which the world has produced. Cave Johnson, the Postmaster General has shown himself equal to the post to which he was appointed. John Y. Mason as Secretary of the Navy, has won esteem of all parties, and as the attorney general brought to the aid of the President the best legal talents of the nation.

To mention some of the acts of Polk's administration, which give it a prominence over all preceding ones, we need but say that he settled the Oregon boundary with Great Britain, on the 49th decree of North Latitude. He consummated the annexation of Texas to the Union. After one of the most brilliant wars ever waged in a righteous cause, he annexed by the treaty of peace, New Mexico, and Upper

California. He reduced the restrictive tariffs of 1842 to the revenue tariffs of 1846 and established the ware housing system, than which nothing has been more beneficial to our commerce. He leaves the finances of the government in the best condition, and the credit of the union higher than that of any government now existing.[189]

Continuing Business with H. Frellsen

On March 13, 1849, Waddill received a letter from H. Frellsen & Co. enclosing a draft on Hugh M. Keary in the amount of $2,200. Keary did not pay it because Ratcliff, Waddill's local attorney for W. Backer, received one thousand dollars from him and gave him time on the balance. There would be a huge disaster if this could not be resolved.

On the same day, Waddill received a letter from his cousin Jane Brand Barnard. She was one of three children of John Waddil's aunt on his mother's side. His aunt was Anne G. Browder, deceased wife of William Brand. She was not doing well as of March 13, 1849. The children had been struggling since her father had been taken advantage of by his young Irish wife, whom he married after Anne died.

Even before that, the children, including Jane, the only major at the time, whose full name was Elizabeth Jane Brand Barnard, had to file suit in 1841 due to actions taken by William Brand, who was serving as tutor to the children in the Estate of Anne G. Browder Brand. He encumbered the minor's property to obtain a loan. The trial court held that they could not recover. Waddill appealed this matter, and the three children were ultimately successful in overturning the trial judgment granting them relief to the detriment of Brand's mortgagers.[190] It was fortunate considering the later loss of all of their father's estate in 1846 to his young second wife. Despite Jane's health, she mentioned to Waddill that she was sending him a gift of a small vase.

In the continuing dealings with Frelson, Waddill sent two drafts to them. One was for $250.00, drawn by W. F. Griffin and endorsed by Olympe Joffrion for a debt Joffrion owed to Frellsen. The second draft involved $6.00 drawn by Jacques Amedee Boyer of Moreauville on O. Ronbieu of New Or-

---

189. DJW, March 11, 1849, vol. 2.

190. *Elizabeth Jane Barnard and another v. James Erwin and another* in *Louisiana Reports: Cases Argued and Determined in the Supreme Court of Louisiana*, Louisiana Supreme Court– Law reports, digests, etc.,Thomas H. Thorpe and Charles G. Gill, vol. 41 (West Publishing Company, 1843) 407.

The Life and Diary of John P. Waddill 195

leans on the property of Winder Crouch, as tutor of the minor children of Stephen Pearce. Marius Gauthier sent the letter. Waddill's normal courier, Fielding Edwards, and his lady were moving near Normand's Landing on Red River.

Waddill learned also that the sheriff of Avoyelles, G. P. Voorhies, was going to be married the next Monday to Mrs. Mitford Wells, widow of W. E. Mitford Wells. Waddill commented that "She is a fine woman in appearance and I think her quite intelligent. She is quite young, not over 24 years of age, if that. I esteem her much."[191]

Pierre Ellinckuysen came to the office of Waddill on March 16, 1849. They had made a proposition to Henderson Taylor about the claim of Angelina Milligan, Pierre's wife, against W. H. Duvall and F. Ricord. They had not yet succeeded. Pierre had bought from James MacEnery $100.08 worth of goods and gave him a draft for the money that was on F. Ricord, syndic of the Estate of Russell Milligan. It was not yet satisfied. As fees, Waddill accepted a draft on Ricord as syndic.

Pierre Ellinckuysen and Angelina had married on June 6, 1848, after the death of her father, Russell Milligan. Russell had married Susan Heddingrant Pearce, in 1826; she died in 1833. Angelina was a child of that marriage. Susan was the daughter of Stephen Pearce, the second son of William Pearce Sr. Stephen had eleven children with Sally Goodwin Pearce. Susan was the second child.[192]

Ellinckuysen was traveling to New Orleans on the next day. He was going to ship to Waddill a No. 2 Cary plow by the first boat for Waddill's use.

March 17, 1849

Waddill and his brother worked hard to get others to join their Sons of Temperance Division No. 44. They met on this date with their new regalia. They also now had collars and rosettes.[193] Waddill's wife made three collars and rosettes for the members. Two new members, François B. DeBellvue and J. Millen, signed up.

---

191. DJW, March 15, 1849, vol. 2, pg. 33.

192. Stafford, *Three Pioneer Rapides Families*, 358.

193. There was a proscribed design for the collars and rosetts. They can be found in the *Book of Degrees of the Order of the Sons of Temperance of North America* at the end of the book under the chapter entitled "Regalia." P.G.W.P.J. Young, 1854.

Food was always a concern for families in the 1840s. Obtaining it, preparing it, and preserving it were constant concerns. Those who could not afford to purchase meat or other foods had to raise it, grow it, or hunt and fish for it. On March 17, 1849, Waddill felt pleased to pay one dollar for three hams of venison. It would be smoked and salted for preservation and would feed the family for a while.

James MacEnery was appointed postmaster in Marksville in 1849. Waddill agreed to sign his bond for $400.00 for serving. MacEnery was the brother of Dr. Donat MacEnery and often spelled his name as "McEnery." Henderson Taylor was Waddill's security.

Waddill continued to keep up with national politics. He was well-pleased when, on its last night in session, the Senate confirmed Edward A. Hannegan, whom Waddill felt was an elegant senator, as minister to the Court of Berlin (Prussia). President Polk had appointed this native of Indiana.

At this time, the Papal States had deposed the Pope, as a temporal prince, and declared themselves a Republic. The *America* brought news that the Hungarians had whipped the Imperialists in several battles lately. Waddill prayed for their success. He noted that the British Parliament neared making her coastal trade free to American vessels. If they would do that, Waddill felt that the United States would reciprocate.

On Sunday, March 18, 1849, Waddill felt dull. He lounged around the house, visiting his wife and children and reading. He was disappointed in Sunday school and felt it was not flourishing. There were only a few children that day.

On March 19, 1849, Sheriff Gradenigo P. Voorhies married Mrs. Mitford Wells, widow of W. E. Mitford Wells. John's brother W.W. served as a groomsman. Waddill wrote again, "She is a fine looking woman, and for my acquaintance with her I esteem her much. The newly married couple has my best wishes for their happiness and prosperity." G. P. Voorhies was a popular sheriff.[194]

Dr. David M. Murdock sent a client to Waddill to defend a case for Mr. Orin Robinson after Joshua Pearce sued him. Waddill charged $25 if he would be successful and fifteen if not. James M. Bell introduced Robinson to him after Dr. Murdock gave Waddill a good reference. Waddill was pleased with himself. His practice was growing more and more each year. His brother was coming along, and his property investments were increasing.

---

194. G. P. Voorhies later served as State Representative in the Louisiana Legislature for Avoyelles Parish.

March 20, 1849

The mail continued to vex Waddill. It was, coming from New Orleans and the east, a total failure. Neither his *Daily Union* of Washington, D.C., nor the New Orleans *Daily True Delta* came to land. He wanted someone to force the contractors to make changes.

Julia and John's three children went to visit her mother on Red River. They intended to stay until the following Sunday. Waddill intended to send William, his brother, for them. The high water was finally receding.

Waddill was handling the negotiations for A. Derivas, who was interested in finding a partner for his newspaper *The Villager*. Waddill wrote to Legras, telling him that Derivas would form a partnership if Legras would pay $320.00.

On March 21, 1849, Waddill received three letters. One was from Archibald D. M. Haralson, an attorney from West Feliciana, who was born in 1816 in Virginia. Haralson had written on February 13, 1849, telling Waddill that he had seized a slave belonging to Gideon M. Glaze to satisfy the judgment of Terrence O. Connell for use of J. P. Waddill against Glaze and wanted to know whether Waddill would purchase the slave at two-thirds of his appraisement, if he were not appraised too highly. Waddill did not get the letter until this day, and the sale was to take place on the first Saturday in March.

Waddill felt that the mail contractors and postmasters between Marksville and St. Francisville were abominable. He could only hope that the department would see to this issue. Waddill may have lost his debt, which was over $500.00, because of the trade delays. If not, it could be another year before he would collect.

March 23, 1849

Waddill was serious about not drinking alcohol. He was unique, being from Avoyelles. He played cards at the residence of William Edwards. They played as partners against E. Lumins Foster and John's brother W. W. The games ended equal, as Waddill would not bet anything, so he lost nothing. John Waddill was opposed to gambling in all of its facets and forms. He would never gamble and stated that to others.

Waddill's brother-in-law Henerie L. Barlow came to the village of Marksville from his mother's plantation on Red River on March 24, 1849. He was an attorney hired to collect as a seizing creditor for his client, Jacques Meindillon, against Emile Chaze. Oliver Normand, a partner of Chaze, obtained an injunction against the seizure. He employed Henderson Taylor and was sending his son, Lewis Taylor, to attend the case. Waddill felt that Henarie would be too much for young Lewis. The case was scheduled for trial on Tuesday before Lewis White, a magistrate from Point Maigre.

Cholera was making many people in New Orleans and the state very sick. Julia came home from her mother's on March twenty-fifth and told her mother that she was sick with a disease similar to cholera. She was cured with cholera medicines. Waddill and Julia discussed the disease that neither wanted to contract.

On March 26, 1849, Dr. B. T. Dulany lost his six-day-old infant child to lockjaw. The community was saddened by this turn of events.

Continuing to make sure his family had food, Waddill purchased a cow for $15.00. She would provide milk for the entire family. The cow was six years old. Waddill was told that the cow was excellent. That night, Julia prepared green peas for supper, and Mrs. Tiller dined with them.

High water remained a problem for the area due to the Mississippi River flooding. On April 15, 1849, Avoyelles seemed to be safe, but flooding on the Mississippi threatened crops there. In Avoyelles, corn, cotton, and cane were in a flourishing state. It appeared to Waddill that the land in the parish was the best for sugar cane in the state. He hoped that property values would go up. As quickly as his hopes rose, however, a frost came that hurt the cotton crop greatly. Many farmers had to replant.

Congressman John Harmanson

John Waddill's friend and congressman, John Harmanson, left Avoyelles on April 19, 1849. He spent the night at Waddill's house on Thursday. Waddill had high praise for Harmanson. He introduced and passed a bill releasing to the State of Louisiana all swamp and inundated land. It amounted to about six million acres of land, all alluvian. Louisiana, due to the Mississippi Delta and flooding, was always growing in size. This magnificent donation was a great benefit to the state.

Waddill considered Harmanson one of the best Democrats in the state. Many spoke of his potential run for governor, but it appeared to Waddill that the Democrats would nominate General Joseph Walker, then state treasurer. Waddill hoped that Harmanson would at least run again for Congress. He was a gentleman of fair intelligence, indomitable energy, and an independent fortune, not rich, but self-supporting. He resided for several years in the parish of Avoyelles where, in 1844, he had first entered political life as a member of the state Senate. In 1846, he was elected to the Congress of the United States from the 3rd Congressional District of Louisiana, and in 1847, he was reelected.

Harmanson's first opponent had been Thomas J. Cooley of Point Coupee. Harmanson beat him by a seven hundred-vote majority. His opponent in 1847 was Neal Lafayette Saunders, whom he beat by a handsome majority also. Harmanson was born in Virginia but was principally raised in Monroe, Louisiana. He married Rachael Selser of Louisiana, by whom he had many children. His family was connected with Edward Livingston and Auguste Davezac, who both served in the Andrew Jackson presidential regime.

Major Auguste Davezac had served Jackson as an aide-de-camp in the Battle of New Orleans, in which he participated with the rank of major. Davezac served as Secretary of the United States Embassy of the Netherlands.[195] When Edward Livingston became Secretary of State, Davezac was appointed chargé d'affaires until 1839. President Van Buren re-appointed him to his old position in the Netherlands, where he served from 1845 until 1850. Davezac married an aunt of Harmanson. He had lived in New Orleans but moved to New York, where he died in 1851.

195. "Auguste Davezac," Wikipedia, https://en.wikipedia.org/wiki/Auguste_Davezac.

CHAPTER 33

THE MAIL FAIL AND PATRONIZING THE PRESS

April 17, 1849

On this day, the mail came in, but brought few or no newspapers. Waddill received two New Orleans *Weekly Deltas*, one a March number, and the other the ninth of this month, and also one *Washington Union*, the March 23 edition. The mails remained very irregular. He subscribed for the *Washington Union*, the New Orleans *Weekly Delta*, the New York *True Sons*, the *Democratic Review*, and DeBow's *New Orleans Commercial Review*, and in some mail deliveries, he scarcely would get a paper. On this day, Waddill paid a newspaper agent by the name of Dearning ten dollars for a subscription to the *Washington Union*, to last two years before ending December 31, 1849. Also, he paid five dollars for an old subscription of his friend J. B. Elam for the New Orleans *Jeffersonian*. This is what he called patronizing the press.

On April 24, 1849, the mail came and brought Waddill a *Washington Union* dated April 10, a *Democratic Review* for April, and a New Orleans *Weekly Delta* dated April 19, 1849. Things were looking up.

This was the month that Waddill papered his dwelling house and bedroom. Julia had been whitewashing and doing all kinds of renovations necessary for spring work. Waddill felt pressed into his wife's service on fatigue duty for several days, but, eventually, he was partially discharged. He had a dry sense of humor.

E. L. Foster, editor of the *Prairie Star* (Marksville), published quite a scurrilous piece against the Democratic Representative in Congress, John Harmanson.

John P. Waddill and his brother-in-law, James H. Barlow, decided to form a legal partnership. They began on April 25, 1849. Waddill believed that the intelligent Barlow, for whom he had much affection, would work well with him. Julia was pleased.

One of Waddill's friends was Henry Monroe Havard, a well-respected citizen who was born in Mississippi in 1812. Being close to the same age, they had developed a close relationship. Havard had moved to Avoyelles after his parents relocated to Rapides Parish from Mississippi. He moved to Tilden[196] in Avoyelles Parish to buy a plantation in 1841.[197] He had married Laura M. Robinson on November 9, 1848. Laura was just shy of nineteen years old when they married. Julia and John attended the wedding held on the plantation just six months before.

Havard was in Marksville visiting Waddill at his office for some minor matters and to talk politics. Both men were interested in reading and studying.

Waddill tried to convince Havard to run for public office. He was qualified and would have support parish wide. He was respected as one who did good for others without credit or expectation of favors returned.

Havard told him that he enjoyed politics, at least the study of ideas and beliefs, and loved to read. He was really a self-educated man. Havard loved the plantation and the area of Tilden. He was satisfied. He had been asked to run for the legislature and other public bodies, but he had no desire to leave his land. His wife of six months was content, and they were happy. He would hold no electioneering. Havard agreed that he would always help Waddill.

The two chatted and even had coffee as the discussion continued. There was racket outside and the sound of horses galloping instead of trotting or walking as normal. Both men heard the sounds of commotion and walked outside the office.

A rider, excited that he found him, shouted at Havard. It was a deputy sheriff. The news was not good. A young man at Bayou Sara, near St. Francisville, had shot Havard's brother, John. It happened ten days before, and the news had just arrived.

Havard questioned whether his brother was dead and, upon finding that he was alive, asked about his condition. The deputy told Havard that he thought the wound was fatal.

Havard knew that his younger brother was a little more outgoing and fun loving than he was. He left in great haste.

Days later, Waddill found out that John A. Havard did not die but had

---

196. Tilden was a farming community near present day Hamburg, near Moreauville. (erroneously stated as near Bunkie). Jefferson D. Robinson was Tilden's postmaster in 1876. See Saucier, *History of Avoyelles Parish*, 120.

197. *Biographical and Historical Memoirs*, 636. Havard and his wife raised six children.

serious wounds. Henry Havard had three children at the time, and he and his wife, Louisa, ended up with four more. John Havard, born in 1815, settled and worked as a planter near Tilden also.

June 1, 1849

Waddill purchased one hundred pounds of bacon from W. Edwards at eight cents a pound. Waddill spread the payment of $8.00 over a period of several weeks. He also paid Louis Beridon for freight on a barrel of sugar and a box of candles.

John and Julia's child, Ida, had been sick for three weeks. She was attacked with a violent fever, which affected her head very much. She was getting better but could not get out of bed. Julia took her out in the carriage to get her fresh air. Although Waddill was worried about her being injured on this ride, they came back safely.

Devotion to God

Waddill had a deep devotion to God. Yet he questioned certain beliefs. He did not hesitate to read or hear opposing views. A look at different times in his life would lead the reader to believe that his constant questioning and study made him stronger in his beliefs. He felt led to write a hymn to God and sent it to *The Villager* for print. The editors thought well enough of it to print it.

Hymn to The Creator of the Universe
1st
As on your starry vault—I look
Where all so beautiful appearance,
I read Oh! God thy radiant Book,
Thy Register of many years,
Each glittering orb that onward rolls
Through space as with the lightning speed
Proclaims that some great power controls
Its flight, and has its course decreed

2nd
Each burning sun whose twinkling rays,
But rarely reach our distance world

Measures rivaling years and days
To rolling planets round it whirled.
And far, oh far beyond my sight,
Throughout the measured realms of space
Unnumbered suns and orbs of light
Within thy universe have place.

3rd
While these I read, I bow to thee,
And let my soul's devotion prove,
That I, untaught by man, will be
The artery of the God I love
My shrine shall be this orb of thine;
My temple Lord! The boundless space
"For all within the vast design
Were made to be thy dwelling place"[198]

---

198. DJW, August 1849, vol. 3, pg. 35.

CHAPTER 34

Politics, Mail, and Death

September 4, 1849

John Waddill shouted to his brother in the office. They had received four *Union* newspapers, one Sunday *Times*, one Baton Rouge *Advocate*, and two *Weekly Deltas*. Finally, they had news from Europe and their own country. The Hungarians appeared to be succeeding against the Austrians and Russians in their war of independence.

W. W. could only chuckle from the other room. He thought John complained too much about the mail and the newspapers. W. W. did admit that his brother was in a much better mood when the mail and newspapers arrived on time.

William Wallace, in fact, simply thought that John complained too much. It had not been that long since he left Tennessee to join John. He was only three years old when his brother left Tennessee, but John had kept in touch with him. The family in Tennessee had been poor, even destitute in some periods. Not having regular mail and newspapers were not in the thoughts of many as problems in their everyday struggle.

It was a political time, and not just internationally. The local Whigs had moved to form a ticket in an effort to beat the Democratic Party. On Saturday, September 15, 1849, the Democratic Party delegates met in convention in Mansura, Louisiana. They nominated the following candidates: Aurelien D. Coco and Louis M. O'Neal for the House of Representatives, Gradenigo P. Voorhies for sheriff, Aristide Barbin for recorder, Marcelin Bordelon for clerk, and Sosthene Riche for assessor. Some believed that Marcelin Bordelon would not accept the nomination. Thomas H. Kimball, who wanted the nomination for recorder, and Louis H. Mayeaux who wished to be assessor, were highly displeased at their defeat before the convention. Waddill expected they would soon think better of it as they were both good Democrats and had long been so.

Waddill was wrong. Although the convention nominated Sosthene Riche, Louis Mayeaux ran anyway. Waddill was happy about the results. On November 12, 1849, the elections for the state and parish officers came off, and in Avoyelles Parish, the results were the election of the entire Democratic ticket, with one nominee falling to another Democrat. Louis M. O'Neal did not win as a House candidate.

William F. Griffin (incumbent) and Aurelien B. (Dominique) Coco were elected to the Legislature, beating the third and fourth place finishers, Julien Deshautelle (incumbent) and James H. C. Barlow. Aristide Barbin was elected recorder, beating Ferdinand B. Coco. Gradenigo P. Voorhies was elected sheriff, beating Adolph D. Coco. Sosthene Riche was elected assessor, beating Louis H. Mayeaux, who was really disappointed. Jerome Callegari was elected school superintendent, beating Thomas H. Kimball. John Pierre Aymond was elected coroner with no opposition.

Waddill was especially pleased with Jerome Callegari, a fine and quite intelligent man. Callegari was born in Rome, Italy, and educated at Venice. He came to America when he was thirty years old and settled in Avoyelles, where he taught school for many years. He married Ellen Scallan in 1834, and they had one son, S. Callegari.[199]

Shortly after the convention in Mansura came notices of several deaths, which saddened the community of Avoyelles. News arrived that Clair Goux, wife of Julien B. Maillett, died near the mouth of Black River at the residence of her husband of congestive fever. She was buried on September 16. Louis Charrier died on September 15 of congestive fever. It spread a certain fear of why these fevers were occurring.

Another sad story came to Marksville when news of the twelve-year-old son of Basil Desselle died on the sixteenth from the kick of a horse. He was struck in the side and lived about one agonizing hour.

On this same day, the previous news of hope for the Hungarians was dampened when their army was crushed by the Russians and Austrians. Arthur Gorgey with twenty thousand of his men were prisoners as of August 1849, and Louis Kossuth, deposed head of state, had fled to England.

On September 21, 1849, Waddill came home with live chickens. He purchased only four bits worth (fifty cents) rather than the three-dollar's

---

199. S. Callegari was born on October 7, 1840, and became a prominent merchant of Cottonort. He later served in the Confederate Army in Company F, 18th La. Infantry. He married Irine Riche in 1875 and had three sons and four daughters. Jerome Callegari died in 1887 at age eighty-five. Stafford, *Three Pioneer Rapides Families*, 100.

worth he was supposed to buy. It really was expensive to feed a family. Having livestock and growing gardens and crops was necessary to make it, even with the successful law practice. Most clients dealt on credit, as Waddill himself did quite often. Commerce throughout the country dealt with credit and notes that would be traded, sometimes with more than two transactions. A client would come to Waddill and agree to pay twenty dollars. Waddill would then use that note to trade with someone else to pay for his purchase. That vendor would hold the note or trade it with someone else. When the notes were not paid timely or were defaulted on, then a lawsuit would be processed. A large part of Waddill's practice consisted of enforcing these types of notes.

Actual currency was not plentiful. The only federally sanctioned currency was gold and silver coin. These coins were called specie. Since specie was scarce, banks would issue paper notes to supplement the money supply. Faith in the issuing bank was paramount since, in theory, the notes could be redeemed for coin. The value of the bank notes was based upon the bank's ability to convert the notes to coin. Without the signing of promissory notes, there would be far fewer commercial transactions, even for small amounts. Many times Waddill would accept vegetables, meat, and other produce as his fee. Food was the commodity everyone needed. If a client could make candles, they could pay with a product that many commercial establishments used for light. It was natural that specie was preferred for transactions, but due to its scarcity, bank notes and promissory notes were important for commerce.

Flooding of the Red and Mississippi rivers was continually a problem. Mrs. Duke, Julia's mother, had to come live with the Waddill family as her house, which was on the property next to the Red River, overflowed. The water had receded, but the ground was very soft, and the mosquitoes were so bad that she could not stay there. The Red was finally in its banks.

It was not just the Red that flooded. Bayou Boeuf caused problems for many planters. Old man Kilpatrick stopped by Waddill's office to tell him that he lost his entire crop of cotton due to inundation of his property. He was proceeding to Point Maigre across Red River to teach school to make a living.

Waddill had some funds to make improvements to his home. He engaged Louis Mayeaux, who was running for assessor at the time, to cut and hew seventy-five feet of cypress, ten inches square, for seven dollars. It would take ten days and Mayeaux would then haul it to Waddill. Mayeaux was electioneering at in the corner of the prairie part of the Parish on an campaign tour.

Statewide Politics, November 1849

General Joseph Walker was elected governor of the State of Louisiana. He defeated Alexandre Etienne DeClouet by 999 votes' majority.

Waddill's friend that he met while serving in the Senate, Leon Chabert, passed through Marksville, Louisiana. He had filed a suit in 1846 on notes that amounted to quite a bit of money. He had just come back from Texas, trying to settle his case. Chabert received a judgment in the amount of $15,812.17 against the Cartwright family.

The defendants had offered to pay Chabert with three thousand acres of land and twenty-five slaves "to dismiss my judgment." He told Waddill with a smile.

Waddill knew that this offer was not enough. After the latest ruling by the Texas Supreme Court, they "had no more defenses."[200] Chabert was nodding confidently.

The Cartwright family was not accustomed to losing. Matthew was the son of John and Polly Cruchfield Cartwright, who moved from Tennessee to the Ayish Bayou District of Texas when Matthew was fourteen. He was born in 1807 and, at one time, owned one million acres in Texas. The Cartwright family started as cotton brokers with a gin and a mill. They would bring cotton to Natchitoches, Louisiana, and transport it down the Sabine River.[201]

December 9, 1849

William Wallace Waddill was a huge help to John with the elder Waddill's burden of practicing law, duties as an elected official, and increased estate consisting of property in different parts of the parish. W. W. had just come back with Julia from a visit to Bayou des Glaises after staying for a few days, checking on their properties.

John was thankful for W. W.'s presence and help. Leaving Tennessee when his younger brother was only three, had not really allowed a close relationship to form. The letters that John Waddill wrote to W. W. and received

---

200. See *Cartwright v. Chabert*, Reports of Cases Argued and Decided in the Supreme Court of the State of Texas, vol. 3. Texas Supreme Court, edited by James Webb, Thomas H. Duval, O. C Hartley, R. K. Hartley (Gilbert Book Company, 1851) 261.

201. Sandra Kardell Calpakis, "Matthew Cartwright," Texas State Historical Association, https://tshaonline.org/handbook/online/articles/fca77.

from him helped to establish a connection, but that was nothing like it was after W. W. arrived. John was relieved of so many responsibilities that he had no problem helping W. W. establish an income. It was a pleasure, but in reality, John Waddill's income was increasing due to W. W.'s help.

Tuesday, December 11, 1849

Waddill felt much guilt about not being able to visit Thomas J. Hickman, without whom John would not have been able to attend college. Hickman helped John in ways that he could never pay back. He wrote to him frequently.

On this day, the letter to Thomas Hickman offered genuine thanks and appreciation. Waddill had heard from Hickman, who was pleased that John was doing well, socially, economically, and politically. Waddill could say only thank you to Mr. Hickman for giving him the opportunity. The plantations and enterprises of the Hickman Brothers were doing well.

December 20, 1849

The law partnership with Waddill's brother-in-law, James H. C. Barlow, was going well. They began to actively seek law books to improve their research. Gideon Bingham sent to them the following law books: *Kent's Commentaries*, four volumes; *Greenleaf on Evidence*, two volumes; *Blackstone's Commentaries*, two volumes; *Pothier on Sales*, one volume; *Story on Bills*, one volume; *Story on Agency*, one volume; *Story on Partnerships*, one volume; and *Story on Contracts*, one volume. Born in 1816, Gideon Bingham was well educated, and made his living as a traveling bookseller. He died about a year later, 1850, in New Orleans.[202]

On December 12, John's brother-in-law, James H. C. Barlow, was attacked with bilious,[203] pneumonia, and pleurisy. He was sick for days but did finally recover.

A day before, William Henarie had visited the Waddill family. He was a cousin of Julia. William was born in 1801 and had married Nancy Ann Choate, born in 1814. They visited with their son, Samuel King Henarie, who

---

202. The Gideon Bingham letters 1840–1847, William L. Clements Library, http://quod.lib.umich.edu/c/clementsmss/umich-wcl-M-4192.4bin?-byte=15370544;focusrgn=bioghist;subview=standard;view=reslist.

203. Bilious was a severe stomach ailment causing nausea. The term is no longer used. http://www.merriam-webster.com/dictionary/bilious

was ten years old. They left for the Red River after staying one night. Waddill was impressed with Nancy's intelligence. He also noticed that William looked older than his years. They lived in Vermilion Parish.

It also appeared that the relationship between Waddill and B. B. Simmes was fully restored. Simmes asked Waddill to support Judge Carrigan for the office of enrolling clerk in the Senate.

CHAPTER 35

The Senate in 1850 and Back Home

On February 1, 1850, Senator Waddill introduced a bill granting Michael and Joseph Torras the "exlusive privilege of keep a ferry across the Mississippi at Shreve's Cut Off in Pointe Coupee and West Feliciana Parishes." On February 7, 1850, he introduced another bill. This one granted "Joseph Kirk, of Kirkwood Plantation, and his heirs exclusive privilege of operating a ferry across the Atchafalaya at the mouth of Bayou Des Glaize."

As one writer stated: "These two measures, which passed the legislature overwhelmingly, placed into private hands the most direct connection between West Feliciana and north-central Louisiana. This helped Waddill increase his own personal patronage, but it came at a cost to many, for the benefit of a few."[204]

April 19, 1850

Waddill and W. W. made a full commitment this day, signing a pledge between each other to depend on no one else but themselves for aid, counsel, or advice, and they mutually pledged, in their most sacred honor, that they would never play any kind of game at billiards, or on a billiard or Bagatelle table, or any game at cards, dice, chess, drafts, or any other game of hazard (except at home or the dwelling house of a neighbor, and then without a bet).

They made their mutual and sacred pledge to each other that hence forth that they would never bet money, or any species of property or rights, on any game or in any manner whatever during their natural lives. Each of them placed their signature on John's diary of volume two, page 53 dated this day.

---

204. Samuel C. Hyde Jr., *Pistols and Politics: The Dilemma of Democracy in Louisiana's Florida Parishes, 1810–1899l* (Louisiana State University Press, 1998), 38–39.

William Bishop, the oldest attorney in Avoyelles, died in April 1850. John P. Waddill respected him greatly. As a young attorney, he often went to Bishop for advice. He never enjoyed going against him. His age and wisdom were hard to overcome when Bishop was on the other side of the courtroom.

Though he was older than all of the other attorneys, Bishop had remained active and progressive. He listed his name in the *Expositor* when it began in December 1842 and continued with *The Villager* when it started up in August 1853. Bishop had served as the attorney for the police jury beginning in 1837[205] until he decided he preferred private practice. Waddill thought that Mr. Bishop would be missed.

He never forgot the speech Bishop made for him at the nomination-of-Senator event. He was passionate, and Waddill's spirits were lifted after the many seeming betrayals that occurred.

The spring and summer of 1850 continued without much different going on in Marksville and Avoyelles. Waddill's law practice was thriving, and he continued to grow in popularity.

Slave Troubles

On August 26, 1850, the community came to a shocking halt. A few days before, two slaves, in two areas, were arrested. One, Calvin, was arrested for killing his master. The other, Moise, was condemned for attempting to rape Mrs. Lafargue, a married lady in the parish. There were rumors that Mrs. Lafargue's husband caught them in the act, to which his wife responded with rape. Waddill wondered if there were more to that story. Sheriff G. P. Voorhies hung both of the slaves on the courthouse square in front of a watching crowd.

Construction of Addition to Waddill's Home

Waddill had the flooring for one room in his house, but now he needed to add on and reconstruct part of his home for the rapidly growing family. He ordered plank from T. B. Tiller and received 892 feet from the mill of Conner and Edwards. No one had heard from Tiller's brother-in-law since the shooting of Gorton. Tiller was very grateful for Waddill getting him off of the murder charges. His business suffered for a while but gradually came back after Phillips murdered Gorton and ran away.

---

205. *Biographical and Historical Memoirs*, 613.

T. B. Tiller had begun to sell some of his assets as a precaution if he decided to move. Some community members had bitter feelings. He sold one lot to Thomas Bell and Thomas Stemman on October 28, 1849.[206] On January 21, 1850, he sold fifty acres to Mrs. C. D. Brashear, who had been declared separate in property at the time her husband was elected mayor of Marksville. C. D. Brashear had business dealings with T. B. Tiller. In an ironic twist, C. D. Brashear and his wife had filed suit against Lewis Gorton for an unpaid debt. On February 2, 1850, the Brashears filed against the Estate of Lewis Gorton to collect rent from Gorton's Landing until the final judgment in the lawsuit.

The flooring cost Waddill five dollars per thousand feet. Mrs. Conner told Waddill that there would be another 1,275 feet to haul. This would be more than adequate to support the entire home. The first haul was delivered on October 9, 1850. The total addition was going to be twenty-six feet long and thirty-five feet deep. Waddill was adding nearly one thousand square feet. Samuel Bass would be his carpenter. He would begin the week of October 14 by delivering the framing of the house he had previously done at the sawmill of Edwards and Conner. Waddill enjoyed the company of Samuel Bass and hoped to speak to him more.

It was during this time that Waddill wrote about the drought in the parish. Waddill had never seen anything like it. He made a note that the last day of rain was July 10, 1850. Three small showers occurred, but that barely caused the dust to settle. The shrubbery in the yard was dying, and the sugar crop was greatly injured. Cotton crops were doing tolerably well, and cotton was bearing a high price at fourteen cents a pound. The corn crop was very light, and corn was now selling at one dollar per barrel.

The Cruel World of Slavery

On October 15, 1850, Waddill wrote of the sale of property of the succession of Mahali Morris, the deceased wife of Valery Broussard. The slaves of the estate were sold except for two, an older woman of forty-five years and her child, a girl, four years old. George Scott, the administrator, did not bring those two out. The rest of the slaves sold for high prices. Most of them were under ten years old. The whole sale brought $5,525.00. Joseph Joffrion bought a family for $1,700. John H. Harmanson bought one man, Charles, for $995.00. William Scott bought a man and a young boy for nearly $1,700.

---

206. Records of Avoyelles Parish, no. 7242 in V-65 r.

Valery and Mahali Broussard, children of Mahali Morris and Valery Broussard, bought Mary, a slave woman and her child for around $1,000. Waddill believed it to be $1,085.

In addition, the undivided half of a crib of corn fourteen feet long, twelve feet wide, and four feet deep was sold for fifty cents per barrel, shuck and all. It was a successful succession sale in the eyes of the parties. Waddill was the attorney for the succession, so he attended the sale to witness.

On October 17, 1850, George Scott brought into Marksville and delivered to Waddill, as the attorney of the estate, the forty-five-year-old female slave, Phoebe, and her daughter, Hannah Jane, about four years old. Waddill was to send them to Marcelin Bordelon's that night. There were several other items of silver and pewter that Valery Broussard inadvertently failed to sell.

Court began a new session with Judge Ralph Cushman presiding on October 21, 1850. Many witnesses did not appear, and the judge issued attachments for them to be fined for contempt. John had several criminal cases to handle. On October 23, Victorin Bordelon Jr. stood trial for stealing hogs and was acquitted. John received $35, and Marcelin Bordelon agreed to pay him.

Judge Farrar came to court to handle recused cases. A special term was held for these cases.

P. H. Toler, the somewhat wayward son of Joel Toler, was charged with assault and battery. Waddill defended Toler, and he was acquitted. John earned $25. John A. Havard was charged for an assault and battery and was acquitted. John's fee for his friend was $25. John P. Waddill was on a roll.

Waddill loved new things, as he always had. He paid H. B. Evans $12 for three daguerreotype pictures. His family was really excited.[207]

December 14, 1850

Waddill, his daughters, Ida and Laura, and his son, Henarie, had the measles. Two of his slaves, Irma and Adolph, had them also. This started on November 12. Waddill's brother-in-law, J. H. C. Barlow, nearly died from the measles. His ears were affected greatly. The epidemic started in the prairie area of the parish, where many were affected.

---

207. It is believed that the photo of John Waddill in this book is a copy of one of these. It may be an ambrotype due to its physical condition, which would mean it was taken later.

January 9, 10, and 11, 1851

The handling of the Joel Toler succession was a massive undertaking. Waddill was helping to settle the estate by selling property. He oversaw the sale of all property except about one thousand acres of good, unimproved land and three slaves for $38,000.00. Sugar crops not sold were delivered to New Orleans. For $133.00, Waddill purchased two hundred barrels of corn in the husk.

Waddill sent Richard, his hand, to Red River with ten pounds of sugar, about a gallon of Irish potatoes, and about five pounds of lard, for the benefit of his mother-in-law, Mrs. E. Duke.

On January 13, 1851, Waddill purchased one bottle of Doctor Wistar's balsam of wild cherry. This was for his wife's serious cough.[208] On January 22, 1851, he paid Dr. Donat MacEnery five dollars in gold for services and one dollar for another bottle of Wistar's wild cherry. Miss Anna Sterling and Miss Eliza Phillips were visiting Waddill on the evening of January 21, along with Doctor D. MacEnery, who was becoming a close friend.

To build an addition or any new construction was a tremendous task. Waddill received from Messrs. Leckie Robert & Co. three boxes of window glass, one ten by twelve inches, and the other eight by twelve. He also received forty-nine pounds of putty. He used Fielding Edwards to forward the $15.00 to pay for this. The freight for Edwards was $11.15. Waddill procured from T. B. Tiller fourteen pounds of finishing brads for $1.00. He also purchased from J. B. Goux six door locks at $1.40 per lock for a total of $8.40.

Gardening was a necessity. On January 14, 1851, Waddill began to sow peas, lettuce, endive mustard, spinach, turnips, cabbage, and many other seeds.

On January 18, 1851, John E. Frith's kitchen burned down in Marksville. The house was saved by the exertions of the citizens of the town. There were nearly one hundred people helping.

After receiving the mail on January 23, 1851, Waddill learned that the St. Charles Hotel,[209] in New Orleans, which cost $600,000, was entirely

---

208. Sold for over one hundred years, this elixir created in 1840 was very popular for coughs and other maladies. *Dr. Wistar's Balsam of Wild Cherry*...(Seth W. Fowle & Sons, 1871), https://books.google.com/books/about/Dr_Wistar_s_Balsam_of_Wild_Cherry.html?id=O9HjZwEACAAJ.

209. Truly a beautiful historic building. "'The Finest Piece of Architecture in the New World': The Old St. Charles Hotel," Old New Orleans, http://old-new-orleans.com/NO_StCharlesHotel.html.

consumed by fire. It was the most magnificent building in the city. The fire started in the hotel, but Dr. Theodore Clapp's church[210] as well as the Poydras Street Methodist Episcopal Church and others were destroyed. Fire engines could not help douse the fire due to its great height.

Samuel Bass

John Waddill developed a closer relationship with Samuel Bass. Except for an error in framing the addition to Waddill's home, he was an excellent carpenter and a great conversationalist. Waddill did not understand Bass's abolitionist bent, but he respected his position. He talked to him as often as possible about his views. Bass had come from his home in Canada.

In Canada, it was rare to see much of slavery. The British Imperial Act in 1833 abolished slavery in the British Empire. There may be a few slaves around, but the institution was frowned upon. In the United States, especially in the South, slavery was routine. Bass worked with slaves.

Waddill and Samuel Bass would keep referring to each other as Mr. Bass and Mr. Waddill. John never felt comfortable calling him Samuel, and since Bass was working for Waddill, he felt obligated to call John "Mr. Waddill."

T. B. Tiller continued to liquidate his holdings in Marksville. On January 6, 1851 he sold to W. F. Griffin fifty acres.[211] Shortly after, on February 21, 1851, he sold his last piece of property to Cornelius Voorhies in document number 7652, recorded in Conveyance Book V-114, Records of Avoyelles. It was at that point that Tiller would begin a new life elsewhere.

---

210. Pastor Clapp joined the Unitarian Movement and became very popular. First "Unitarian Universalist Church,"Old New Orleans, http://old-new-orleans.com/NO_FirstUnitarian.html.

211. Records of Avoyelles Parish, no. 7560, conveyance book V-11.

CHAPTER 36

Teaching William Wallace Waddill the Law

W. W. Waddill was a quick learner. If John had to guess, he would have stated that W. W.'s first choice was not to be an attorney. He was not sure what William's real desire was, but John knew that his younger brother wanted to emulate him.

On April 18, 1851, W. W.'s efforts as a lawyer-in-training led to his collection of a fee of $25 from A. G. Pearce as tutor for Sarah A. Robert. It was welcome in the office.

W. W. enjoyed the company of Samuel Bass, also. He felt like he could talk to him about anything without being intimidated. Bass would stop by the law office to visit when he came to town. The law firm continued to do work for Bass as he kept doing small jobs for the Waddill family. On April 21, 1851, Waddill paid to John N. Deaver for Bass a sum of twenty dollars on the debt he owed to Deaver.

Disappointing news came when Mr. Alphonse Cazabat quit teaching in the Marksville Academy. Mr. John McDowell, the principal of the institution, went into the country to employ another teacher. This saddened Waddill, because Alphonse was a good teacher, although he had strange ways about him, and Waddill did not know if another could replace him easily. It turned out that Mr. Cazabat was mentally ill, the cause of his termination.

One of Avoyelles' citizens, Mr. Julien Jules Goudeau, age twenty-one, born 1829, son of Julien Goudeau, from the Bayou Rouge Prairie, arrived at Marksville on his way home from the Military Institute of Kentucky,[212] where he had been going to school for about thirteen months. John was excited to see him and felt some pride. Young Julien looked well and improved physi-

---

212. The Military Institute of Kentucky was opened in 1845 as a military preparatory school. It remained there until a fire burned it down in the early twentieth century. http://www.kmialumni.org/menu.html.

cally, but Waddill did not think that Julien studied very hard. His father was born in 1806 and was married to Marcelline Decuir. They had ten children. The couple had considerable property and had about twelve slaves.[213] The elder Goudeau would die on September 24, 1852. Julien Jules eventually moved to Marksville and worked as a horticulturist. His wife Henrietta Edwards Goudeau, whom he married on February 23, 1852, bore five children.

Mrs. E. Duke, Julia's mother made a matrimonial agreement with William A. Alexander, who would be her third husband. He was from Rapides Parish.

W. W. came in very handy, even though he was not yet a lawyer. He served as a witness to Waddill's settlement of two lawsuits filed for James and William W. McElroy of Allen County, Kentucky. William helped in many ways, besides in the law practice. On April 27, 1851, W. W. went to Alexandria to obtain a school-teacher for Waddill. He stayed two nights at Mrs. E. Duke's. He was not successful in hiring a teacher. W. W. did buy for Waddill a pair of tortoise shell side combs for Julia, for which Waddill reimbursed W. W. one dollar.

Summer was coming, and mosquitoes would be a problem. Waddill bought from A. Voinché twenty yards of brown linen mosquito bar for two dollars cash. He also paid E. Reynaud ten dollars towards getting cloth for his coat. He employed Mayer, the tailor, to make him a marmot coat at five dollars and a Marseilles vest for $3.50.

The drought was getting bad for Avoyelles Parish. No rain since March 10, 1851, caused Waddill not to plant too much corn in the prairie, but he was planning to try on his property at Bayou des Glaises. Waddill wondered how he could keep up with his law practice, his political job, and the farming enterprises in different areas. And at the same time, his young daughter, Ida, had been ill for four days. His family was not exempt from illness. The bills from medical care kept piling up. Of course, Waddill would sacrifice anything for the good health of his family. He paid Dr. D. MacEnery ten dollars in gold on April 30, 1851. It was obvious that gold was the preferred method of payment for anyone providing services. The common method of transferring promissory notes was much more risky. These transfers often resulted in lawsuits upon default.

On April 30, 1851, Waddill was extremely excited. The next day, Thursday, the girls of the Marksville Academy were preparing to give a recital to the public, especially the parents of the students, to entertain them with music

---

213. Julien Jules Goudeau, www.ancestry.com.

and speeches. They were to recite a range of original poetry. John wrote a verse for Miss Mary Botts, which would be read in public for the first time. Waddill could not help but be pleased that the public would hear his oft-written poetry, even though it was simply in a school recital. Mary E. Botts was nearly sixteen years old and the only child of John Botts and his wife Mary Custard. They lived in Marksville and married on October 1, 1832. Major John Botts was born in Virginia, moved to Kentucky, and settled in New Orleans and eventually Avoyelles in 1824. He had served as a major in the War of 1812 under Generals Hall and Harrison. He was somewhat of a hero in Avoyelles, and a well-respected planter. *The Villager* ran a lengthy obituary on his death.

> Died, at his residence, in this parish, July 22th, Major John Botts, born April 12, 1784. The date of the notice above shows that the birth of Major Botts was nearly contemporary with that of the American Republic. He was born when Washington had just founded the nation. The child of 1784 has seen a people, who had been free scarcely two years when he was born, grow and occupy one of the largest places in the history of the world. To be born at the same time that a nation was, and to die leaving that nation one of the greatest on earth is a happiness which but few enjoy.
>
> Major Botts was born in Virginia. Before his majority, he left the paternal mansion, and immigrated to Kentucky, whose uncultivated pathless forest still resounded with the exploits of Daniel Boone, the intrepid pioneer, the wonderful hunter.
>
> 1812 came, Major Botts saw the struggle between the United States and England renewed, a struggle which, at the time of his birth was in every one's recollection, and like all the gallant young men of that period, he hastened to join the standard of his country under Generals Hall and Harrison. In 1819 he established himself in New Orleans, which was then a village of such humble pretensions that no one suspected it would ever reach its present greatness. Finding his prospects gloomy there, the young Virginian came and established himself in Avoyelles, a parish at that time, very young for it has been colonized only a little more that eighty years. That was in 1824. Energetic like all the pioneers of the American race, he devoted himself to the cultivation of cotton and on the twenty second of July last, thirty-four years after his arrival in Avoyelles, he expired, leaving a large fortune acquired by hard labor.

His death is then that of one of those pioneers, who began American civilization with the sword, and with the plough. It is even like a broken medal of the grand epoch of Washington, and those medals are rapidly passing away! Major Botts is not dead entirely. He leaves his wife, the worthy and noble companion of his days of struggle and of his success. He leaves also a daughter, well known throughout the parish. Of her we say nothing, for her virtues are stamped upon her countenance and respect forbids us parade them before the public gaze: but we can say that she is the wife of a man who is one of a class, the most brilliant and popular of the American race; that, in leaning upon him, she has chosen a valiant arm, a loyal soul, who, in these times of political hatred and divisions, has the esteem of all parties.

In conclusion, we will say that the daughter of Major Botts is worthy, and should be proud to hear the name of him to whom applies so well the beautiful verse of V. Hugo:

"*Les vrais coeurs de lion sont les vrais coeurs de peres.*"[214]

Construction Payments and Other Transactions

Although Samuel Bass had completed the work on the home of Waddill, he had received a promissory note for the final payment from Waddill. On May 7, 1851, Waddill paid Bass fifty dollars on this note.

Thomas J. Hickman remained an important person in Waddill's life. He had spoken to William W. Waddill often of how much Hickman helped him. W. W. finally met him and could see why his brother respected him so much. He handled some of Hickman's legal issues. On May 7, 1851, John Waddill paid $5.80 for Thomas Hickman, five dollars for the depositions of D. Coco and Valery Bordelon Jr., and for the clerk, Aristide Barbin, the balance of eighty cents.

As Waddill kept improving the home addition, he paid Fielding Edwards, his middleman, ten dollars for the freight for bedsteads and chairs. It was brought up on the steamboat *Rockaway #2*. This steamboat was built in 1850 and eventually sunk at Bayou Sara in 1855. It was a Mississippi River to Red River steamboat, hauling mail, commodities, and other merchandise.[215]

---

214. From the Editor of *The Villager*, July 31, 1858, pg. 2.

215. "Steamboat Postal history," The Historical Shop, http://www.historicalshop.com/sitecontents/steamboat/steamboatph.htm

John Waddill was nearing completion of his home improvements. He paid Henry Steinman $1.50 for work in papering a bedroom. Mr. Kirk made a mantelpiece for his sleeping room. He also finished the gutters and put them up. Waddill gave John Kirk eighty cents to pay F. B. Barbin for a piece of cypress lumber for gate posts. John Kirk was paid fifteen dollars for his work on the house. Waddill believed he overpaid him.

Electricity

One of the benefits of having his brother around, as Waddill saw it, was that W. W. would help with entertaining the children when John was busy. On May 27 and 28, 1851, J. W. Ball gave a lecture in Marskville, endeavoring by precept and experiment to explain the mysteries of electricity. His performance impressed all of the family, including W. W. and John. W. W. went to both performances along with his older brother.

Thomas, John's son, went to the first night's demonstration. Julia attended the second one.

On May 14, 1851, John received from Leckie Robert twelve sacks of corn, one barrel of hams, and seventy-two pounds of dried apples. Richard, Waddill's man, hauled them home. The family and slaves would be fed well for a while. The bacon that Waddill purchased from Mr. Goux and had brought him earlier did not appear healthy. It was from pork shoulders.

In an interesting event, Clement Carmouche employed Waddill to file a petition before the police jury to liberate a slave, Claire. He would get twenty-five dollars if successful and twenty if not. This was a required process for an owner to set a slave free.

Julia went to her mother's residence on the Red River with the intent to go to Alexandria for the purpose of visiting the family of her uncle, Samuel W. Henarie. Waddill was not very happy about it, but gave her thirty dollars for her expenses, which he felt with economy would be much more than she needed—at least he hoped so. All of the children stayed with Waddill and W. W. The children appeared to have the mumps, which was going around in Marksville during June 1851. John and Julia had a slight disagreement on whether to let their son Henarie stay with Julia's mother. Waddill did not permit it.

W. Alexander, Waddill's step-father-in-law, went to Waddill's house to check on all of them. Waddill's son, Thomas, had the mumps, but he recovered well. Waddill's worries were due to Thomas having the measles, scarlet fever, whooping cough, and the mumps. He then figured that Thomas had been vaccinated through sickness of each of these for most childhood dangers.

James H. C. Barlow, Waddill's brother-in-law, also went with Julia to travel to Alexandria. He was now practicing law there. They both knew that W. W. would soon take the bar exam and begin the practice with his brother, Waddill.

Finally, on June 10, 1851, a heavy rain with severe gale winds came to Avoyelles. It was the first rain since March 8. Planters were happy. Waddill had set out ten rows of potatoes. They did not look well, so he planned to plant more. As W. W. and Dr. MacEnery went a-bathing,[216] the latter made it clear he was "excited with drinking."

In an effort to help William Alexander in his law practice, Waddill rented from Mrs. Susan B. Stirling a small house to be used as an office. P. H. Toler had it before. The rent would be three dollars per month.

John Waddill was a stickler for professionalism. He paid extra to have his petitions and filings on higher grade paper than normal. He purchased Cass paper, much more expensive than plain paper, to file his pleadings with the clerk. J. L. Generis carried it in stock for him. Waddill would order a ream at a time.

Local Indians

The local Indian population was significant. They did not have much influence but managed to enter the local market with some products. Waddill would purchase eggs from local Indian girls who would come to the town to sell chickens and eggs. On July 1, 1851, he purchased fourteen chickens from them for $1.50.[217]

Waddill was hired to represent the estate of Berlin Childress. On July 5, Appolinair Bordelon finally adjudicated the property of the estate to Mrs. Berlin Childress. Mr. Berlin Childress had requested that the property be purchased in his wife's name, Nancy Childress. The property was in the name of Bordelon's children, and he was the tutor of their estate. Berlin and his wife had two children, Minerva and Anna. Nancy was born in 1812. Berlin was born in 1801 in Mississippi. Anna married Brant Marshall.

Waddill continued to do business with Fielding Edwards, who had a good reputation for following through with his middle-man orders and ship-

---

216. "a-bathing": a common term for swimming.

217. These Indians were probably part of the Tunica-Biloxi Indian Tribe, who have an established reservation today on the edge of the corporate limits of Marksville. They could also have been remnants of the older Avoyelles Indians.

ping of goods. On July 28, 1851, Waddill gave a letter to Fielding directed to Norment, Cooper & Co., enclosing thirty dollars. Norment, Cooper & Co. was a merchandising company out of New Orleans. The funds were to purchase one barrel of pork, one keg of lard, one keg of paint, five gallons of varnish, and a barrel of vinegar. This company had access to warehouses owned by E. H. Flint above and below the falls of Red River.[218] Waddill hoped that he would soon finish all of the improvements to his home.

The night before, John and Julia dined with Judge Gervais Baillio and "his lady" at their residence in Hydropolis.

Democratic Politics, July 7, 1851

On this day, the Democrats held a meeting and appointed delegates to the Democratic state convention to meet at Baton Rouge on the second Monday of July. The purpose was to nominate candidates for Congress in the district that included Avoyelles Parish and for the Auditor of Public Accounts.

On July 15, 1851, Waddill and his wife, with the whole family and W. W., went with the family of Henderson Taylor to Bayou du Lac and spent the day at a fish fry. It was a Tuesday, but everyone needed a break. They caught plenty fish. At the same time, the inhabitants of Marksville, or at least a large group, had gone to the village of Plain Dealing,[219] Louisiana, near Chalybeate Springs. The water had some healing agents, and it was quiet near the Arkansas border. There, they had a picnic.

On July 22, 1851, Waddill settled with A. C. Armstrong in full for the following items: a scythe and a snathe (the handle of a scythe), two ivory combs, two pen stocks, and the repairing of his watch. He gave him a fifty-dollar Tennessee bank bill and owed him one dollar after the discount on the bank bill. Thomas H. Kimball painted for Waddill as his house reached near completion. Waddill paid him $10.50, which Waddill felt was five dollars more than he owed him. Two days later, Kimball finished the painting. On that day, Waddill went to the home of William Alexander on the Red River for the evening.

---

218. *The Times Picayune*, August 29, 1851, pg. 1.

219. Plain Dealing was originally settled by George Oglethorpe Gilmer, who, with his son, purchased 5,000 acres. It was in the area that the United States had forced the Caddo Indians to abandon after they had been settled 1,000 years. https://en.wikipedia.org/wiki/Plain_Dealing,_Louisiana.

Thomas, his son, was sick with fever, and Waddill was worried. W. W. was a great help staying with him when needed. Waddill wanted to expand the practice and needed books to help W. W. learn the law. He ordered the fifth volume of the *Louisiana Annual Reports*, giving the clerk of the steamboat *Romeo* the order on August 6, 1851. Waddill was impressed that on August 12, 1851, it arrived on the *Romeo*; he paid $7.50. If only the mail was as sure. On August 8, the family came home from the Red River. William had been sick but was recovering. He had not been so sick that he had to stay in bed much.

On Sunday, August 10, 1851, the preacher Mr. D. Kinnear, from the Opelousas District of the Methodist Church, and "his lady" came to Waddill's house.[220] He preached at 10:00 a.m. and at 8:00 p.m.

On June 30, 1851, the commercial establishment in New Orleans of Peet, Simms & Co. ceased business with Philip Simms, Eleazer Peet, and John Lerethe. The two partners, Eleazer Peet and Philip Simms, continued to do their wholesale dry goods business on their own account as Peet, Simms & Co. at 25 Magazine Street agreeing to settle the accounts between themselves.[221] Waddill had business dealings with this firm through Fielding Edwards. On August 23, 1851, he sent $750.00 for Edwards to give to Philip Simms on behalf of James L. Edelen of Maryland.

The last bit of painting on John and Julia's house was done on August 23, 1851, and Waddill paid Thomas Kimball in full. Henry C. Steinman finished papering the house.

Food for the family continued to be a concern, and even with William's help, their property and livestock did not provide enough for all of the family and slaves living with the Waddill family. Over a week's time in August, Waddill purchased eight more chickens for eighty cents. Joseph Bonnett was paid fifty cents for eggs. He also purchased two dollars' worth of beef, mutton, and butter. He purchased coffee and, from an Indian, thirty cents worth of chickens. Fresh chicken made a good meal.

On August 25, 1851, John attended the sale of the property of the succession of Mrs. Ann A. Kimball on the Bayou Rouge Prairie. The property sold for upwards of $15,000.

On August 28, 1851, Miss Sarah Jane Robert married Mr. William Vernon. They were both minors. John's friend A. G. Pearce allowed the wedding at Oakwold on Bayou Rouge. The next day, John purchased from A. Voinche

---

220. "1851 Methodist Church Appointed Preachers," Louisiana Genealogy Trails, http://genealogytrails.com/lou/1851_methodist_church_preachers.html.

221. *Times Picayune*, July 8, 1851, pg. 3

a pair of suspenders after Julia commented on his pants sagging at the wedding. They cost one dollar.

William Edwards came by the Waddill home on August 31. He was quite excited. William Conner and he had repaired their steam sawmill and began operations the previous Wednesday. It was working well. They were getting business coming in and finishing much quicker. Waddill was happy for his friend.

Teaching W. W. the law was a pleasure to Waddill. His brother continued to learn and help with collections of fees. John loved to teach, to instruct, and to learn more by teaching. On September 17, 1951, the Louisiana Supreme Court licensed William Wallace Waddill as an attorney.[222]

W. W. had helped Waddill in so many ways, not just in his practice. It was great to have a family member living with John and working with him.

---

222. RAPCC, no. 4298, book PP, pg. 738, September 17, 1851.

CHAPTER 37

Politics Heat Up

September the 1, 1851

This day Alexander G. Penn of the Parish of St. Tammany called on the Waddill brothers at their office. He was the Democratic candidate for Congress from the third district of Louisiana, which included Avoyelles. He had replaced John Henry Harmason as the congressman for the area.

He had no opponent as yet. Mr. Watterson of the Livingston Parish had been nominated by the Whigs but declined the nomination. Waddill wrote: "He [Mr. Penn] had gone to Mansura, to the Democratic Convention there held today for the purpose of nominating: 1st a Candidate for the Senate, for Avoyelles and Rapides. 2. Two Candidates for the House of Representatives for the state; 3rd a sheriff; 4th a candidate for assessor; 5th a coroner."

The delegates in the Convention, as Democratic candidates, nominated the following: For the state senator from Avoyelles, William F. Griffin; for representatives John J. Taylor and Sosthene Couvillion; for sheriff, Aurelien B. Coco; for assessor, Martin Couvillion; and for superintendent of public schools, Fabius Ricord.

Louis H. Mayeux was dissatisfied with the nomination for assessor, and he determined to run himself for the office of assessor. If he did, Waddill felt that the Democrats would beat him badly, as they had at the last election. Waddill presumed that would satisfy him. Waddill once thought that Louis H. Mayeux was a good Democrat, but he doubted it now.

September 1, 1851

Waddill paid A. Denis ten dollars on a bill of sixteen dollars, which he had against Waddill for work on his wagon.

Apparently, the bad blood in politics did not affect Waddill's personal relationship with Louis Mayeux. He purchased beef from Louis on the same day.

September 6, 1851

Colonel Thomas C. Porter of New Orleans was in Marksville. He was the Democratic candidate for auditor of the state. He did not win the race, but he became the U.S. Customs collector at the New Orleans Port. He was credited in the *Picayune* of December 9, 1856, for sending the newspaper a report of the Secretary of the Treasury for the period ending June 31, 1856.

Waddill received the news of the defeat, capture, and execution of General Narciso Lopez by the Spanish-controlled Cuban Government. His men had all been killed or captured. He landed in Cuba on August 11 with 486 men for the purpose of aiding the revolting creoles of Cuba in achieving their independence. "After he landed they never rendered him any assistance, consequently his little band, through as heroic as that of Leonidas, the Spartan king, could not contend against 18,000 soldiers opposed to them."[223]

September 12, 1851

Benoist W. Kay was at Waddill's house this day. Waddill wrote: "Mr. John McDonnell [McDowell] left here last Sunday for New Orleans. He has gone there employing a lady to teach Music in his female academy. He is to be back by Sunday. Red River was very low. Navigation was almost wholly stopped at snaggy point.[224] Travelers are daily passing, from the mouth of Red River to Alexandria. This began the first sign of a true benefit for the landings in Alexandria over those at Marksville." Waddill hoped that this would not change the nature of importance between the communities.

September 15, 1851

Waddill went to Alexandria to attend the Supreme Court, which sat September 16. This day, the Supreme Court met, but only two judges, George

---

223. Though unsuccessful, many in the United States resented the execution of Lopez. Today, Cuba's flag is the banner that Lopez used in his rebellion. https://en.wikipedia.org/wiki/Narciso_Lopez.

224. Snaggy Point is no longer called that. It is near where the new Red River Bridge is on Highway 107 in Avoyelles Parish, just north of where the Civil War Fort DeRussy is located.

Eustis[225] and Pierre A. Rost,[226] were present. Judge Isaac Trimble Preston[227] was sick, and Judge Thomas Slidell[228] was absent.

September 17, 1851

This day, Judges Eustis, Rost, and Preston appeared in their seats. Court was opened and judgment rendered in a criminal case from Natchitoches.

The court appointed the following: H. M. Hagains, James F. Flint, and Henderson Taylor as a committee to examine Applicants for the Bar. They examined Mssrs. Sanford, Smith, Gardiner and my brother, William W. Waddill, and reported to the Court favorably.

The said Applicants were examined in open court by Judge Eustis, Chief Justice of the State of Louisiana, and they, being found competent, were all admitted to practice Law in the various courts of the state. Judge Eustis and Rost passed through Marksville on their way to the Mississippi and visited several of the local attorneys.

William W. Waddill was one of them. John Waddill was pleased.

October 1, 1851

Waddill visited with Samuel Bass and paid him $2.50, the final payment on the note that he had given Samuel for his work on the family home.
During this period, news spread about a potential repeal of the Missouri Compromise. Bass could only hope that this country, his adopted land, would see slavery as he did and one day soon free every man and woman, regardless of how it affected planters.

---

225. "George Eustis (1796–1858)," Celebrating 200 Years: The Bicentennial of the Louisiana Supreme Court, 1813–2013, http://www.lasc.org/Bicentennial/justices/Eustis_George.aspx.

226. "Pierre Adolphe Rost," Wikipedia, https://en.wikipedia.org/wiki/Pierre_Adolphe_Rost.

227. "List of Justices of the Louisiana Supreme Court," Wikipedia, https://en.wikipedia.org/wiki/List_of_Justices_of_the_Louisiana_Supreme_Court.

228. Ibid.

CHAPTER 38

John P. Waddill and William W. Waddill Practice Law

The brothers continued their general practice, handling many types of cases. On October 4, 1851, Waddill was retained by John Robinson in a suit before the Justice of the Peace, Guillot. Waddill's business associate, Fielding Edwards, brought the case against him for obstructing the road to Normand's Landing. It was dismissed on an exception but would be heard later upon removing the procedural issue. John's fee was $7.50, and the case would be heard the second Monday of the month.

Premature Death

It always bothered Waddill when anyone would die, but it especially touched him when the deceased was young. Miss Mary Cullom, age thirteen, died on October 5, 1851. She was the daughter of Francis Cullom, and the cause of death was pneumonia. She was a fine student of Mr. and Mrs. McDowell. Her sister, Emily, was also sick, but the family had high hopes for her recovery. Dr. G. E. Elmer treated both of them. Dr. Elmer was acknowledged as the head of his profession. Avoyelles was fortunate to have him.

Miss Burroughs and Miss Stephens, both students at the school, were also very sick at this time. Miss Stephens had been taken home by her brother-in-law, the young Calliham.

On the Red River, Mrs. Robinson, wife of Rowland Robinson, was also dangerously ill. Ralph Cushman's wife was just recovering from an attack of congestive fever.

During this time, there was a continued drought on the prairie. The atmosphere was full of dust, and there was little or no vegetation. Only wild basil and other hardy plants were making it under the harsh sun. The drought continued, but it did not seem to affect cotton. The crops on the bayous in the parish were doing relatively well.

Court Proceedings

Two of Waddill's clients received prison time in Avoyelles Parish. François Dubroc and John Zeline each got one year in the penitentiary. Augustus Bartell got ten days in the parish jail for assault and battery. Norbert Bordelon was acquitted of the same charges.

On October 26, 1851, the former mayor of Marksville, C. D. Brashear, came back from Texas looking for a home. He was quite sick with fever. He had purchased a small plantation near the Trinity River. It was somewhat south of Red River and entirely in Texas.

That Saturday, Mrs. Lucinda Simmons, widow of Don Louis Goudeau, came to see John Waddill. He wanted to leave the office early to rest, but he could not turn down any business. She had married Goudeau when he was fifty-seven. He died at age sixty-five.

She had some assets that were her separate property, but her deceased husband, Don, had debts that he undertook that she could not pay.

Waddill looked over all of the numbers and the property of the community and gave her advice that seemed to relieve her. They had married on September 14, 1843, when she was twenty-nine, believing that she was getting too old to be single. They had been married only eight years when Don died. He had property that valued, at the most, $1,800.00. His debts exceeded that.

Waddill recommended that Mrs. Simmons renounce the community. She would lose the property but also gain relief of all debts. It was Waddill's opinion that this would be her best avenue.

Mrs. Simmons took Waddill's advice and retained him to do the work, saving her much worry and debt. They had no children, so there was no risk of heirs having to assume debts.

General Pierre Couvillion and John L. Taylor dined with John Waddill on October 28, 1851. They enjoyed a fine meal and talked politics, and Mr. Taylor slept at the Waddill home that evening.

Education

Waddill's step-father-in-law, William Alexander, wanted to help with the building for the female academy run by Mr. McDowell. He commenced raising the house designed for it on October 29, 1851.

The McDowell's invited several guests for dinner at their home. Judge R. Cushman, J. L. Generis, James MacEnery, Aristide Barbin, William Alexander, and Alfred Mayer were present for the meal. They helped with finances and manpower to assist in the school building.

The next day, Waddill visited Dr. Elmer and C. D. Brashear in hopes of receiving more help on the project. After his visit, he received a letter from Stephen F. Milligan, who had left for the Gold Rush and was writing from California.

Waddill had great respect for William Alexander. William had filed suit against the steamboat *Little Tour* and owners for a skiff before Joseph Guillot, magistrate of the Second Ward in Avoyelles Parish. Miss Mary Jane Barlow was with him as a witness. Mary Jane was Julia's sister. Alexander won the suit for twenty dollars plus court costs.

CHAPTER 39

Deadly Politics

November 3, 1851, was the day of elections throughout the Louisiana. The Democratic candidates supported in Avoyelles Parish were the following:

For state auditor: Thomas C. Porter

For Third Congressional District: A. G. Penn

For state senators, Rapides and Avoyelles: W. F. Griffin and Thomas O. Moore

For House of Representatives, Avoyelles: John L. Taylor and Sosthene Couvillion

For sheriff: Aurelien D. Coco

For assessor: Marin Couvillion

For parish school superintendent: A. Lafargue

The Democratic ticket succeeded throughout the parish. Aurelien Coco was elected sheriff by a small majority of twenty-nine votes. After the election, about 8:00 that night, Augustus Bartell stabbed Coco,[229] the sheriff elect, and as many supposed, John E. Frith. Frith had been abusing Coco and W. F. Griffin, the candidate for Senate, during the day.

Just before Coco was stabbed, Frith came out of his grocery in a very excited manner and abused Coco and Griffin, but principally Griffin. Onlookers said that Frith shoved Coco with his hands, and Coco struck him with a stick, a tremendous blow that knocked Frith down. He struck him three or four times afterward and was on him when Hayden Edwards pulled him off.

---

229. A. B. Dominique Coco was known as "A. B." The B stood for Boldinid a nickname in the Coco family, resulting from their ancestor's family name, Boldino.

Augustus Bartell caught him by the head while Edwards held him, drew him back, and, as those present observed, cut him several times.

Thomas Adams caught him by the throat and choked him, so it was said. Waddill was not present. This all happened in Marksville near the recorder's office. Although he completely denied it, the reports show that Firth stabbed Coco in the abdomen.

On November 4, 1851, at about 11:00, Aurelien Dominique Coco died of his wounds received the previous night. He was one of the most promising young men in Avoyelles Parish. Waddill said of him, "He was an educated, noble souled young man." He left a wife and three children. He would be a loss to the whole parish. Even at his young age of twenty-six, he had twice been elected to the state legislature of Louisiana.

The funeral of Aurelien D. Coco was held on November 6, 1831. It was the largest that Waddill had ever seen in the vicinity. Nearly three hundred persons were in attendance. The funeral service was very imposing as two priests officiated.

Martin Rabalais, the cousin of Aurelien D. Coco, was sent to Alexandria for Andrew J. Isaacs, district attorney, for the purpose of having an examination of those who aided in the death, preparatory to counseling them for trial.

The whole matter was a sad affair, and Waddill felt that there was no doubt but that all who participated in the death of Mr. Coco would give all of their earthly goods if he were alive and well.

Isaacs and James H. C. Barlow arrived on November 10, 1851, for the purpose of prosecuting those who killed Aurelien D. Coco. On November 8, 1851, the examination of Thomas C. Adams and John E. Frith, charged with the murder of Coco, was concluded. Mr. Adams was bound over to appear at court in a bond of $2,000. Mr. Frith, without full examination, was by his own consent bound over for his appearance at court with a bond of $10,000.

There was no further examination of Augustus Bartell. He was bound in a bond of $12,000. The relatives employed Waddill's brother-in-law, James H. C. Barlow, to prosecute those charged with the murder of Mr. Coco. This was considered normal at the time.

This was a troubling time in Marksville and throughout the parish. It was shocking to most of the citizens that something like this would happen over politics. It was not odd that ill words were spoken and even that shoving and pushing occurred. The occasional fist-fight could also be expected. The people of the parish took politics very seriously. Yet to know that the sheriff-elect on the night of his victory would be stabbed and die from the injuries sent shock waves throughout the community. Rumors of lynching spread. The courthouse, which had been deteriorating, became the place to meet for the public. Its condition became even more noticeable. Some of the citizens had already committed to improvements. Waddill had committed $120 at $10 per month to help replace the courthouse. The police jury would assist if enough was raised.

During this time, Waddill's slave Mary gave birth to a girl, and both were doing well. W. W. went to New Orleans for an order, which Waddill had placed from H. Frellsen & Co. for one keg of lard, one keg of butter, one barrel of mess pork, one barrel of flour, one barrel of Irish potatoes, and one barrel of onions. Waddill gave W. W. thirty dollars to be placed on the order. Waddill asked his brother to deliver a letter to Alfred Kearney & Co. of New Orleans for wire and cement. He left Normand's Landing for the journey.

On his account, Waddill made a payment of five dollars to Dr. MacEnery. He also paid $9.90 to E. Reynaud on a draft drawn to John by Samuel Bass.

Regular troubles continued. Waddill had sent Richard, his very trusted slave, in his wagon to the Red River to help Jeffrey, his mother-in-law's slave, harvest corn. They had not returned timely. About 4:00 in the morning, they arrived at Waddill's home without the wagon, which had been disabled about a half mile from his home.

The whole family, except John, left Waddill's home to go to the Red River to visit Mrs. Youngman, an aunt of Julia, whose whole family came to visit with Mrs. Kennedy. John visited General Pierre Couvillion, who was very sick with pleurisy. Even in his sickness, he commented on the murder of Coco. "I cannot believe that this is happening in our community. What has become of electioneering?" Waddill, still saddened by the events, could only nod in agreement.

On November 18, Waddill traveled to Alexandria, arriving at Mr. Kay's on the Red River. He just learned that his mother-in-law was moving with Mr. W. Alexander to Gray's Creek in Rapides Parish. Mr. Alexander owned a small plantation there. He caught up with them five miles from Alexandria. They had stopped to rest. Miss Jane and W. Alexander were on horseback, and Waddill's mother-in-law with the children were in a carriage. He traveled with them about a mile just to visit. They parted ways as Waddill headed back to Alexandria.

On November 19, 1851, Waddill joined the Oliver Lodge of Alexandria as an apprentice mason. He was now a Free and Accepted Mason.

When Waddill arrived home, he heard very sad news. General Pierre Couvillion died. Waddill's own words described him: "He was a man of uncommon strength of intellect, and was highly esteemed in his Parish & indeed wherever known in the state." He was only forty-seven when he died. General Couvillion had filled many important offices in the state. In 1833 or 1834, he was elected to the State Legislature from Avoyelles. He was afterward re-elected several times. In 1844, he was honored with a seat at the 1845 Constitutional Convention. In 1845, he was elected to the State Senate to begin serving in 1846. His term ended in 1847, and he refused to run again. It was then that John P. Waddill was elected. Couvillion left a large family and a larger circle of friends to mourn his sudden and untimely death. He was wealthy.

Samuel Bass was paid in full on November 22, 1851, when Waddill gave him twenty dollars. He felt that he overpaid him but did not complain. Bass gave Waddill the note as paid in full. On this day, Waddill did not feel like having a discussion. He was still stunned from the murder of the sheriff-elect Coco. Bass was also disturbed by the situation. A few days later, Waddill realized he had not paid Bass in full, but only the note. He still owed him sixteen dollars and paid in full all that he owed him on December 17, 1851. Waddill felt a bit guilty.

On November 21, 1851, Waddill came back from his becoming a Mason. He kept detailed accounts of his expenses. They are as follows:

For a green cloth Paleto	$16.00
a beaver hat	5.00
a Caddy of tea	3.00
Ear ring, comb, and velvet for my wife	5.15
mending carriage	5.00
tobacco	2.50
quills, rings, watch key, razor, cigars and shaving	4.25
board and horse feed	5.25
ferriage at Alexandria	1.50
Masonic Expenses	25.00
one pair of cotton socks	1.50
	$74.15[230]

---

230. DJW, November 21, 1851, vol. 2 pg. 93.

These figures showed how expensive it was even to go by carriage to a town only thirty-five miles away and stay only one night or two.

On December 21, 1851, the chimney in Waddill's home was finished. He paid Thomas L. Ralph the sum of sixteen dollars, with $22.50 for the balance on the brick itself paid to L. Beridon.

CHAPTER 40

Christmas 1851

The day after Christmas, Waddill received Marie Couvillion, the widow of Pierre Couvillion, at his office. She desired to be appointed administrator of his estate. He also filed a petition to be appointed natural tutrix of their children. On December 29, Waddill took an inventory of the succession of General Pierre Couvillion.

W. L. Casou slept at Waddill's house on December 28. He was a good friend. Casou had petitioned the legislature to legitimate his four children, namely, Fanntarie W. Casou and Caroline C. Casou by his wife Nancy Miles, and Francis Marthas Casou and Susan Elizabeth Casou by his wife Frances Glass, widow of Hugh Nelson.

Making sure that Waddill had enough light in his office was always a problem. He ordered candles, his preferred choice over lanterns. He received them shipped in forty pounds per each box.

Waddill almost wished for the drought weather of the summer and early fall. Now it was raining so much that the Red River had risen over ten feet. Bayou des Glaises had risen quite a bit. It was navigable until the junction. The rains erupted into storms, some so heavy that fencing in the prairie and other parts of the parish blew down.

More Politics

The Louisiana State Legislature planned to convene on the third Monday in January 1852. There was a Senator to elect in place of General Solomon W. Downs,[231] whose term expired with the adjournment of the present term

---

231. General Solomon W. Downs practiced law and was known as a duelist. He was wounded in his lung in a duel, leaving him in a weakened condition. He was later instrumental in outlawing duels in Louisiana. Downs's body was buried in 1854, in what became a vacant field. In 1937, his remains were relocated to a prom-

of Congress, March 4, 1853. General Downs served in the U.S. Senate from March 4, 1847, to March 4, 1853. He was replaced by J. P. Benjamin, whom the state legislature appointed. General Downs was from Ouachita Parish and had been appointed Brigadier General of the State Militia in 1843. He was once a candidate for vice president with General Lewis Cass from Michigan, but they failed to get the nomination of the Democratic Party. Downs also served as a delegate of the 1845 Constitutional Convention for Louisiana. In the Louisiana state legislature, the Whigs had a majority of seventeen on joint ballot. They would be electing the new senator.

In that Congress, specifically the House of Representatives, the Democrats and Whigs from Louisiana each had two members. On January 1, 1852, John L. Taylor, one of Avoyelles's representatives, visited John Waddill. He was doing well. Waddill and he talked politics and spoke about W. L. Casou's business in the legislature and about his children.

From the heirs of John Dugouf, Thomas McMahon purchased the house and lot adjoining Waddill's office lot in Marksville. Waddill was pleased. He was even more excited the next day.

Birth of Waddill's Daughter

January 2, 1852, Julia gave birth to a baby girl, Mary Florence. Both of them did well. On the same day, Waddill filed a petition for Marienett Mayeux, the widow of Pierre Couvillion, to invoke a family meeting for the purpose of adjudicating the property to her. On January 15, 1852, Waddill filed the petition to homologate the proceedings of a family meeting adjudicating the property in community to her.

On January 8, 1852, Waddill settled some claims with the estate of Joel Toler. He obtained notes of that succession amounting to a little over $3,400.00. Waddill had worked long and hard on this estate. His payment was to be considerable.

Continued Reading of Current Events

On January 14, 1852, Waddill subscribed to the *Union and Democratic Review*. It cost twenty-one dollars, but he felt compelled to do it because of his thirst for knowledge. On January 16, 1852, he subscribed to the *Edin-*

---

inent spot in the Riverview Burial Park in Shreveport, which was once part of his plantation. See *The Monroe News-Star*, February 26, 1937, pg. 7.

burgh, London, Westminster, and North British Reviews* and *Blackwoods Magazine*. That was $7.50.

Land Holdings

Waddill hired James McCauley, deputy surveyor, to survey the 407 acres of land that he had purchased in Big Cane. The surveyor told Waddill that this land was first quality. He paid McCauley ten dollars.

Waddill went to the store of A. Voinche on January 17, 1852. The purpose was to weigh two hogsheads of sugar that A. Voinche bought from William Clopton. They weighed as follows: number one 1, 1,120 pounds and number 2, 1,141 pounds. The total came to 2,261 pounds. Waddill represented Clopton.

Marcelin Bordelon had returned from New Orleans with the corn that Waddill had ordered previously. Waddill had given him thirty dollars and owed him $7.50. Waddill also purchased a barrel of Irish potatoes from Daniel R. Eldred and paid him $2.50.

Waddill agreed to file a possessory action against George Barron on behalf of Sylvert Bordelon for a fee of twenty dollars.

Many Deaths

On January 19, 1852, Amos Fisher, an old resident and planter on Bayou Rouge, died at his residence. In addition, Sam, a slave belonging to William F. Griffin, died in Marksville of pneumonia. On January 27, Oilo Sophia Taylor died at the residence of her brother-in-law, Henderson Taylor. She had pneumonia and was only thirty-nine. Waddill described her as:

> an excellent woman, intelligent, amiable, and affable. Her husband was at the time of her death in Baton Rouge attending to his duties as a member of the Legislature. She would be missed. She kept her beliefs of faith for about ten days, with Christian patience and fortitude. Mrs. Taylor was for several days perfectly aware of her approaching dissolution, and having an unalterable and firm faith in the Christian religion, she resigned herself to her Father without a murmur and died without a struggle. She was surrounded by her children and kindred and as she passed into eternity. Her eyes rested upon those whom she had known and loved from her childhood, who standing over her with eyes dimmed with sorrow, proved to her

that those true hearted companions of her joyous hours stood by her unchanged in that most terrible of all her trials, the hour of her death. She leaves besides her husband, six children to mourn her loss three daughters and three sons.[232]

Before John Waddill gave up alcohol and tobacco, he had a recipe for beer. He shared it in his diary. "For a five gallon dimijour, boil about three ears of corn until it is swelled and soft and put it in the dimijour. Then mix cold water and molasses together until it is very sweet and fill the dimijour with it. In three or four days you will have good beer. When the beer is out, sweeten more water and pour on the corn. You can have good beer there in a day or two."[233]

232. DJW, January 20, 1852, vol. 2, pg. 97.

233. Ibid.

CHAPTER 41

THE LODGE
MAY 1, 1852

As a Protestant, John P. Waddill did what many men have done. He joined the Masons in 1851 and stayed fairly active in the organization. He found that the business and social contacts were beneficial, and hesaw no harm in belonging. He did think some of the traditions and secrecy a bit far-fetched but overall felt it was to his benefit to belong to the organization.

On May 1, 1852, John traveled to Alexandria on the steamboat *Post Boy*. It cost three dollars, and that seemed high, but the trip was so much quicker than on horse or buggy. It was safer also. He was going to watch S. W. Henarie take his degree of Fellow Craftsman in the Oliver Lodge this evening. There would be many men present to watch this event and to congratulate Henarie. He hoped there would be as many the following evening.

Waddill rose to the degree of a Master Mason, a high honor. The event would be held in the same lodge, Oliver Lodge, in Alexandria, Louisiana. The night was not a disappointment. Again, a good group of men assembled at the lodge.

Waddill was in Alexandria for three days. He missed his family, but he was able to make a fee on May 4 while away from them. It was from Whitely M. Sasser as agent of Edward H. Durell, administrator of A. Rivarde Sindry Estate. This was good since the entire round trip to Alexandria and night stay on the 3 and 4 cost a total of $42.46. This was for passage fees, cash to the Oliver Lodge (ten dollars), hack hire, cigars, and other incidentals.

While there, he had a shave and trim of his hair. He hoped his wife would like it. Perhaps the three days away, including overnight for two, would cause a bit of a strain.

Upon his return, Waddill was tired but happy to be home.

He arrived home very late and was up the next morning to go to work at his office. He was enervated. He needed sleep, but two days later, Julia

Waddill fell ill. Waddill thought it was acidity of the stomach. He hoped it was not related to the days he was gone. Normally, Julia was very strong in his absence.

Thomas H. Waddill, John's son, commenced school at Mr. McDowell's schoolhouse on May 10, 1852. On May 16, Charles J. Hallberg was invited to give a message in the schoolhouse. A widow lady named Cropper was employed as a music teacher.

Waddill hoped his son would be as fortunate as he was in his education. Waddill placed a heavy emphasis on learning and never stopped reading and studying. He and others hoped that the school would be a success. It was encouraging that Thomas began reading Caesar's *Commentaries* in Latin on May 17.

Thomas was the first-born child and first son of John and Julia. He was born in 1842, and beginning by reading in Latin and starting his Classic education at age ten was a good sign. Thomas Hickman Waddill would go far, Waddill thought.

On May 17, Julia was still sick. When Waddill asked her how she was, however, she told him that she felt better and stronger.

On May 7, Waddill had received a letter from his cousin, Jane E. Brand, wife of Major J. G. Barnard, of the U.S. Corps of Engineers. Based upon the letter, Waddill thought that her husband was partially insane. She told Waddill about their intent to move to a northern state. Jane feared that her constitution would not be strong enough for the climate.

Based upon records found in Massachusetts, the couple moved there, and Barnard served in the Union Army. Jane died on February 28, 1853, listing her father's name as William Brand. He later served as the Chief Engineer of the Army of the Potomac.[234] He had a distinguished career in the Union Army.[235]

The pastor who preached at the academy spent the night at Waddill's home on May 17, 1852. Reverend Charles J Hallberg[236] was in the Masons.

---

234. "Official Records of the Rebellion: Volume Eleven," chapter 23, part 1: *Peninsular Campaign: Reports of Brig. Gen. John G. Barnard*, http://www.historyofwar.org/sources/acw/officialrecords/vol011chap023part1/02020_15.html.

235. "John G. Barnard," Wikipedia, https://en.wikipedia.org/wiki/John_G._Barnard.

236. Charles J. Hallberg was part of the Louisiana Conference of the Methodist Church. He was born in the West Indies and was of Swedish parentage. He was part of several Louisiana circuits, including Alexandria. While on circuits, Methodist

In fact, he was a Royal Arch Mason and gave Waddill a long lecture and teaching on Free Masonry.

The next day, May 18, 1852, Waddill's good friend, former partner, and sitting judge, Ralph Cushman, came to visit Waddill on a personal issue. Apparently, he had concerns about his son, Walter.

Cushman had found his son to be unsteady and weak in moral conduct. He hoped Waddill could find the time to speak to him. Cushman was traveling to Opelousas the next day to hold court. His daughter, Marjorie, was going with him. He hoped Waddill would make the effort soon.

Waddill encouraged his friend and told him he would do anything that he could to help. Cushman also told Waddill that he would continue to financially support the new Protestant church building.

William Alexander, Waddill's step-father-in-law, was building the new Methodist Protestant Church. It would be forty feet long and twenty-five feet wide. The ceiling would be sixteen feet high. Each of its twenty-four pews would seat nine people with a half-foot of seating area. They first raised the rafters on May 14, 1852.

May 22, 1852, was Henarie Browder Waddill's second birthday. Waddill thought that he would be a fine promising boy.[237] Two days later, Waddill sent W. W., his brother, to make collections for their law practice. The collections had to occur on occasion because so much of their work was paid by promissory notes.

All at the same time, Waddill planted sweet potatoes even though there was a severe dry spell. It had rained on Bayou Boeuf and Bayou des Glaise, but the prairie drought continued. A splendid rain finally fell on May 25. The clouds came from the northwest and interrupted the hoeing of the rows of potatoes. The corn planted was also flourishing.

Waddill was doing well, and W. W. was helping a lot. Their friend and fellow attorney Henderson Taylor's son, Seth Lewis Taylor, was to marry Miss Mary Ely on May 27, and the Waddill family, including William, was invited. It was to be at the Taylor home in Hydropolis on the Avoyelles prairie. They attended the wedding and reception and enjoyed themselves. The long

---

preachers would go from area to area to preach. He died on July 29, 1870, at age fifty. "Charles J. Hallberg: 1820–1870," Louisiana Conference, The United Methodist Church, http://www.la-umc.org/obituary/1548266.

237. In 1865, Henarie Waddill attended the Louisiana State Seminary of Learning and Military Academy (the forerunner to LSU) through 1867. He became a teacher, which would have pleased his father. He died March 6, 1905.

ride home in the carriage was exhausting. Henderson Taylor, "his lady," two daughters, Miss Tammy Satterfield, and Edward H. Satterfield were leaving the day after the wedding for a summer trip to the northern and eastern states. They would not return until the end of September. Miss Ellen Taylor was going to a boarding school in North Carolina. Before leaving, Henderson Taylor paid Waddill and William Alexander $100 for his subscription toward building the Marksville Protestant Church. They headed to New Orleans for the first leg of the journey.

John Waddill heard that five days prior Rowland Robinson was stabbed in the breast by William Galligher, a brick layer. Waddill could not understand why emotions of individuals controlled the actions of people, especially in a murder.

William Waddill came back home with only five dollars collected. He got extremely wet from the rain. He stayed overnight at Johnson P. Grimball's. Johnson was to credit the account of Grimball, owed to Waddill in notes, for the one night stay.

On May 27, Waddill helped W. Alexander raise scaffolding around the church. He also hauled weatherboarding from the shop to the church for Alexander. By June 5, 1852, they finished weatherboarding the church. It was lathed and ready for shining.

The law practice of Waddill and Waddill took on the claims of Dominique Coco and Dr. L. Moncla, who had a claim against Nelson Durand, totaling $842.91, a substantial sum of money. They agreed to take the debt that Durand owed to the heirs of Pierre Leglise. His property was to be seized and sold. The day before the sale of the property, Waddill received a letter from Durand stating his claims against Pierre Leglise, through his heirs. It was too late as the property was being sold.

May 29, 1852

Madam Enoch Marcelle came to see Waddill. She wanted to retain Waddill to file for separation of property from her husband.

Waddill remembered trying this some five years ago, and she never finalized it. He wanted to be sure it was different this time.

Her estate had been reduced by her husband's inaction and imprudent ways. She had to go through this now, before all of her funds disappeared.

Despite his weariness, Waddill accepted the retainer. He had hoped to be able to help her earlier and hoped she would not change her mind this time. Marcelle had one child with him, Lucinda, and did not want to be made destitute.

Later that week, Fabius Ricord dislocated his leg, having wrenched and strained the tendons and muscles, so as to loosen and slip the kneecap. When Waddill saw him on May 30, 1852, he was doing well and pain free.

Waddill wrote that his corn and sweet potatoes were doing well. He had an acre and a quarter of sweet potatoes.

On June 3, 1852, John and Julia entertained the wives of A. G. Pearce and James Horace Marshall, friends and business associates of John. Mrs. A. G. Pearce was Sidney Elizabeth Kay, the great-granddaughter of Dr. Enemund Meuillon[238] and Jeannette Poiret LaMothe. She brought her daughter Virginia, who was born in 1838 and only fourteen years old.

Mrs. James Horace Marshall was Eliza Eugenia Pearce, the first cousin of Alanson Green (A. G.) Pearce, and was born on April 8, 1826, to Joshua Pearce, the uncle of A. G. She had married James Horace Marshall in 1848. James Marshall, born in Avoyelles Parish on March 2, 1817, was the grandson of Dr. Enemund Meuillon.

Waddill could not believe how much Eliza had grown. She was eight years younger than James, but he had seen her last in 1840 at the residence of Leander F. Ardry, of Rapides Parish. She was nearly fifteen then, and both she and John were single at that time. John and Eliza were two of the attendants who waited on W. H. Duvall and Miss Malvina Pearce at their wedding held at the Ardry residence. Malvina was the daughter of Stephen Pearce and his first wife Sally Goodwin, who died in 1829. Malvina was born on October 16, 1822.

Waddill noticed how attractive Eliza was even in 1840. This was only a month before John would marry Julia. The other bridesmaid and groom were Julia Malvina Barlow (Waddill's future wife) and James S. Edelen. It had been twelve years since Waddill had seen Eliza. He wrote she was now married with five children. The parents of W. H. Duvall were now dead, as was Mr. Ardry.

Fielding Edwards had been the keeper of Gorton's Landing since shortly after Gorton's murder. He was well trusted to handle many financial transactions. Waddill sent fifty dollars by the way of Gorton's Landing to H. Frelson & Co. as a balance due to Bress Frellsen & Co. from John Pierre Normand.

---

238. The Sons of the American Revolution Chapter in Central Louisiana, based in Alexandria is named after Enemund Meuillon. In 1777, Dr. Meuillion was living in Point Coupée and listed as a 2nd Lieutenant of the Point Coupée Militia. In 1779, he participated in the expeditions of Governor Bernardo de Glavez to capture the British forts and posts at Manchac and Baton Rouge. He later served as the Spanish Commandant of Post El Rapido until the Louisiana Purchase. "Dr Enemund Meullion," Find a Grave, http://www.findagrave.com/cgi-bin/fg.cgi?page=gr&GRid=22613945.

Waddill wrote a letter and carried it with the funds to Fielding Edwards along with five dollars for an order for $13.75 to Leviman, Wills & Peak for freight. The order was for a sack of coffee, keg of lard, and sack of salt.

More National Politics

On June 7, 1852, Waddill learned that the Democratic National Convention had nominated General Franklin Pierce of the state of New Hampshire as their candidate for President of the United States. In 1837, General Pierce had been elected to the U.S. Senate from New Hampshire, and in 1842 he resigned. He was a Brigadier General in the Mexican War and acted under the command of General Scott. W. R. King of Alabama was nominated for vice president.

On June 26, Waddill's order came to Gorton's landing. John paid the freight for the sack of coffee, keg of lard, and sack of salt. The family had a picnic in the hills near Marksville. Waddill's friend and business associate, Fielding Edwards, became quite sick from a diseased liver. Dr. Poret was treating him. Waddill felt badly for Fielding and shared that with his close friend and confidante, Reverend Charles J. Hallberg. On June 29, another friend of John's, Oliver Mock, was close to death from a disease of the stomach and bowels. Dr. G. E. Elmer went to Bayou des Glaises to treat him.

Julia's grandfather had a slave by the name of David. Nearing death, her grandfather decided to free him. David took the name of David French and lived as a free man in Avoyelles Parish. On June 30, 1852, he came to visit Julia and brought a present of a dress to Julia's daughter and a knife to their son, Thomas. Once again, Waddill could not help but think about his friend Samuel Bass and his views on slavery. Waddill enjoyed the visit greatly and was happy to see Mr. French doing well.

BOOK IV

The Constitutional Convention 1852

Samuel Bass and the Freeing of Solomon Northup

Death of John P. Waddil

CHAPTER 42

THE CONSTITUTIONAL CONVENTION OF 1852

The State Legislature in 1852 passed an act calling upon the people of Louisiana to vote on April 12 on whether they would call a convention of delegates to amend the state constitution. On that day, the convention was carried by a large majority, yet not one half of the legal voters cast their votes or attended the polls. An election for delegates was to come occur on June 12. The people of Rapides and Avoyelles spoke of voting for Waddill as the Democratic candidate for the Senatorial District. Waddill cared nothing for the office and furthermore feared that, in consequence of absence, it would greatly injure his practice as a lawyer. While he was in the state Senate for four years, his practice greatly decreased. If he would be selected as a candidate, and if the people wanted his services, he would let them elect him, but he would serve them only until after July Court. He decided he would not electioneer.

June 14, 1852
The Election for Delegates to the Convention

Two days prior to the election, Julia, William, and many of their friends went to Bayou du Lac to have a picnic and fish fry. They caught but few fish, and Waddill had a little fever. He was not feeling well for the election. The election was held to select delegates on the fourteenth. Dr. R. H. Sibley[239] and Waddill were elected for the Senatorial District of Avoyelles and Rapides. Joseph Joffrion and John H. Boyer were elected as delegates from the Parish

---

239. A well-known and loved physician who was known for his generosity, Dr. R. H. Sibley was born on August 21, 1792, and died on April 14, 1853. *The Times Picayune* ran a notice of his death and referred to a visit to New Orleans only a week earlier, "looking as hale and hearty as ever, and possessing his usual flow of life, cheerfulness and conviviality." *Times Picayune*, April 21, 1853, pg. 2.

of Avoyelles. A. J. Isaacs[240] and W. W. Whittington were elected as delegates of the Parish of Rapides. Stephen Vanwickle, Bennett B. Simmes, and Matthews were elected as delegates from the Parish of Pointe Coupee. The whole number for the state was 129 for the convention.

June 16, 1852
The Whig National Convention

The 1845 Constitution of Louisiana was not considered very democratic with all Judiciary officials appointed, not elected. In his *A History of Louisiana,* Alcée Fortier wrote that, "The Constitution of 1845 was not considered to be sufficiently democratic and, not- withstanding the opposition by Governor Walker, a convention was called to change it."[241]

John P. Waddill was passionate about the people having a right to vote, so he decided to run with this as his main cause and was elected June 14, 1852. He was earlier elected to the Senatorial District of Rapides and Avoyelles. He had help from a man his age, or a year younger, by the name of Michael Ryan. Ryan had been elected as a state representative from Rapides in 1851. He, like Waddill, studied the law, tutored as a clerk, and left teaching to become an attorney. He was an Irishman who moved to the United States at age twenty-two, in about 1836. He taught languages at Spring Creek Academy on the Calcasieu River.[242]

Michael Ryan was somewhat of a rebel, and Waddill accepted his help with a wary eye. Ryan did not seem to be too loyal to the Democratic Party and tended to affiliate with the Whigs too much in Waddill's view. Maybe Waddill's reticence was due to the fact that Ryan was born in Ireland and not a natural citizen.

The convention delegates served for one month, from July 5, 1852, to July 31, 1852. Although it did not have everything Waddill wanted, he supported the constitution's adoption. Samuel Bass wanted Waddill to oppose mentioning

---

240. In May of 1853, A. J. Isaacs ran against J. H. C. Barlow, John's brother-in-law for district attorney in the Rapides District. Isaacs won, but Barlow ran and won in the next election. He later became a judge in Rapides.

241. Fortier, *A History of Louisiana*, vol. III, *1808–1861*, 251.

242. Michael Ryan served two sessions in the legislature, 1852–1854 and then was elected to the State Senate for four years. https://legis.la.gov/legisdocs/members/h1812-2016.pdf.

slavery in the constitution. Waddill owned slaves and could not avoid that fact. In the 1850 Slave Schedule prepared as part of the U.S. 1850 Census, Waddill owned six slaves, three men and three women. The ages of the men were thirty, eight, and one. The women were ages forty-six, twenty-seven, and fifteen.

Waddill traveled from Marksville on *The Caspian*, a steamboat, and headed to Baton Rouge. He landed at 12:00 a.m. in the capitol. He was already tired.

It became evident that most of the delegates would be in favor of changing the selection of judges from appointment by the executive (governor) to election by the people.

Duncan F. Kenner was elected president of the body as a Whig on the day that John Waddill was seated. The constitution was proposed effective July 31, 1852, and would be voted on in November to replace the 1845 Constitution.

One of the key issues was to put in place the election of judges. The appointment process was not effective.

Waddill was exuberant in his effort at the convention. He solicited the help of fellow delegate John B. Cotton, who also graduated from Augusta College in 1847. He had become a lawyer by reading with his brother, V. F. Cotton, and being admitted to the bar in 1848 in Alexandria, where he studied. He later moved to Lafayette to practice in that area and the New Orleans area.[243]

Waddill worked tirelessly, taking his mind off not being home and missing the work on his fields and at his law office. All of that would have to wait. He had more important work to do. It would be only a month. Perhaps even less, he thought.

When the delegates presented this proposal on judges, Waddilll was quite pleased. The delegates also proposed that in lieu of the governor appointing the Supreme Court, the chief justice should be elected at large by the voting citizens in this state. As to the four associate judges—they would be elected from regions as the state's four districts showed. This included selected senatorial districts.

As to the lesser courts, the delegates proposed that voters elect them also, but to allow the legislature to determine the districts and the procedures for these elections.

243. By Henry Plauché Dart, *John Blackstone Cotton, 1824–1881: A sketch of his life and times prepared in connection with the presentation of his portrait to the Supreme Court of Louisiana* (New Orleans: Hauser Printing Company, 1915). With this new provision in the constitution, he later was elected the first judge of the newly created Sixth District on May 17, 1853.

John was quite pleased. The delegates listened and asked a few minor questions and adopted this section with a vast majority. Avoyelles Parish would be in the third district for the Supreme Court, consisting of the parishes of St. Tammany, Washington, Livingston, St. Helena, East Baton Rouge, East Feliciana, West Feliciana, Pointe Coupee, Avoyelles, Tensas, Concordia, Lafayette, Vermilion, St. Mary, St. Martin, and St. Landry.[244]

One of the provisions of the constitution that pleased Waddill was the limitation of the criminal jurisdiction of the Supreme Court to questions of law only. This would prevent the upper court from interfering with findings of fact in the lower courts. The convention left it to the legislature as to whether the issue of civil cases for limitations to findings of fact or law.[245]

There were many other changes, some of which Waddill did not particularly agree. The minimum age of the governor would be twenty-eight years of age rather than thirty-five. Waddill had reservations about that.

> I suspect that even though it is only a seven year difference, in maturity and wisdom, it is my belief that a 35 year old is much more qualified than a 28 year old man.

At the end of the session, one of the most discussed issues involved the secretary of the Senate and the clerk of the House and their ability to communicate in French and English. Many in the southern part of the state and in Avoyelles, Pointe Coupee, and St. Landry[246] spoke French as their primary language. Waddill really could not speak conversational French, although he understood some French, but many in the northern parishes did not and had many questions about how to word this section. Waddill would strive to learn French later.

The idea came from President Kenner himself. He suggested that the clerk be conversant in French and English, not in its writing. That should be simple enough to go through the selection process.

---

244. Article 64 of the Louisiana Constitution of 1852.

245. Article 62 of the Louisiana Constitution of 1852.

246. Evangeline Parish was not yet in existence, as one of the four parishes settled by direct French descendants rather than Acadians in "Le Grand Dérangement," (Avoyelles, St. Landry, and Pointe Coupe, being the others). Evangeline came from lands in St. Landry in 1910.

The delegates agreed to this without much grumbling. Each member would be allowed to address either chamber in French or in English.[247]

All in all, the convention was brief, and the business of changing the State of Louisiana had begun. Waddill was pleased. He was also ready to go home. At half past ten on July 31, 1852, the convention adjourned *sine die*. Waddill did not like all of the provisions but felt that the new constitution was much better than the 1845 Constitution. He took the steamboat *Cleona* on August 2, 1852, and arrived home at noon. He disembarked at Gorton's Landing and really felt home.

On August 6, 1852, four days after returning from Baton Rouge, C. Pasquier & Co.[248] of New Orleans shipped to Waddill one barrel (forty-two gallons) of molasses; 186 pounds of hams of bacon; and two hundred slabs of bacon sides. The cost of the goods, besides freight, was $52.50.

---

247. Article 101 of the Louisiana Constitution of 1852.

248. C. Pasquier & Co was a New Orleans commercial company located at 11 Bank Place. There was notice in the April 2, 1852, *New Orleans Times Picayune* that a light draught steamer would be going to Bayou Rouge and Bayou des Glaises for their goods. D. Glasscock was the master.

CHAPTER 43

The Trial for the Murder of A. B. Coco, 1852

Oliver Mock's widow hired Waddill to handle the deceased's estate matters. Elizabeth Havard, his wife, asked for the administration. Mr. Mock had five children and was married twice. He did not marry Elizabeth V. Havard until February 26, 1851. They had moved to Avoyelles Parish where Mock had patented four tracts of land, eighty acres in 1845, forty-six acres in 1845, and two adjacent tracts of eighty acres each in 1848. In 1850, he was listed as owning twenty-one slaves. He died in August 1852. Elizabeth was from Mississippi, where their marriage took place one year before his death.

Julia Waddill's cousin, Samuel W. Henarie, stayed at the Waddill residence from August 3, 1852, to August 17, 1852. This was simply a family visit. He brought "his lady" and son and left that day for Alexandria, where they resided.

August 19, 1852, Mr. W. Alexander, Mrs. Alexander (Julia's mother), and Julia's three siblings, Mary Jane Barlow, E. Jane Duke, and Spencer Mayo Duke, left the Waddill home for Grey's Creek in the Rapides Parish, where they resided.

On August 25, Julia, Florence, (their youngest child), William (Waddill's brother), and Irma, their house servant, went to White Sulphur Springs in Catahoula. They were going for ten days to visit family and to rest. Julia's health was not good. Waddill described her as quite lean. They came back on September 5, 1852.

Before they left, John and W. W. put the finishing touches on the bookcase of their office. They also placed their books on the shelves. Waddill was quite pleased. He thought it might be worth forty dollars.

On September 4, 1852, Julien Baptiste Maillet, a local grocer, sold out his stock of goods in Marksville. The sale was by auction. Two days later, Daniel R. Eldred came to Waddill for advice on his rights in the partnership between him and McCauce. Waddill charged ten dollars.

Trial of Murder, 1852

On July 31, 1852, the day before Waddill came back from the constitutional convention, John E. Frith and Augustus Bartell were indicted for the November 1851 murder of Aurelien B. Dominique Coco. The trial was moved to Point Coupee Parish for a change of venue. On October 5, 1852, John E. Frith was acquitted.

All the evidence and brutality of the murder shocked Waddill. These men brutally stabbed Coco on the night of his victory for sheriff. He died of his injuries in the next day or two. Thomas C. Adams was indicted for aiding and abetting, but during the trial, he was discharged. The lawyers for the defendants had raised the issue of self-defense, and the juries accepted that version. Many in Avoyelles Parish were jolted and shocked. Waddill had respected Coco and was deeply saddened by such a waste of life over political differences.

September 1852

Waddill's slaves needed quarters. He noted in his diary,

> On September 7 Richard, one of the slaves started building a small house for the slaves. It was framed by W. Alexander's Negroes Aaron and Solomon who did the framing and covered about a third of it. It is the following dimensions—Length 15 feet—Width 13 feet—height of the house—8 feet from floor to ceiling . . . I bought 3000 shingles to cover it with. The shingles were not of good quality to cover the structure. I have not paid him for them. I had of my own shingles, 700 or 800.[249]

Waddill had traveled to Alexander's home to ask for assistance. Alexander allowed his slaves to help. Waddill had done legal work for Alexander previously. He prepared a few property transactions that Alexander was well pleased with in the performance and costs.

Waddill had enough slaves that required him to build a home for them. He had one that would be able to begin it but would need help with framing it. Waddill's slave, Richard, had told him that Alexander had two slaves that could help.

Richard mentioned Aaron and Solomon. Alexander allowed them to help until Friday of that week. It would amount to four days. One of W.

---

249. DJW, September 7, 1852, vol. 4 pgs.12–13.

Alexander's slaves also built a bookcase for Waddill. The "negro" house was begun on August 23, 1852.

Waddill purchased the lumber from Mr. Fielding Edwards at Gorton's Landing on the Red River. Waddill noted in his diary the lumber and costs as follows:

700 feet weather boarding	$7.00
350 feet inch plank	$3.50
200 feet scanting	
3 by 4 – 10 feet long	$2.00
100 feet 4 by 5	$1.00
108 feet posts 4x 8	$1.08
68 feet plates 4x6,	
17 feet long	$0.68
26 feet plates 4x8	
13 feet long	$0.26
65 feet joists 3x4	
13 feet long	$0.65
100 feet inch plank	$1.00
22 feet inch & a half plank,	
14 feet long	$0.22
54 feet 12	$0.54
100 feet inch and a quarter 10	$1.00
200 feet rough edge plank	$1.50
Total	$20.43[250]

Richard and Mr. Alexander's men began building the quarters. The length was fifteen feet, the width thirteen feet, the width of the gallery eight feet; the enclosed part of gallery was ten feet; the height of the house was eight feet. It took three thousand shingles, which Waddill purchased from R. W. Kay. As he mentioned previously in his diary, the shingles were of poor quality, and he could not use 700–800 of them. He finished the cabin on September 11, 1852.

September 25, 1852, was the day that Waddill took the money collected from Roderic Ferguson, the amount of $13.15. This was for T. B. Tiller, who moved several years after his brother-in-law shot Gorton. Tiller owed Waddill $15.50 on a bill for collecting from R. B. Marshall.

---

250. Ibid., pg. 12.

On September 28, 1852, Waddill paid James Rey, postmaster, two dollars to subscribe for one year to the *Saturday Evening Post* for Miss Mary Jane Barlow and three dollars for a one-year subscription to *Harper's Magazine* for his wife, Julia. The next day, Madam Pierre Couvillion paid on Waddill's bill the sum of fifty dollars for the succession of Pierre Couvillion.

Waddill noted that Julien Goudeau died on September 24, 1852. He described him as a very worthy and wealthy Creole citizen of Avoyelles. He died of carbuncle at his residence in Bayou Rouge on the prairie.[251] It appeared that the illness did not last long. The boils under the skin were very painful, and he lasted only four days upon the onset. Some two weeks previous to his death, his daughter Julianna married Lucien D. Coco of Avoyelles.

Waddill was pleased to hear that Judge John H. Overton resigned his office of judge of the 15th Judicial District Court due to accepting an appointment of the New Orleans and Opelousas Railroad presidency at a salary of $4,000 per annum. Waddill was simply impressed at the enormity of the salary and happy for his friend. Overton moved to New Orleans and started his new duties. Waddill also heard the sad news that Judge Isaac T. Preston of the Supreme Court drowned in Lake Ponchatrain after an explosion on a steamboat. Waddill considered him a man of superior talent and erudition.

International News

Waddill wrote in his diary about the loss of the Duke of Wellington. He called him the Iron Duke, as he was known. "He was considered by many as one of the ablest generals of modern times. His greatness renown and glory were acquired at the Battle of Waterloo, where he was general-in-chief of the

---

251. A carbuncle is a red, swollen, and painful cluster of boils that are connected to each other under the skin. A boil (or furuncle) is an infection of a hair follicle that has a small collection of pus (called an abscess) under the skin. Usually single, a carbuncle is most likely to occur on a hairy area of the body such as the back or nape of the neck. But a carbuncle also can develop in other areas of the body, such as the buttocks, thighs, groin, and armpits. Most carbuncles are caused by *staphylococcus aureus* bacteria, which inhabit the skin surface, throat, and nasal passages. These bacteria can cause infection by entering the skin through a hair follicle, small scrape, or puncture, although sometimes there is no obvious point of entry. http://www.webmd.com/skin-problems-and-treatments/guide/carbuncles-causes-treatments.

allied armies of Russia, Austria, and England when the defeated the French under the great Napoleon Bonaparte."[252]

On October 3, 1852, Miss Pamela Kay, her brother Charles, and her sisters, Mary, Cordelia, and Leona, visited the Waddill family. They dined with them.

Henderson Taylor returned to Marksville on October 7, 1852, after the acquittal of John E. Frith of the murder of Aurelien B. Coco. F. Cullom and his son E. N. Cullom also arrived. William Edwards and Chaz had come in the night before.

Criminal Violence

Waddill could not understand the rash of violence going on in his small town and Avoyelles Parish. On October 8, 1852, Peter Wilson was put on trial for the murder of Webb. The jury could not agree, causing a mistrial.

On October 9, 1852, Valaire Dauzat was put on his trial for stabbing Edmond Couvillion. The jury found him guilty, and he was sentenced to three months imprisonment in the parish jail and an additional month if he did not pay the cost of prosecution.

The Death of T. B. Tiller

On October 16, 1852, came news that T. B. Tiller, who lived in Marksville for many years but had moved to Pine Bluff, Arkansas, died. He died of cholera at Natchez. He was sick on board a steamboat and died just before they landed him. He stayed in Marksville a while after the killing of Gorton by his brother-in-law but eventually moved. Waddill was saddened by the news of his death.

---

252. DJW, September 24, 1852, vol. 4, pg. 35.

CHAPTER 44

Charles Étienne Arthur Gayarré

Charles Étienne Arthur Gayarré was a Louisiana historian. Born in 1805, he lived to be eighty years old. He was a Creole attorney and politician.[253] He was a U.S. Senator, elected in 1834 as a Jacksonian Democrat. He stepped down immediately due to illness. He wrote *The History of Louisiana*, which, in its final 1866 version, turned out to be over two thousand pages covering 1539 to 1866. The entire set is available online at the University of Chicago.[254] He was a wealthy man until the Civil War, in which he lost a fortune. He continued to live on his earnings from writing.

Later in life, after 1853, Gayarré became very cynical due to the Regular Democrats ignoring him over some one else for a diplomatic post. He also thought that blacks would never be the equals of whites, believing that the system of the antebellum South was the best form of society. He wrote satire until his death, claiming that Louisiana politics was corrupt.[255]

On October 17, 1852, Waddill met up in town with William Alexander. He had great respect for Mr. Alexander. He helped Waddill in his selection to the Constitutional Convention and thought they had a relationship that would continue through their lives. William Alexander was the elected state representative for the area.

He told him that Charles Gayarré was coming to speak on *The His-*

---

253. He also served in the House of Representatives for one year in 1844 and served as Secretary of State 1845–1853. "Charles Gayarré," Wikipedia, https://en.wikipedia.org/wiki/Charles_Gayarré.

254. http://penelope.uchicago.edu/Thayer/E/Gazetteer/Places/America/United_State/Louisiana/_Texts/GAYHLA/home.html

255. Stephen M. Klugewicz, "'Unfit for the Age': Charles Gayarré, the Conservative as Satirist," The Imaginative Conservative, http://www.theimaginativeconservative.org/2013/03/unfit-for-the-age-charles-gayarre-the-conservative-as-satirist.html#.

tory of Louisiana and the Democratic Party. Both William and John were members of the Marksville Protestant Church. They were more than acquaintances.

The crowd was large for the small community of Marksville. Gayarré did not disappoint. He spoke of aristocracy with humor and pride, claiming that equal rights were a myth and that God himself ordained the aristocrats.

"For anyone to believe that the poor should be equal to the rich, there is no sense in this," Gayarré preached.

He continued:

The system we have in this State of electing our leaders has reached a point of nonsense and corruption. I was once a part of it. A few power brokers sit in a back room and decide whom the Democrat is to be to hold the post. I know our forefathers did not intend this to be the system. This small group determines whom we elect? I say no! Maybe we should limit who can vote to the property owners. Then at least we know what to expect and who to elect. Instead the Regular Democrats nominate someone and expect us to follow their lead.

Gayarré's knowledge and wisdom impressed Waddill. In fact, he was inspired. The only problem was that Waddill believed in the party system and loyalty to the party. In Avoyelles Parish, he was one of those who nominated and decided who should run. It was a system of weeding out those who had not been properly loyal to the party and proved to hold the values of those who cared. Waddill did not like the idea of only property owners voting, and believed it did not match the ideology and concepts of the founders of the country.

Waddill was inspired yet a bit confused. Later in life, Gayarré would reject the Regular Democratic Party and espouse the aristocracy as the best means of government. Waddill could never have accepted this even though it would have benefited him as part of the landed gentry. Waddill never believed himself to be an aristocrat.

The thoughts caused Waddill to stop and reflect. He had always been one who thought long and hard about issues, wrote about them in his diary, and pondered those thoughts. He had changed positions before. This speech was inspiring and depressing at the same time.

Waddill would continue his studies to broaden his views. On October 8, 1853, he subscribed to the publications *Blackwood's Magazine*, the London *Westminister*, *Edinburgh Review*, *The North British Review*, and *The Quarterly*

Review.[256] *Blackwood's Magazine* was to rival the Whig-supporting *Edinburgh Review*, which too were in contrast to the moderate *The Quarterly Review*.[257]

It was past time for Waddill to start studying opposing views. This would either change him or strengthen his resolve to remain a Democrat.

On October 21, 1852, the Democratic Party planned for a barbecue in Mansura, to be held on October 30, 1852. On November 1, Waddill attended the Whig barbecue held at Julien Deshautelle's home. Waddill noted that there were more Democrats present. T. B. Thorpe[258] was the speaker there. He was entertaining and humorous. A ball was to be held there that night. The Whig candidate for president was Major General Windfield Scott of New York. His vice president candidate was William A. Graham of North Carolina.

Waddill was a Democrat and voted for Pierce and King. Judge Ralph Cushman and Dr. D. MacEnery went to the Red River in order to attend the polls in Point Maigre on election day. Waddill paid five dollars for his share of the expenses of the barbecue at Marksville on October 18, for support of Charles Gayarré's speech.

Shortly after this October talk, Franklin Pierce won the presidential race of 1852 in a resounding defeat of General Scott. The Whigs won in only four states on November 2, 1852. On November 5, Waddill paid five dollars for his share of printing tickets for the presidential ticket choice and to reject the new constitution. He paid this to Alcibiade Derivas. Waddill became a loyal Democrat and ended up opposing the constitution he helped to write. It passed, however, and became the new constitution for the State of Louisiana. He also paid Zenon G. Guillot five dollars for his share of the Democratic barbecue at Mansura on October 30, 1852. He gave it to A. Lafargue, who had put up a considerable sum.

---

256. DJW, October 8, 1853, vol. 4, pgs. 56–57.

257. "Blackwood's Magazine," Wikipedia, https://en.wikipedia.org/wiki/Blackwood's_Magazine.

258. Thomas Bangs Thorpe, "Reminiscences of S. S. Prentiss," *The American Whig Review* 15 (January 1852): 92. He also wrote "The Big Bear of Arkansas," available at http://twain.lib.virginia.edu/projects/price/bear2000.htm. This was written in the humorous vein of the time period.

CHAPTER 45

Samuel Bass and John P. Waddill

November 15, 1852, Waddill was walking to the courthouse when he saw Samuel Bass. Mr. Bass was a strange fellow, a Canadian who rarely, if ever, socialized with anyone. He may have been the only person Waddill knew who openly opposed slavery. "Why was he here?" Waddill wondered. Tom, Waddill's slave, a decent man with all the emotions of any young man, had been with Waddill for several years and was with him that day. Bass and Waddill greeted each other and made small talk.

Samuel Bass and Waddill had some interesting discussions when Waddill ran for the Constitutional Convention. His thoughts on slavery ran contrary to most every person that Waddill knew. Waddill often worried about Bass's safety.

Bass was a carpenter by trade. He had a very good reputation and began working on Waddill's home on October 14, 1850.[259] He started the framing at the sawmill of Edwards and Conner. He also made two pairs of steps for Waddill's office on October 16, 1850. For his work on the house, he paid Bass the following: October 30, 1850, $10.45; December 14, $2.00; January 12, 1851, $50.00. On January 18, 1851, Waddill noted that Bass put up the steps to his house but complained that it had been days since he showed up for work. Waddill hired another carpenter, John Kirk, on November 19, 1850.

Waddill remembered the progress on his home as Bass continued walking away. On February 19, 1851, Waddill noted that Bass finished "ceiling the store room in my house. Yesterday Mr. Kirk finished ceiling my front gallery. Today he is boxing or casing the gallery posts." Waddill paid Bass twenty dollars on March 8, 1851 and figured that his balance was $116.55 from the total of $200 charged. Waddill gave Bass a note due with 8 percent interest.[260]

---

259. DJW, October 18, 1850, vol. 3, pg. 38.

260. Ibid., March 9, 1851, vol. 3, pg. 44.

Waddill had developed a relationship with Bass that would continue until Bass died. They spoke frequently, and he was well aware of Bass's beliefs about slavery.

In an interesting turn of events, Waddill represented Samuel Bass in a lawsuit against William H. Bassett. On March 21, 1851, Sheriff G. P. Voorhies collected $43.19 in cash for Samuel Bass and $15.62 in cost receipts and tax receipts, which was the balance Bassett owed. The relationship between Bass and Waddill strengthened as they got to know each other even better.

By March 31, 1851, Waddill had pretty much settled all of Samuel Bass's debts, and he paid Waddill for his fees. The final settlement occurred on April 24, 1851. Their friendship developed beyond business. They did not socialize but did have great conversations when they had the chance. Waddill enjoyed the challenge that Bass provided, especially in the area of abolition.

CHAPTER 46

Politics, November 1852

Reverend Charles J. Hallberg came on his circuit again to Marksville. Waddill paid him ten dollars. Five was from Henderson Taylor and five from himself. John also paid him one dollar for a book titled *Remains of Mrs. Cross*. The book was based on the life of Elizabeth Cross, who, with her husband, William Cross, was a devoted missionary to the South Pacific. While in Tonga, an island in the South Pacific to the east of Australia and west of South America, Mrs. Cross drowned in a canoe accident while trying to reach a remote village.[261] Her death occurred in January 1832.[262]

Politics and News

Waddill subscribed to the *Democratic Review* by sending six dollars to pay his subscription for 1852–1853. He sent it to G. N. Sanders. This started out as the *United States Magazine* in 1837 and changed its name to the *Democratic Review* in 1852. It was published until 1859. Its motto was "The best government is that which governs least."[263]

On November 27, a Democratic meeting was held at Waddill's office. Those present appointed delegates to meet the Democratic delegates from the other parishes in the state in convention at Baton Rouge to nominate candidates for governor, secretary of state, attorney general, treasurer, and state superintendent of free public schools.

---

261. It was noted in *The Wesleyan Magazine*, vol. 56 (January 1, 1833): 56.

262. More details are given in Andrew Thornley, *A Shaking of the Land: William Cross and the Origins of Christianity in Fiji*, trans. Tauga Vulaono (Institute of Pacific Studies, 2005).

263. https://en.wikipedia.org/wiki/The_United_States_Magazine_and_Democratic_Review

On December 5, 1852, Julia and their youngest child, Florence, went to Rapides Parish to her mother's residence. The purpose was to be present at the wedding of Julia's sister, Miss Mary Jane Barlow, to Mr. Green Huie. He had a reputation for being clever, intelligent, and very well off financially. The wedding was scheduled for December 9, 1852.

On December 27, 1852, voters cast ballots in the statewide election under the new constitution for governor, lieutenant governor, treasurer, secretary of state, attorney general, and state superintendent of free public schools. Each parish held elections for Senate and House seats.

The democratic candidates were these:

Paul O. Hebert	Governor
W. W. Farmer	Lieutenant Governor
A. L. Heron	Secretary of state
Isaac E. Morde	Attorney General
Charles E. Greneaux	Treasurer
James N. Carrigan	State school superintendent

For the Senate in Rapides and Avoyelles
William F. Griffin & Mitchell Neal
For Representative Avoyelles
Abraham M. Gray & John H. Boyer

The Whig candidates were: for governor, Louis Bordelon, lieutenant governor, John Ray, secretary of state, D. Avery, attorney general, R. N. Ogden, treasurer, George C. McWhorter, and school superintendent, T. B. Thorpe; for Senate, James T. Flint and James M. Wells; for representative, Avoyelles, Adolph D. Coco (Dr. Thomas Waters was nominated, but declined just before the election).

On December 28, news arrived that for the Senate, both Democrats won. In the House, Gray won, but Adolph Coco, Whig, beat Boyer, the Democrat.

Soon after that, Waddill heard that the entire state Democratic Ticket won every statewide election. Waddill was quite happy.

CHAPTER 47

MEETING WITH SOLOMON NORTHUP

On January 1, 1853, Henry Northup hired John P. Waddill to help free a slave, who apparently was a free man. Waddill noted in his diary the following:

> Today I was employed by Henry B. Northup, sq., of Sandy Hill, Washington County, State of New York, to bring suit against Edwin Epps, to reclaim from slavery a free negro named Solomon Northup, who had been kidnapped in the City of Washington, in 1841[264]

After hiring John P. Waddill for his legal services, Henry Northup had the capacity to obtain a writ to have the sheriff obtain the body of the presumed slave, Platt, who was Solomon Northup. The writ would take some time to prepare. John P. Waddill did some research as to whom this person was that wrote the letter from Northup to his relatives. He knew of only one person who had the view that would have cause to write the letter. They asked around town about where Samuel Bass had worked and found out that he had worked at Bayou Boeuf, where Northup was working in the summer of 1852.

John Waddill worked until midnight on the petition and planned to file it on the third or fourth of January. He hoped to have a hearing by January 4. On the third of January 1853, the sheriff went to the plantation where Solomon worked with Bass, with Henry Northup in Waddill's carriage.

That day, the sheriff took custody of Solomon Northup. He was held for one night in the parish jail at Marksville, right near the courthouse. This jail had been built after the police jury appropriated five thousand dollars to build it in 1847,[265] so it was fairly new but still sparse and inhospitable. When Waddill spoke to Solomon, something seemed out of the ordinary. Northup

---

264. DJW, January 1, 1843, vol. 4, pg. 53.

265. *Biographical and Historical Memoirs.*

spoke excellent English, surprising for a slave. This alone was almost proof enough, without Henry Northup's evidence, of Solomon's free status.

Northup told Waddill of a small gathering soon after Christmas Day, for which William Pearce, through his son, Alanson, had asked Epps for permission to allow Northup to play for a "slave dance" at Pearce Plantation on Bayou Huffpauir. This was less than a week prior. It was intended for the family and the slaves. The Pearce family had one of the larger property holdings in Avoyelles Parish. The home was built about fifteen years earlier, in 1838, near the time John P. Waddill began his law practice. Alanson Pearce was about three years younger than Waddill, but they had become very close over the years. The Pearces had a reputation for being kinder toward their slaves than many other slave owners, especially Epps, who was known to have a hot temper. Pearce had about forty-eight slaves at Oakwold at this time.[266]

Most plantation owners gave the slaves three days off at Christmas. "Slave dances" were common during the Christmas Season. The event at Pearce Plantation was held on the evening of December 29, 1852.

The night of the gathering was mild with a huge bonfire built to allow outdoor dancing near the Bayou Boeuf banks. It provided warmth, light, and deterred mosquitoes even in December. Watching the slaves dance and the property owners mingle and dance seemed surreal.

When Northup mentioned A. G. Pearce, Waddill acknowledged knowing him. It was four days after Christmas. In fact, it was during this last week on Wednesday. Northup was on his way back to Master Epps when Mr. William Pearce asked him to stay for the night to play for the slaves to dance. Master Epps had given him permission to utilize Northup's services playing the fiddle. Of course, Northup agreed. "They danced until daylight."[267]

Northup mentioned that Epps let him keep the small earnings from his music playing. That was one of the few privileges he granted Northup. Epps decided how it was to be spent, though.

Waddill thought of the great risk Bass had taken to write the letter. He felt compassion toward Northup about the kidnapping and serving as a slave for twelve years.

Waddill knew that some locals would not appreciate his participation in freeing a "negro," despite his rights as a free man, but he was overwhelmed by his fortune to help this freeman regardless of the community's attitude.

266. Ibid.

267. These facts of Northup playing that night are confirmed in Solomon's own writing. See pg. 222 of *Twelve Years A Slave*.

CHAPTER 48

Relationship with Samuel Bass and the Freeing of Solomon Northup

On August 11, 1853, Samuel Bass came to Waddill's office to have a will prepared. There were not many attorneys in Avoyelles Parish that Bass would trust to prepare this document to leave what little he had to those closest to him. In fact, Waddill would be the only one. Bass was a known abolitionist, rare indeed in the South, and certainly in Avoyelles Parish, Louisiana. Waddill hand wrote a will to allow Samuel Bass to copy it. It was in olographic form, which required the testator to have it signed, written in his own writing, and dated. For that, he had to come back later that month. This was only eight months after Solomon Northup had been freed. On August 29, 1853, Waddill finished it. Samuel was very sick. Waddill still felt affection for Bass and went to his house at 11:00 p.m. This is when Waddill actually wrote it as Samuel Bass dictated it. Bass then signed it and dated it. It was no longer in olographic form since Waddill actually wrote it. It was in the Louisiana will form known as nuncupative under private signature.[268]

August 30, 1853 Samuel Bass died at the home of Justine Tournier, a Free Woman of Color. His disease was pneumonia. At age 48 he had a wife and four children. They had been separated from his wife for 12 to 15 years. He complained only that she had such a temper as to preclude any man from living with her. Her maiden name was Lydia Catlin Lane. She was living near Prescott, Upper

---

268. Louisiana law has changed over the years. Today, there are only two forms, legal (typed, witnessed and notarized) and olographic (handwritten). The original will was found in the RAPCC, book C, f. 90, September 2, 1853. The entire original probate proceeding to file the will has been stored by the clerk in the office safe in Marksville after it was located.

Canada, or Ogdensburg. Her brother resided in Ogle County, Illinois near Daysville. Aunis Martin in that vicinity has his land titles and many other valuable papers in her possession. Samuel had told Waddill that Freeman Woodlock, his brother in law, knew where Aunis Martin resides. His two daughters, Catherine and Martha Bass are in Manchester, New Hampshire at work in a cotton factory. He also appointed William Sloat[269] of Avoyelles as his executor.[270]

Samuel Bass dictated the will due to his weakness from pneumonia. The witnesses were John P. Waddill and Dr. Donat MacEnery. John P. Waddill and W. W. Waddill handled the estate proceedings. He left all of his property in Upper Canada and the State of Illinois to his four children from the issue of his marriage with his wife, Lydia Catlin Lane. Bass asked that this property not go into the hands of his executor but be divided equally among his children, by the courts of Illinois and Canada. Bass left to his beloved friend, William Sloat, all of his "property, money, rights or credits situated within the State of Louisiana." Bass asked that he be given a decent "Christian burial." Bass affirmed that in the presence of the witnesses, John P. Waddill read the will to him. Alcibiade Derivas was an affiant to one of the statements, confirming that the will was in the handwriting of John P. Waddill as Bass dictated it to him. He was the third witness to the will.

Justine Tournier was a mulatto, whose proper name was Agustine Tournier, born after 1801. She was called Gustine, which is probably why Waddill referred to her as "Justine." She gave birth to Helena Tournier in 1847, as a child of Samuel Bass. Census records of 1880 shows that Helena's father was from Canada, the home of Samuel Bass. She was later called Ellenor and Ellen. Helena Bass married John Cass on March 24, 1868, in Avoyelles Parish. Ellen was the mother of Mary Cass, who married Thadius Hudson, Claude Hudson's father. Claude Hudson became the great-grandson of Samuel Bass. She died in 1922 as Ellen Bass Cass at the age of seventy-six in Rapides Parish.

269. William Sloat was referred to by Waddill in two separate notes in his diary prior to this. The first reference was March 25, 1850, when Waddill referred to paying W. Sloat $100, which was all that he owed him. The second reference was on September 28, 1852, when Waddill sent his slave Richard to Edwards and Sloat at Gorton's Landing. Fielding Edwards had taken over Gorton's Landing after Gorton was killed. Apparently, William Sloat was a handy man who worked with Edwards at Gorton's Landing and on his own with odd jobs.

270. DJW, August 30, 1853, vol. 4, pg. 55.

Bass did not know that he would die the day after he signed his last will and testament. Timely, yet sad. It was sad for Waddill too. He felt a kinship with Bass in that they both helped to set Northup free. Waddill was paid for his work on the case, but Bass was not, nor did he want money. His inspiration was of a much higher order. Bass knew that slavery was wrong, much more for a free man made a slave. Bass would help in any way that he could. Fifty dollars was a good fee for the thirty-nine-year-old attorney, John P. Waddill, whose peers would never consider a pettifogger.

August 30, 1853, was only eight months after Henry Northup came to see John P. Waddill to ask him to represent Mr. Northup in a claim to free a slave who, as a free man of color, had been wrongfully enslaved. A slave named Platt sent a letter to New York, the home of Solomon Northup. It eventually landed in the hands of Henry Northup. Apparently, Platt was actually Northup. Samuel Bass posted the letter for Northup at the post office in Marksville at great risk to his personal safety. It was actually addressed to Mr. William Perry or Mr. Cephas Parker, friends and associates of Solomon Northup. It was signed "Solomon Northup."[271]

Bass helped Northup by sending letters of his story to shopkeepers that Northup remembered who might help. They in turn contacted Henry Northup, a member of a white family who had actually owned Solomon but set him free. Henry Northup came to Louisiana, identified Solomon, and then retained Waddill to help free him in a court of law, in the 13th Judicial District, Avoyelles Parish, before Judge Cushman. Bass made sure that he was nowhere near the courthouse to avoid accusations, which would be true. He lay low after risking his personal safety by posting letters on behalf of Solomon to help rightfully gain his freedom.

It is strange how seemingly insignificant facts can lead to solutions to problems that seem unsolvable. When Henry Northup came to Waddill, he had a letter written to Parker and Perry, who were store owners in Saratoga, New York. This letter stated only that Northup was on a plantation that was on Bayou Boeuf, which was a very large area. Waddill and his brother, W. W. Waddill, who was working with him, would have to travel the area in hopes that they could discover a slave who was going by a different name, proving almost impossible to locate one slave when there may be more than one thousand.

In *12 Years a Slave,* Solomon Northup wrote about the conversation be-

---

271. See pg. 212 of *Twelve Years A Slave.*

tween Henry Northup and Waddill as they began to discuss politics. Abolitionists came up. Henry Northup suggested that Waddill may not be familiar with this type of political position by any individual, and John brought up one person he knew, his old friend and carpenter, Samuel Bass. At that moment, Waddill asked for the letter again, read it, and looked at his brother. "Where did Samuel Bass work last summer?" he asked. "I don't know," W. W. answered. Waddill suggested that W. W. go find Bass, who turned out not to be home but at the River Landing.

Perhaps it was serendipity, because W. W. found Bass at the landing, and after discussion, learned that Bass did work on a home on Bayou Bouef and that he was the one who wrote the letter. He admitted this reluctantly but did so knowing that he had to do it.

The lawyer in Waddill would not allow an injustice. Fifty dollars would be his fee.[272] Henry Northup told Waddill about the New York law.

"In an act passed by the State of New York on May 14, 1840, in an effort to provide a legal process to protect free citizens from being kidnapped or reduced to slavery, it is the duty of the Governor of New York to take measures satisfactorily to return him to his freedom."[273]

Waddill had to do his due diligence in reviewing the paper work. He did not want a free man to be enslaved, yet he would follow the law and all that it required. He also knew that this could affect the slave trade and certainly did not want that to happen, if free people were being sold as slaves.

As he checked the papers, Henry Northup was designated the person to obtain Northup's freedom as the New York act stipulated.[274] The original letter from Northup was in August of 1852, and Henry Northup left to go to Washington, D.C., in December. It was no wonder that Solomon was nervous about his risk of sending a letter.

Henry Northup arrived via steamboat at Red River at 9:00 a.m. on January 1, 1853, which was a Saturday. Not only was Saturday a workday, Waddill paid little attention to bringing in a New Year. Henry traveled to Marksville and found John P. Waddill. Solomon Northup described Waddill in his book as:

> a legal gentleman of distinction, and a man of fine genius and most noble impulses. After reading the letters and documents presented

---

272. DJW, January 4, 1853, vol. 4, pg. 25.

273. See pages 225–26 and Appendix A of *Twelve Years A Slave*.

274. Ibid., 226–27 and Appendix B.

him, and listening to a representation of the circumstances under which I had been carried away into captivity, Mr. Waddill at once proffered his services and entered into the affair with great zeal and earnestness. He, in common with others of like elevated character looked upon the kidnapper with abhorrence. The title of his fellow parishioners and clients to the property which constituted the larger proportion of their wealth, not only depended upon the good faith in which slave sales were transacted, but he was a man in whose honorable heart emotions of indignation were aroused by such an instance of injustice.[275]

Given the short time that Solomon Northup knew John P. Waddill, his characterization of him was very accurate. It is also interesting to note how Solomon described Marksville in 1853.

Marksville, although occupying a prominent position, and standing out in impressive italics on the map of Louisiana, is, in fact, but a small insignificant hamlet. Aside from the tavern, kept by a jolly and generous Boniface, the courthouse, inhabited by lawless cows and swine in the seasons of vacation, and a high gallows, with its dissevered rope dangling in the air, there is little to attract the attention of the stranger.[276]

Although not totally accurate, Solomon could not see the entire town and all of its businesses. It is interesting that this was the impression of both Northups. Waddill had never heard the name Solomon Northup, not knowing they called him Platt. He had a slave named Tom, who did not know his name. Since the letter was dated at Bayou Boeuf, he figured that this must be Solomon's location, but it was a huge area.

William Wallace Waddill, who was working with John P. Waddill, agreed to go up and down the bayou in John Waddill's carriage to begin on Monday, January 3. That would have taken some time. The following is a direct quote from Solomon Northup's *12 Years a Slave*:

The arrangement being adopted, however, there was nothing further to be done until Sunday had elapsed. The conversation between

275. Ibid., 228.

276. Ibid., 228–29.

Messrs. Northup and Waddill, in the course of the afternoon, turned upon New York politics.

"I can scarcely comprehend the nice distinctions and shades of political parties in your State" observed Mr. Waddill. "I read of soft-shells, hunkers, and barnburners, woolly-heads and silver-grays, and am unable to understand the precise difference between them. Pray, what is it?"

Mr. Northup, refilling his pipe, entered into quite an elaborate narrative of the origin of the various sections of parties, and concluded by saying there was another party in New York, known as the free-soilers or abolitionist. "You have seen none of those in this part of the country, I presume?" Mr. Northup remarked.

"Never, but one," answered Waddill laughingly. "We have one here in Marksville, an eccentric creature, who preaches abolitionism as vehemently as any fanatic at the North. He is a generous, inoffensive man, but always maintaining the wrong side of an argument. It affords us a deal of amusement. He is an excellent mechanic, and almost indispensable in this community. He is a carpenter. His name is Bass."

Some further good-natured conversation was had at the expense of Bass' peculiarities, when Waddill at once fell into a reflective mood, and asked for the mysterious letter again.

"Let me see, l-e-t m-e s-e-e!" He repeated, thoughtfully to himself, running his eyes over the letter once more. "Bayou Boeuf, August 15- post-marked here. He that is writing for me—"

"Where did Bass work last summer?" he inquired, turning suddenly to his brother. His brother was unable to inform him, but rising, left the office, and soon returned with the intelligence that "Bass worked last summer somewhere on Bayou Boeuf."

"He is the man," bringing down his hand emphatically on the table, "who can tell us all about Solomon Northup," exclaimed Waddill.[277]

---

277. Ibid., 230–31.

That very day, W. W. Waddill and Henry Northup sought out Samuel Bass, John's old friend and associate, and found him at Red River. Bass's initial response was one of cynicism and caution when asked if he wrote a letter for a "colored man."

Bass responded, "Excuse me sir, if I say that is none of your business."[278]

Although Bass knew W. W. Waddill as the brother of John, he did not know Henry Northup and was extremely cautious in answering their questions. The conversation, after a while of reflection, was as follows:

"I have done nothing to be ashamed of. I am the man who wrote the letter. If you have come to rescue Solomon Northup, I am glad to see you."

"When did you last see him, and where is he?" Northup inquired.

"I last saw him Christmas, a week ago to-day. He is the slave of Edwin Epps, a planter on Bayou Boeuf, near Holmesville. He is not known as Solomon Northup; he is called Platt."[279]

Now the mystery was solved. Waddill made Solomon Northup plaintiff, and Henry was the guardian, with Edwin Epps the defendant. It was a petition of replevin, directed to the sheriff, commanding him to take Solomon into custody to be detained until the decision of the court.[280] Waddill filed the original petition, which is still in the courthouse records of Avoyelles Parish. He wrote the petition with passion.[281]

> That said plaintiff Solomon Northup is a free mulatto, griffe,[282] or colored person, about forty-five years of age, born of free parents in the County of Washington and state of New York on of the United States of American, in which slavery at the time of the birth of said Solomon, nor since, did not exist, it being what is called a free state . . . that since the year A.D.1844 or there-abouts, one Edwin Epps a resident and citizen of the Parish of Avoyelles has fraudulently and forcibly detained your petitioner the said Solomon Northup in servitude as a slave, knowing him to be free, and said Epps has endeavored to fraudulently conceal the name of the said Solomon, one of your petitioners

---

278. Ibid., 231.

279. Ibid., 232.

280. Ibid.

281. RAPCC, no. 2712, book G, f. 274, January 3, 1853. Henry Northup and Solomon Northup were made plaintiffs.

282. A "griffe" is a half black, half mulatto, or three-fourths black person.

by calling said Solomon, by the name of "Platt". . . that since the said Epps has had your petitioner so in his service, your petitioner's services are worth two thousand dollars, which said petitioner claim as wages and damages, and two hundred dollars per month, or at that rate, for services and damages until the said Solomon is decreed, & set free from the time this suit is served.

Waddill also alleged that Epps would conceal or send out of the jurisdiction, so he asked for sequestration and to be retained by the sheriff until the suit was decided. John P. and W. W. Waddill filed the petition. John Waddill signed as security for cost.

Judge Ralph Cushman signed an order on the same day ordering that the bond be set at $500.00 and that a sequestration be issued as Waddill had prayed for. It would be for only one night and day, and then Northup would be freed.

Although Henry Northup heard rumors of Bass leaving, and Solomon never saw Samuel Bass again, Bass had not left Marksville, but he remained in hiding as much as possible. Solomon Northup wrote of the cooperation of the interested parties in Avoyelles Parish as follows:

> This apprehension had the effect of expediting matters considerably. The sheriff, who lived in one direction from the village, was requested to hold himself in readiness immediately after midnight, (of Sunday Jan. 2) while the Judge was informed he would be called upon at the same time. It is but justice to say, that the authorities at Marksville cheerfully rendered all the assistance in their power.[283]

When the sheriff questioned Solomon and was satisfied, Solomon was asked if he recognized the man with him, Henry Northup. He looked and shouted, "Henry B. Northup! Thank God!—Thank God.!"[284]

On January 4, the parties met. Epps had H. Taylor as his counsel. Along with Waddill and Henry Northup, they met with the judge and sheriff. After hearing all of the evidence, Taylor informed his client that he was satisfied.

---

283. Northup, *Twelve Years A Slave*, 233–34.

284. Ibid., 235. In the movie made from the book, Solomon hollered, "Mr. Parker." The movie-makers obviously had reservations about the audience knowing who Mr. Henry Northup was since he had not been introduced in the movie prior to this scene.

No trial would be necessary. A paper was drawn up, and Epps acknowledged he was satisfied of Northup's right to freedom. It was signed and filed on January 4, 1853.[285]

Although John Waddill wrote a mere few lines in his diary, this was meaningful to him. He also gained a new respect for Samuel Bass. Solomon Northup was a free man and would never return to Avoyelles Parish.

---

285. Ibid., 241–42 and Appendix C.

CHAPTER 49

A. G. Pearce

January 19, 1853

Waddill saw Lemuel Pittman, whose wife just died. He was going to see Henderson Taylor to hire him to oppose the application of Burnes to administer his wife's estate. Taylor convinced him otherwise.

"I told him that he better let it alone, and try to prove up what he had paid out of his own funds for Mrs. Pittman, his wife," Taylor told Waddill.

Waddill was aware of the two not having equal estates. Her expenditures went beyond her means. Taylor was correct in his advice. As administrator, Pittman would have conflicts trying to get reimbursed. It was soon after that that Waddill filed a petition in the clerk's office for the sale of the property of Mrs. Susan M. Pittman. It was to be advertised on Thursday in *The Villager*. The estate was on Bayou Boeuf.

January 21, 1853

John P. Waddill saw his friend A. G. Pearce that day in Marksville. Alanson was quite happy. His farm had produced 230 bales of cotton last year.[286] He mentioned that Epps was not happy about the slave, Northup, being set free.

Waddill mentioned that he had to see Mrs. Toler on business on January 27. She had thirty bales this last year with just two hands. A. G. invited Waddill to stay the night at Oakwold.

On January 24, 1853, Colonel Paul O. Hebert was sworn into the governor's office at his plantation in the Iberville Parish.[287]

---

286. In 1853, cotton was selling for eight to nine cents per pound. A bale weighed about 500 pounds. One bale would fetch about forty-five dollars.

287. "Paul Octave Hébert," Wikipedia, https://en.wikipedia.org/wiki/Paul_Octave_H%C3%A9bert.

Waddill had to pay Henry C. Steinman twenty dollars to make a new cover lining and otherwise repair his and Julia's carriage. He finished the carriage on January 25, 1853.

January 22, 1853

Adolph Frank sold Waddill twenty pounds of beef for a dollar. On the same day, Julia and W. W. spent the day at the home of Fabius Ricord. On the twenty-sixth, Waddill bought from E. Reynaud a saddle blanket at $1.40; from S.N. Goux, a watch key at $1.00; and from H. C. Steinman, a martingale and bridle reins for $1.25.

January 27, 1853 on Bayou Huffpauir

Waddill was heading to the home of Joel and Eliza Toler. He intended to deliver the note of G. Sadler to her for $805.00 due in 1854. He would stay overnight with his friend Alanson G. Pearce at Oakwold, the home built in 1835 by A. G.'s father, William Pearce Jr.[288]

The connections were close. The Toler's had a plantation on Bayou Huffpauir (HuffPauir) near the Pearce's Oakwold. Patrick Henry Toler, the Toler's third son, had begun to run the plantation. Joel Toler had donated the property for the Bayou Rouge Baptist Church, of which Peter Tanner was a founder and deacon.[289] Grimball Addison Robert, also a Bayou Boeuf planter born near Cheneyville, was the young half-brother of Mrs. Epps's father.

Waddill did not, but Alanson had a bit to drink as it was cold January 27, 1853. They stayed up late talking. Waddill mentioned that W. F. Griffin was coming home on February 6, 1853. Waddill expected him to say that not much was going on in the legislature.

Joel Toler died in 1853, and the Toler family hired Waddill. On March 14, 1853, W. W. Waddill returned from Opelousas to file suit on behalf of Eliza Toler as administrator for the case of *Samuel W. Henaire v. M.W. Preston, C.C. Preston and George Hill* for payment of two notes. The notes were for $495.00 each, with 8 percent from January 9, 1853. W. W. made a twenty-dollar deposit with the court for cost to accrue on the suit.[290]

---

288. DJW, January 27, 1853, vol. 4, pg. 28.

289. Northup, *Twelve Years A Slave*, 146.

290. DJW, March 14, 1853, vol. 4, pg. 37.

January 29, 1853

Waddill's order through the steamboat *Dellman* for forty-five yards of matting to be used for carpet came in. He also received a barrel of bacon, box of candles, and a keg of lard. The matting was twenty-five cents per yard for $11.25. He also received two barrels of Irish potatoes at $1.75 per barrel for $3.50.

Robert Bowman was a mechanic and builder of wooden cisterns. He built them in Avoyelles and Rapides and built up considerable wealth. He never married and had no children. He became ill in late January 1853 from typhoid pneumonia. John knew him as an older man with great talent for the work he did.

Dr. Timothy Carroll was the ward of Avoyelles Parish and the State of Louisiana. On January 29, Bowman died. Dr. Carroll employed Waddill to handle the administration of the succession. He did have nieces who were very poor. Waddill hoped that they would get the inheritance worth about $10,000. One of Waddill's first duties was to attend and finalize the sale of land to William Brown from Bowman.

February 1, 1853

On January 31, 1853, David Rose and others committed to the Marksville jail a man by the name of Baker, upon the charge of having shot Hiram Harvey of Bayou des Glaises twice with a revolver. Baker was the aggressor. Harvey, it appeared, neither attacked Baker nor defended himself when attacked, as he was unarmed. One of the balls took effect in the hand, and the other entered the abdomen, near the top of the hip, and lodged somewhere in the body. Word spread that Harvey was dangerously wounded.

Waddill received an interesting letter from Senator William F. Griffin delivered by John H. Boyer. He wrote that the legislature was doing very little. The auditor did state that warrants were being issued for payment from the state for witness fees in the *State v. John E. Frith and Augustus Bartell* murder case in the killing of A. B. Coco. The feelings toward John E. Frith were still fresh in the minds of Avoyellean citizens. Coco was respected and had just won the sheriff's race when he was stabbed and died. It was good that the state finally was paying the citizens that testified.

February 2, 1853

Waddill always made sure that his slaves were well-fed and housed. He also clothed them. He bought two pair of pantaloons for Richard at $1.25 a pair from John B. Goux and bought cups and saucers.

Waddill's long-time client Daniel R. Eldred hired him for the purpose of employing F. P. Hitchborn to go to Tensas Parish to collect from Thomas M. Griffin a judgment over $1,000, which Waddill had obtained on his behalf in Avoyelles Parish. Eldred agreed that he would give Hitchborn one hundred dollars if he succeeded and fifty dollars if he used fair and legal exertions and did not succeed. Waddill felt confident that the imposing Hitchborn would succeed.

Rev. Charles J. Hallberg came to Waddill's home for dinner on February 3, 1853. He left for Bayou des Glaises immediately after to get his horse and collect some money due him. He arrived at the residence of R. W. Kay at 5:00 that morning with his lady. He had been appointed to another circuit, near Shreveport, this year. This was a bit sad for Waddill. He had gained great respect for Rev. Hallberg.

Waddill paid him five dollars for Mr. Kay, and he also paid him eight dollars for the following books: Gibbon's *Decline and Fall of the Roman Empire*,[291] Mosheim's *Church History*,[292] and Ousley's *Old Christianity*.[293] There were nine volumes in all: six of Gibbon's volumes, two of Mosheim, and one of Ousley. He came back from Bayou des Glaises on February 7. Before he came back, Mrs. Hallberg visited Waddill's home on February 5. Mrs. A. G. Pearce and her sister-in-law called at the house but did not get out of their carriage. They were in a hurry to get home. They dropped off at the Red River, Gorton's Landing, with A. G. Pearce, John Ewell, and Mr. Daniel R. Eldred to go to New Orleans.

More Land for Waddill

John P. Waddill was now expanding his estate. On February 15, he received by letter two patents from the United States Land Office deeding to

---

291. English historian Edward Gibbon published his first volume in 1776 and followed with five additional volumes published by Strahan & Cadell, London. The last volume was in 1788–89. It is still used today by historians. https://en.wikipedia.org/wiki/The_History_of_the_Decline_and_Fall_of_the_Roman_Empire.

292. Johann Lorenz von Mosheim was born in approximately 1694 and died in 1755. https://en.wikipedia.org/wiki/Johann_Lorenz_von_Mosheim

293. Gideon Ousley wrote '*Old Christianity*' as a fervent anti Papacy writer. See *British and Foreign Evangelical Review*, vol. XXIX (London: James Nisbet & Co.; Edinburgh: Oliver & Boyd) 282.

him the following property: "Lot No. 5, being the North East Quarter of the South West Quarter of fractional section 40 in T3N R3E in the district of lands subject to sale at Ouachita, Louisiana; and the South Half of Lot Numbered 2 of said section 40, in T3N, R3E, in the same land district, containing a total of 80 acres." For the patents, he would have to pay the land office at Ouachita. On February 23, Waddill gave W. F. Griffin, who was heading to Baton Rouge, fifty-six dollars for entering Waddill's name for the "Southeast quarter of the Northwest quarter of Section 40 in T3N-R3E, in the land district formerly subject to sale at Ouachita and Red River, Louisiana."

February 26, 1853

Waddill began working on the succession of Pierre Couvillion, his good friend. He obtained all of the names of the children of the marriage between Pierre and Marrinett Mayeux. They were viz: Pierre Couvillion, Gregoire Couvillion, Arsenne Couvillion, wife of Sylvert Couvillion, Olivier Couvillion, Rose Couvillion, Olive Couvillion, and Augustin Couvillion.

He noted that Couvillion had a lot of children. Then Waddill heard about Madam Adrienne Couvillion dying and being buried on March 1, 1853. She raised sixteen children. Her full name was Celeste Mayeux.

Clothes were a constant expense for Waddill. He paid his tailor, Mayer, $6.75 for a pair of cloth pants and fifty cents to put a pocket in his coat. He had just paid Foust three dollars for making a pair of shoes for himself and thirty cents to mend his son, Thomas's, shoes.

William M. Lambeth was a sugar cane plantation owner on the Red River. He was from New Orleans but had more than one hundred slaves on several sites. Waddill noted that he was on his death bed on April 2, 1853. He died on April 3, 1853. A review of his will, written in New Orleans, showed that he had no children or wife, and only one sibling, a sister, Frances Bernard Pitts. He left her $500 per year.

Waddill's friend F. P. Hitchborn, who had become an attorney, was handling the estate of John H. Harmanson, Waddill's good friend and political ally. At the same time, the wife of George Barron had died and left a will. St. James Bordelon had come to Waddill to annul the will, or prevent enforcement. Adelaide Bordelon and George Barron had no children. She left all the property to her husband but voided that in the will if there were no children of the marriage. On April 1, Madame Joseph Mayeux hired Waddill to sue George Barron to annul the will of his wife Adelaide Bordelon, made in his favor.

Waddill purchased from W. F. Griffin a half-ream of foolscap paper[294] for the drafting of petitions in court. He also purchased *English Notes* by Matt F. Ward.

The subscriptions for paying for the building of the Methodist Church were coming along well. F. P. Hitchborn paid twenty-five dollars, and R. J. Tanner had completed his payment. William Gober also paid his subscription of fifteen dollars. John went with Julia and their two youngest children, Henarie and Florence, to the Myrtle Grove Plantation on the Red River, William Alexander's estate. Mary Jane, Julia's sister, and Mr. Green Huie were also there and doing well. They left and traveled home on wet roads. The route from Foulk's Landing on Red River took from sundown to near 8:00 p.m.

In May of 1853, H. C. Barlow, Patrick H. Toler, and Andrew J. Isaacs, incumbent, ran for district attorney for Rapides and Avoyelles. Toler was the only one with a residence in Avoyelles. H. C. Barlow won in a rematch with Isaacs. Toler was not very happy. He hired Waddill after the loss to be his agent. He decided to leave Marksville for the Texas gold mines.

---

294. "foolscap": any of various sizes of writing paper; esp., in the U.S., a size measuring 13 by 16 inches. http://www.yourdictionary.com/foolscap

CHAPTER 50

Life in the 1850s

Mrs. T. B. Tiller moved back to Marksville from Pine Bluff, Arkansas. Her husband had died of cholera. On the same day, Waddill received a solar lamp that he would try to use in his office. It burned whale oil and was supposed to be brighter than the normal lamps and certainly the candles Waddill used. William Edwards delivered to him a five-gallon can of sperm oil at $1.75 per gallon, totaling $9.75 on June 9, 1853. Included in the order were 165 pounds of Rio coffee[295] at nine-and-three-fourths cents totaling $16.08; and a barrel of choice sugar 251 pounds at seven cents for $17.57. Waddill also paid fourteen dollars for two mahogany card tables. His wife loved them. The storage and freight for the card tables alone was $2.25.

On June 28, 1853, Henderson Taylor and A. J. Taylor came back from Texas after a two-month absence. They had decided not to move to Texas. Waddill was joyous that his friend and opponent in court would be staying.

Politics

Marksville was the host for the meeting of Democrats for the purpose of sending delegates to the Democratic convention at Baton Rouge on July 18, 1853. Waddill was disappointed when only eighteen people showed up. They passed resolutions instructing the delegates to vote for W. F. Griffin as their first choice for their candidate for Congress.

At this time, Freeman P. Hitchborn traveled to New Orleans for legal business. Waddill needed to send cash to his commission merchant, Payne and Harrison. With Hitchborn, Waddill sent $550.00 to be deposited to

---

295. Rio coffee came from large plantations near Rio de Janeiro. It was a high quality. See Stanley J. Stein *Vassouras, A Brazilian Coffee County, 1850–1900, The Roles of Planter and Slave in a Plantation Society* (Princeton University Press, 1985), 48–49.

his account with them to allow for payments on goods as needed. Waddill received the letter of confirmation of receipt from Payne and Harrison on July 21, 1853. On that day, his first order was received from his merchant. Waddill received from Payne and Harrison the following bill of articles, which Hitchborn purchased for him on July 18, 1853.

1 bbl. best flour	$6.25
2 boxes No. 1 soup-96 lbs.	$7.20
3 lbs. refried borax	$1.12
5 lbs. flour of sulphur	$0.40
10 lbs. bicarbonate of soda	$0.80
20 lbs. of alum	$1.20
To Box & for drayage	$0.75
Commissions for purchasing	$0.44
	$18.16

Alum could be used for pickling, water treatment, cooking, tanning hides, and medicinal purposes. This first order from Payne and Harrison went well, and their commission was not great. Waddill was pleased with them.

Health Concerns

Many times the death of a person and sickness within the family would cause Waddill to take extra precautions. Such was the case when Rosaline Vitrac of Hydropolis died of congestive fever at the age of forty-five. She never married. Her nephew hired Waddill to handle her affairs. During this time, Waddill's mother-in-law and four of his children and several slaves were all sick with chills and fever. Waddill did not take this lightly. They all began to heal, much to his relief, after several days.

After they all recovered, W. W. Waddill and Julia left four of the children with her mother and they proceeded to Sulphur Springs in Catahoula near Little River. The springs were known for their curative powers.[296] Waddill gave his wife and W. W. sixty dollars for expenses. They left on August 7.

---

296. White Sulphur Springs was a famous resort in antebellum times. The state board of health discovered the springs to have dangerous levels of bacteria, which shut down the prosperous resort area in 1911. It was in Catahoula Parish, but now is in LaSalle Parish, which was formed from Catahoula. It is off Highway 8, twelve miles southwest of Jena. http://www.thepineywoods.com/sulphur.htm

Samuel Bass

On August 11, Waddill wrote out a form of an olographic will for Samuel Bass to be copied as his own. For that will to be valid, it had to be written in Bass's handwriting, dated and signed. Waddill charged him ten dollars. It was good to see Bass again. He told Waddill that he did not feel well and would like to take care of this soon.

Waddill told him that this would be done soon. Waddill would write it out and visit him to finalize as he copied it. The next day Waddill visited Bass at his home. Bass was in bed feeling worse. Bass could not even sit up. He asked Waddill if he could come again.

Waddill assured him that he would be back. Waddill felt a little ill with fever also. He had chills that night and fever all night long. Waddill took Calomel for the fever. This sickness lasted three days. On August 15, 1853, he took another dose of Calomel and a good dose of castor oil. Dr. MacEnery came by to check on him. On the sixteenth, he felt better and was taking quinine. Waddill was not better. In the evening, it got worse, and he took another hard chill. Dr. MacEnery came again, and he prescribed blue mass.[297] They placed cold water on his face to lower the fever. On the seventeenth and eighteenth, John took quinine and began to feel better. On the nineteenth, he took another dose of Calomel. It was the twentieth when Waddill took a dose of castor oil that finally worked.

Ten days, later Samuel Bass died. Waddill was one of the last people to talk to him, and despite Bass feeling weak, John got him to sign his will prior to his passing.

More News of Death

The bad news did not stop with the death of Samuel Bass. Miss Eugenie Coco was attending school at a convent on the Mississippi River. She had what the family believed to be yellow fever. She died at the residence of her father, A. B. Coco, who had been stabbed and killed in November 1851 after winning the sheriff's election. Their home was in Hydropolis.

---

297. Blue mass was a common remedy for many ailments, including constipation. It varied in ingredients, but generally contained 33 percent mercury, 5 percent licorice, 25 percent Althaea, 3 percent glycerol, and 34 percent rose honey. https://en.wikipedia.org/wiki/Blue_mass

On September 1, 1853, Waddill's wife and brother came back from Sulphur Springs. Julia had been sick since Sunday.

Even the court adjourned on October 5, 1853, until December due to the yellow fever breakout among people gathered together.

On October 8, 1853, Waddill sent ten dollars to Leonard Scott of New York to pay for his one-year subscription to the *Republicans of Blackwood's* Magazine, and the *London, Westminister, & St. Edinburgh Review*. He sent a ten-dollar bill from the Bank of Charleston, South Carolina.

Political Betrayal, October 15, 1853

John O'Quin made a speech at Mansura. He was an independent Democratic candidate in opposition to Joseph Joffrion and George Berlin, the regular Democratic nominees for the state legislature. Waddill was for the nominees.

That morning, Lewis Texada left Waddill's house for Rapide Parishs, where he resided. He was a candidate for the Senate in opposition to Michael Ryan. They were both Democrats. Mr. Texada had always been true to the democracy. He had forever abided by the nominations; Michael Ryan had not done so. In 1847, he ran against the regular Democratic ticket, Mr. T. O. Moore and Meriday Neal. He was beaten. David Martin, editor of the *Louisiana Democrat*, wrote a humorous burlesque on the canvass, satirizing Ryan in a most unmerciful manner.

October 17, 1853

Waddill learned by the mail carrier from Rapides that James T. Flint, an eminent young lawyer who resided in Alexandria, died of yellow fever at his residence on the night of the fourteenth. He also learned that Willis Bouner and Jessee A. Bynum, both planters of Rapides, had died within the last few days, the first of yellow fever and the second of some other disease. Jessee A. Bynum was, for a long time, a prominent member of Congress from North Carolina. Waddill knew him to be a man of extensive information, especially political.

Yellow fever had been horrible in all of central Louisiana. Waddill knew too well how bad it could be on a population. In 1850, the cause of yellow fever was not known. It would not be until the early 1900s before scientists discovered that mosquitoes spread the dreaded disease.

Devastating News

On October 17, 1853, John Waddill heard that his benefactor and friend, Thomas J. Hickman, had died. Waddill noted in his diary:

> Today I have learned that Thomas J. Hickman, a wealthy planter of Rapides died a few days since, with the Yellow Fever. Mr. Hickman was an excellent man, and was one of my first and warmest friends. When I was poor and had not a cent, and was pursuing the study of law, he came to my aid with money, and made his home, my house, until I obtained license for practice. He never asked me for repayment but once and that was not until I had made money enough to pay him without feeling it a hardship. He leaves a widow and six or more children. He married the daughter of General Gaiennie[298] of the Parish of Natchitoches.

Waddill was deeply saddened. He had worked for Hickman and his brothers when he first moved to Louisiana from Tennessee. It was Thomas who encouraged him to go to Augusta and who supported him. He came back to Louisiana, and Hickman encouraged him to study law, once again supporting him. Yellow fever was a horrible way to die, and he felt saddened that he could do nothing about it.

At the same time he experienced these feelings of sadness due to the loss of such a good friend, Waddill was confronted with the pain of politics and betrayal. He learned that the Honorable William F. Griffin and Judge Ralph Cushman were supporting Michael Ryan for the Senate instead of Lewis Texada. He could not see why they did so. He hoped that Texada would get two thirds of the votes in Avoyelles Parish and show to the world that all sense of decency had not departed from the voters yet. Waddill wanted for Texada a fair field and no foul play. It hurt Waddill that these two very close friends and associates of his would betray the party line.

There was more sadness in Marksville. Just as the sheriff informed the public that three prisoners in his custody for murder escaped by obtaining the

---

298. General François Gaiennie was the general of the State Militia. He was a Whig politician who served in the State Legislature. In 1839, he was killed in a duel by General Placide Bossier, a Democratic opponent who had defeated Gaiennie in a State Senate race. See the story of the duel in Steven M. Mayeux, *Earthen Walls, Iron Men – Ft. DeRussy, Louisiana, and the Defense of Red River* (University of Tennesee Press, 2007), 275–76.

jail keys, they walked through the unlocked doors. In addition, two "negroes" also made their escape. Waddill thought it was carelessness. That evening, news of William McDowell Jr.'s death saddened the community. He was the son of William McDowell, the schoolmaster, and was only seven years old. He had a lingering illness from fever.

The next night, Thomas T. Toler and others brought into Marksville one of the prisoners who had escaped. He was a Pole and was imprisoned for murder and robbery. He appeared to be a terrible villain.

On October 25, 1853, Michael Ryan of Alexandria arrived in Avoyelles. He was a candidate for the state Senate for the Avoyelles District. They now had four candidates for that office, two Democrats and two Whigs: Democrats Lewis E. Texada and Michael Ryan and Whigs James M. Wells and William Edwards.

On October 26, the day after a conference with Judge Ralph Cushman, Michael Ryan went down on Bayou des Glaises to see the Honorable William F. Griffin, who was a zealous supporter of him for the State Senate. Waddill would keep this in remembrance.

On November 5, there was a mass meeting of a portion of the Democratic Party at Mansura, who assembled to select a candidate for the Senate for the parishes of Rapides and Avoyelles, to fill the place of Mitchell Neal, whose time had expired. William F. Griffin, residing in Avoyelles, held his seat as senator for two more years; therefore, the candidate had to be nominated for Rapides Parish. There were two Democratic candidates, both residing in Rapides Parish: Michael Ryan, a native of Ireland, and Lewis E. Texada, a native of Rapides. Michael Ryan received the nomination. His nomination was brought about in the most unjustifiable and corrupt manner. Mr. Texada undoubtedly had a greater number of delegates of the Rapides nominating convention in his favor than had Michael Ryan. But David Martin, editor of the *Louisiana Democrat*, published in Alexandria under the heading of "voice of the precincts," prejudiced the minds of the citizens in Avoyelles in favor of Ryan being the choice of Rapides instead of Texada. Avoyelles Parish district Judge Ralph Cushman and Avoyelles Senator William F. Griffin went strongly for Ryan and used every exertion to have him nominated. William F. Griffin, although a sugar planter and greatly behind with his crop, not having commenced grinding, quit his little plantation on Bayou des Glaises and came up to the prairie to assist Ryan and electioneer against Texada.

Ryan, for the purpose of securing the nominations, distributed through the parish from $700 to $1,000. At grogshops, he got men to electioneer for him. He also gave breakfasts and suppers for voters. When the nomination came in, he obtained ninety-eight votes, and Mr. Texada obtained fifty-five. Mr. Texada spent nothing in electioneering. He gave A. Derivas fifty dollars in Waddill's presence to print some papers for him. He and Martin Rabalais, and Waddill, made a Democratic barbecue in Mansura, for which they paid sixty dollars—Texada paying twenty dollars, John paying twenty, and M. Rabalais and others paying twenty. Judge Cushman, some time before the nomination came off, told Louis Bonnett that Ryan had the nomination of the parish of Rapides. Mr. Bonnett, from Cushman's statement voted for Ryan's nomination, Waddill believed.

November 7 was Election Day. Waddill paid to Dubertraud, the barkeeper, five dollars to be treated out in the name of the Democratic candidates. The Democrats carried their state tickets and Michael Ryan, for the Senate, got twenty-four votes majority over J. M. Wells. The Democrats also elected George Berlin, one of their candidates for the legislature. Their other candidate, Joseph Joffrion, was beaten by Leon Gauthier, the Whig candidate. John O'Quin, the independent Democratic candidate, was badly beaten, the Whigs not voting for him as he says they had promised. The Whigs elected their candidate for sheriff, Adolph Coco, over Martin Couvillion by two votes, some said, but the returns showed an eight votes majority for Coco. The Whigs elected James H. Barbin as clerk over Fabius Ricord, Democrat, by 192 votes. The Democrats elected A. G. Morrow assessor and Belizuire Dupuy coroner. The Democratic state ticket ran far ahead of the Whigs: Perkins, Democrat for Congress won by a 101 majority; Greneaux, for treasurer, by a 102 majority; Marks, for auditor, by a 96 majority; Carrigan, for school superintendent, by a 100 majority.

The Whig candidates opposed to these were Preston Pond, Hawthorn, John E. King, and Larmon. Larmon died before the election.

The election in Avoyelles Parish showed that all was not right. Prominent Democrats did not electioneer for the representatives or parish officers. William F. Griffin went and voted at the Big Bend Box, Bayou des Glaises, but did not stay five minutes there, thus abandoning the election to the Whigs. Waddill was disappointed in Griffin and Cushman. He would talk to them later.

CHAPTER 51

EDUCATION OF WADDILL'S CHILDREN

John P. Waddill continued to do whatever he could to help his children get the best education possible. Avoyelles Parish was progressive in that area. By August 28, 1853, after a year of working on it, Marksville had a female school that Waddill felt could vie with any in Louisiana. The instructors kept the peace and harmony in the school. The girls were strictly attended to by their teachers early and late in the day. When they walked out, a teacher always went with them. The moral standards were high and strictly enforced and encouraged.

Mrs. McDowell was the principal of the female academy, and there were few, Waddill thought, who could be more qualified. The academy taught reading, writing, arithmetic, along with philosophy, astronomy, and English grammar. The pupils made great progress. Not only Marksville, but also the whole parish area was satisfied and proud of the institution.

The school previously had a problem, but Mrs. McDowell had again taken charge of the school with renewed health and energy. The expectations were great, and Waddill felt that she would be successful. She was amiable, polite, and intelligent. No lady had more qualities calculated to draw toward the attachments and win the love and esteem of her pupils. Waddill felt that none could advance the young ladies faster and give them a more lasting impression of the branches taught to them than she could. She possessed a thorough and compassionate education. By a rapid and steady stream of instruction, she had the power of installing into the minds of others whatever she knew.

On July 29, 1853, Mrs. McDowell had an examination of her female scholars. It was very well done, and the school did itself great credit. In the evening, Mrs. Seipel and her musical scholars of the female academy of Marksville held a concert in the Protestant Church.

Waddill wrote:

If no factious opposition from interested or malicious views is made, this academy will become one of the first in the state, and as all of the means possessed by Mr. McDowell are embarked in the school, it has become permanent. In Avoyelles, education has, at length, taken firm root, and the minds of the rising generation, are becoming enlightened and expanded by its influence. The seed has been sown, and the soil has been found capable of the highest culture. The Free school system went into operation in the later part of 1848, and studded our Prairie and Bayous with primary institutions of learning. These soon set the minds of the youths of the parish in ferment of excitement of to obtain knowledge.[299]

Earlier in the year, the Legislature approved the Louisiana State Seminary of Learning and Military Academy. Governor Hebert appointed Waddill as a trustee of the Learning Academy. The Senate approved this appointment. This was recorded in the April 30, 1853, edition of the New Orleans *Picayune*. This ultimately opened in Pineville in 1860, and its first Superintendent was William Tecumseh Sherman. This school eventually moved to Baton Rouge and became Louisiana State University.[300] Waddill's interest in education never waned.

December 9, 1853

F. Edward had shipped from New York a carriage that Samuel W. Henarie purchased for John P. Waddill. John paid the shipping, which amounted to twenty-seven dollars. This was going to be a carriage comfortable for John, Julia, and all of the children. On the same day, W. R. Leckie and his wife and family arrived in Marksville to make it their home. They rented F. P. Hitchborn's home for fifteen dollars per month. Hitchborn purchased Patrick Henry Toler's brick office in Marksville to practice law.

Daniel R. Eldred and his wife and William Alexander dined with the Waddills on December 10, 1853. Eldred and F. Agrippa Robert wanted to hire Waddill to defend them in a suit brought by the Carrollton Bank against them.

299. DJW, August 28, 1853, vol. 3, 26–27.

300. "Louisiana State Seminary of Learning & Military Academy," Wikipedia, https://en.wikipedia.org/wiki/Louisiana_State_Seminary_of_Learning_%26_Military_Academy.

Christmas at the Waddill's Home 1853

On Christmas Day, the Waddill family stayed home and had no company. The day was cold and so cloudy that the sun had not been seen all day. It had rained all week.

The Wednesday before, the sugarhouse and mill and about fifty hogsheads of sugar, belonging to the honorable William F. Griffin, situated on Bayou des Glaises, were destroyed by fire. How the fire caught, no one knew. William Robinson had been sleeping in the sugarhouse up to that night, but owing to the severe cold weather, he slept that night at the dwelling house. Some believed that the sugarhouse and sugar mill were insured for $4,000. This was a high price as the sugarhouse was an old house, and only with perjury added to it could it be valued so highly. The sugar mill was a secondhand one costing Mr. Griffin only $200. He had thirty or forty hogsheads of sugar to make, many believed, the cane being in the field.

On the eve of January 1, 1854, Julia and John spent the night at the home of the Alexanders on their Red River plantation. On January 1, they had a roasted turkey and other good things for dinner. It was exceptionally cold weather on the travel there. Both John and Julia suffered much while traveling to the river. It was on this day that John and Julia's daughter Mary Florence had her second birthday. Dr. G. E. Elmer's wife gave birth to a child on the same day, January 1, 1854.

Waddill went to the clerk's office and ordered a copy of the account and judgment in the case of *Alanson G. Pearce, under tutor, and Eliza Robert, wife of Daniel R. Eldred vs. Joseph B. Robert*, costs to be paid by Daniel R. Eldred and F. Agrippa Robert. It was for the purpose of examining the case of the Carrollton Bank against Daniel R. Eldred and wife, Franklin Agrippa Robert, and Sarah Robert, widow of William Vernon. Waddill wrote: "I believe the defendants will succeed. I will charge five hundred dollars to defend the suit against the three heirs."

The weather continued to be abnormally cold for two weeks. On January 7, it was extremely raw and had sleeted, creating an overnight freeze.

Fiftieth Anniversary of the Battle of New Orleans

John Waddill was thoughtful on this day, January 8, 1854. He noted in his diary:

To day is Sunday. It is the anniversary of the great battle fought between the British army commanded by Sir Edward Packingham and the American army commanded by General Andrew Jackson, in 1815, just below the city of New Orleans in the state of Louisiana. The Americans were victorious. Their loss was not over six killed and some seven wounded whilst the English lost in killed above over two thousand of their troops. It was a decisive victory; as it taught the Americans that in arms they were equal to any soldiers in the world, and it showed the English and the other European powers, that they could not in future hope to trample with impunity on the people of the United States of America. Thirty-nine years have since elapsed and we have had no other war with England or other European power, and long may we remain in peace with them. We have now become a powerful nation; our population is about twenty six million, including slaves.

Our commerce extends through every ocean and sea in the world. We have even penetrated the heretofore-inseparable barrier of the empire of Japan, by their laws and customs made and continued for many centuries, and have had audience of their great dignitaries and expect soon to be in close commercial alliance with that country. Commodore Perry is now near the ancient empire and will there remain with the United States squadron under his command until the spring or summer.[301]

In the first part of this month, the police jury granted $500 to levee the Wild Cat Bayou and build two wooden bridges on the bayous along the road from Foulk's Landing to the hills on the north side of Red River. William Alexander, Pierre Ricoulie, G. John, and P. J. Aymond were appointed commissioners to let out the work.

Waddill was worried about his friend Dr. Donat MacEnery. He was still in a state of intoxication. He had been drunk every day since Christmas. He was a man of fine intelligence, having a good education, and was a regularly graduated physician. This terrible propensity he had to get drunk was ruining him, and all of his fine qualities and intellectual culture came to naught making his drunkenness appear even more debasing and be more degrading than if he were an ignorant man. His drunkenness was not like that of most men, for he became so beastly drunk that he could not enjoy himself. He even became very filthy in his habits. Waddill was his true friend and could not stop worrying.

---

301. DJW, January 7–8, 1854, vol. 4, pgs. 129–30.

CHAPTER 52

Sale of Land, 1853

John and Julia Waddill felt blessed in their financial situation. It had been rough when they first married, but Waddill was diligent in his practice and quickly developed a reputation for integrity and hard work. Whenever an opportunity arose, Waddill purchased property under the theory that each family should be diversified. His experience as a young man in Tennessee, raised on a farm, and working for the Hickmans and Elam in Rapides and Catahoula Parish, respectively, helped him to understand how to make a profit on land, especially farming.

He had considerable acreage near the Red River with two tracts of two hundred acres each and six slaves, three of whom were adult. He also had land on Bayou Rouge in Section 5 T1S-R5E that comprised 133 acres. It was becoming hard to manage his properties, especially due to the separation in miles and his burgeoning practice.

He explained to Julia that he believed that they should sell the property on Bayou Rouge. They had made money, but it was becoming more and more burdensome. Waddill's practice with W. W. was growing larger as his brother really caught on to the practice. Sean Descant was interested in the property and had offered $1,200 dollars. The Waddill family could put that aside and have plenty to educate their children and live comfortably.

Julia responded as she always had, and he appreciated her thoughts even though she rarely disagreed. She did agree. Waddill reminded her that it was important to have some cash set aside. No one knew when his time would come.

Waddill often heard her speak about who would die first, and he loved the banter. She was such a beautiful woman in many ways. Their children were growing fast. Julia thought that this was not the first time he talked about selling property. Waddill seemed to be always buying property throughout the parish. Every once in a while he would sell, but he was mostly buying property as an investment.

The next day, he notified Sean Descant that he was ready to sell his interest in the Bayou Rouge property. Descant purchased the 133 acres from John P. Waddill on October, 8, 1853, in the presence of Adophe Lafargue and L. H. Couvillion. Aristide Barbin served as the official recorder of the documents in the Avoyelles Parish Clerks Office. The property was located just west of present day Cottonport, which was incorporated in 1888.[302]

Julia was correct. At the height of his land ownership, John P. Waddill had owned over 1,500 acres in various parts of the parish. He patented two tracts of land from the United States, comprising forty acres each in April of 1854. He did not stop there. He purchased from Pierre Recoully 128 acres on the Red River in October of 1854 and 117 acres from William Alexander in December 1854. Waddill's last transaction was to purchase, by patenting from the State of Louisiana, a small seventeen-acre tract just north of the Red River in May 1855. He purchased one on the southern portion of the parish that included a piece in St. Landry. He also had property in the southeastern portion of the parish. From 1840 to 1855, Waddill purchased fourteen significant tracts of land and rarely sold any of it.

His law practice gave him the opportunity to discover land available at little cost, and he took advantage of it. He knew that land would help support his family.

---

302. In 1808, Joseph Ducote married Marguetite Bordelon and cleared a cane break on Bayou Rouge, where he built a home about a quarter of a mile from the present center of the town. This is where he and his new wife lived. In 1835, he donated a lane to the small one-room schoolhouse that was built on his property. In 1850, there were about fifty white families and the same number of slaves within a four square-mile area. See Saucier *History of Avoyelles Parish*, 269–70.

CHAPTER 53

BUSINESS DECISIONS

Waddill had to supply clothing for his children and for the slaves. Some could be hand sewn, but others had to be purchased. It cost Waddill eighteen dollars for two pair of pantaloons. He paid the money to his tailor, Mayer, in Marksville.

The legislature was in session. W. F. Griffin was the senator for Avoyelles and Rapides. He announced that he was now chairman of Parochial Affairs.

On January 25, 1854, news arrived that the electric telegraph was in operation from Harrisonburg, via Alexandria, to Shreveport. This impressed Waddill greatly. The announcement came at the same time that the Red River was lower than normal. The level was so low that no boats could pass the falls at Alexandria. Communications would be limited to the electric telegraph, at least from Alexandria upriver. Waddill wondered how much more technology could be invented.

John and Julia sold a small portion of their property. It was the portion adjoining Dr. G. E. Elmer near the Waddill home lot. Waddill's practice continued to grow with new business and clients coming from all over. William H. Washington of New Bern, North Carolina, visited John, and they had a nice chat. He had heard of Waddill's reputation in legal matters and as an honorable man.

Sophronia Davis's father, Major William E. Davis, had died, and she needed legal counsel. Washington wanted Waddill to handle the affairs and hire assisting counsel.

Waddill accepted and asked about his business in North Carolina. Washington explained that he had a cotton and turpentine plantation. The turpentine farming[303] was very profitable. They made about $400 per hand in this.

---

303. Turpentine farming was a booming industry during this time period. It was made from the fluid obtained by the distillation of resin from live trees, mainly

Washington's property was in Craven County. He had been elected twice to the State Senate, 1848 and 1852, to be the senator from Craven County, the 13th District.[304] He was also appointed by the governor on March 2, 1853, to serve as a director on the North Carolina Railroad.

March 5, 1854 – Slave Issues

Waddill had purchased a female slave named Mary in New Orleans from Charles F. Hatcher on February 23, 1854. Since that day, she took a severe fever and had been afflicted with a bad cough since February 25. John had given her flaxseed tea and other remedies. She appeared somewhat deranged in intellect, though it may have arisen from fever and cold in her head. He feared her cough was an old and a permanent one.

On March 6, Mary was no better. She appeared very nervous. Waddill gave her calomel and rhubarb the night before. This worked well. On the 7, Waddill sent for Dr. Elmer to attend to Mary. On the 8th, Mary still had some fever and was hysterical.

The next day, Mary was very hysterical and acted, in Waddill's words, "like a crazy person." Dr. Elmer gave her asafoetida, morphia, and other things. He had given her a cough mixture, principally tarterized autimony,[305] gum arabic, etc. He also gave her a solution of Hartshorn[306] (or ammonia, camphor, etc.). She was a little better, if any.

On March 11, Mary was still sick. Waddill wrote to Charles F. Hatcher, in the care of William H. Foster, informing him that the slave appeared unsound. She exhibited signs of insanity or mental derangement. Waddill

---

pine. It had many uses, including preserving ropes and rigging on sailing ships and caulking the seams between timbers in the ship's hulls. http://daysgoneby.me/turpentine/

304. "North Carolina State Senate 1850–1851," North Carolina in the 1800s, http://www.carolana.com/NC/1800s/nc_1800s_senate_1850-1851.html.

305. A home remedy in the time period for severe cough. See *Homoeopathic Pioneer*, vol.1 (January 1, 1845).

306. Hartshorn was a nineteenth-century remedy made from carbonate of ammonia distilled from the shaved or powdered horns of a male deer. Hartshorn and smelling salts could be mixed with water and drunk as a restorative. "The Connection Between Vinegar and the Fainting Couch: 19th Century Customs," https://janeaustensworld.wordpress.com/tag/regency-medicine/

had Dr. Elmer attend to her, and she was but little better. Further, Waddill requested Mr. Foster to tell him to take her back and let him know whether he could get his money back from Mr. Hatcher.

On March 23, 1854, an outbreak of measles infiltrated the Waddill home, and the slave, Mary, became even sicker with their effect. Waddill gave Mary ipecacuanha,[307] which was an expectorant.

John's good friend, Henderson Taylor, invited the Waddills to the wedding of his daughter, Clara C. Taylor. The groom was Edward Henderson Satterfield of Hamburg. The officiating minister was the Reverend Calvin A. Frazee of Opelousas, a cousin by marriage.

Satterfield was born in 1811 in South Carolina. He was a large slave owner and operated a plantation. He had about fifty slaves in 1850. He was forty-three, and Clara was barely twenty-one years of age. Their daughter, Alice, was born the same year, 1854.[308] Alice died as a very young girl.

Each March, the Waddill Law Office had to pay its taxes. In 1854, Waddill paid his parish taxes in the amount of $6.88. His professional parish tax was $9.33, and the same for W. W. Waddill. Waddill's practice continued to prosper. On March 28, A. Lafargue, F. Borde, A. Durand, J. O. Prostdamme, and L. F. Roy employed Waddill to defend them in the case of the state against them for drawing a lottery. Henderson and J. L. Taylor were also retained. Each one of them paid each of the lawyers seventy-five dollars. Waddill would earn $375.00, a huge fee for him.

J. B. Kirk employed Waddill to defend him in a prosecution for selling spirituous liquors without a license. Waddill charged twenty-five dollars.

---

307. An expectorant made from the dry root of Cephaelis ipecacuanha, a plant from Brazil. https://en.wikipedia.org/wiki/Ipecacuanha.

308. In 1857, Satterfield sold his plantation to Thomas Jeferson Spurlock. It was a credit sale and after only two of the ten equal payments that was to total $165,000.00, with payments beginning in 1857, the Confederates burned the plantation to prevent the Union from its benefits. Spurlock defaulted. In 1865, Satterfield planned to purchase thirty-eight of his slaves for $37,385 and move them to Texas. The war ended shortly thereafter and Satterfield sued to get his money back. This case went to the Supreme Court on the claim that the slaves were free and could not be sold. Satterfield lost his claim. Spurlock's debt was reduced by the $37,385.00. *Louisiana Reports: Cases Argued and Determined in the Supreme Court* vol. 74, pg. 327.

The Citizen

Waddill subscribed to the pro-slavery newspaper *The Citizen* published in New York. John Mitchel,[309] a fervent Irishman who had been sent to the British penal colony in Ireland Island, Bermuda, established this paper. Waddill paid five dollars for the subscription and had William Waddill mail the letter with the money by giving it to the postmaster, James Rey Jr.

Finally, after years of working with A. G. Pearce and others on the succession of Joel Toler, Waddill received his legal fees of $200 on May 4, 1854. John had collected and disbursed $10,000 for the estate. It had taken a while to settle everything. He had just paid a judgment against Eliza Toler, by Agnes Cappel in the amount of $900. He paid it to Jaques Aristide Cappel.

309. John Mitchell had been a fervent proponent of Irish nationalism and was found guilty under the British Treason Felony Act of 1848. Deported to the penal colony in Bermuda, he never lost his passion. Many of those sent there died, mostly from yellow fever. He survived and was sent to the Van Diemen's land, which is now Tasmania, Australia. On his journey there he wrote his "Jail Journal," in which he repudiated British policy in Ireland and wanted a more radical brand of nationalism. He escaped and settled in the United States, where he established the radical Irish newspaper, *The Citizen*. He advocated the defense of slavery by attempting to expose his ideas of hypocrisy of abolitionists arguments. He believed that slaves were treated better than the Irish workers of British companies. https://en.wikipedia.org/wiki/John_Mitchel.

CHAPTER 54

WILLIAM WADDILL LEAVES AVOYELLES

On a sad and joyous day, William W. Waddill left John P. Waddill's home for Harrisonburg, in Catahoula, Louisiana, where he intended to locate and practice law. John felt blessed to have William in Avoyelles the years that he did after leaving him in Tennessee. He enjoyed teaching William the law. John was relieved of many duties in his practice and home life because Waddill's family adored William. They felt safe with him and enjoyed his company. Having him live at his home was a blessing. Waddill would miss him.[310]

John believed that William was an excellent young man and attorney. He knew he would do well. William had an excellent new library of law books worth between $350 and $400. He was free from debt and had about $120 in cash and plenty of clothes.

William Wallace Waddill left by steamboat on July 1, 1854. He was twenty-five years old. John rode in his carriage to see his brother off at Gorton's Landing. William took the steamboat *Pista*. On the same day, Julia went to visit her sister, who was with her husband, Green Huie, at the residence of their mother, Mrs. Alexander, on the Red River. Julia returned on July 2, with John making the same trip two days in a row to pick her up. She had brought their two daughters.

Death in Rapides

On July 6, 1854, Waddill learned that Thomas "Doc" Culbertson Jr. of Alexandria shot and killed James F. Murray,[311] the mayor of Alexandria and a

---

310. After John P. Waddill died in 1855, William moved back to help the family and to close out John's estate. He remained in Marksville, becoming active in Marksville politics and owning a successful law practice.

311. James F. Murray had a wife and one step-child, Judith A. Beatty, age four.

Rapides planter. He was shot at a public dinner on July 4. The examination of Culbertson took place on July 15, where he was committed for trial at the next district court. There was so much concern for potential for escape that he was sent to New Orleans with special funding of the Rapides police jury to hold until the trial.[312] Murray had served as a 1st Lieutenant of the Rapides Guard.[313] Citizens had talked of taking the law into their own hands, but that impulse died down after Culbertson was transferred to Orleans.[314]

Last Diary Entry by Waddill

Waddill never let go of his political thoughts. He knew that the Whig party in 1854 was losing strength. The Whigs had been failing in elections. He thought that the Free Soilers, the anti-slavery party, would not be long-lived. The nascent Republican Party had not yet made its big step in electing officials. He wrote:

Effect of Secession to the North;
Let us look to the North;

Freesoildom is wealthy, active, strong and has been up to this time been united for political effect. But freesoildom is chiefly dependent for it's prosperity upon commerce manufactories, government patronage, and southern trade. Take these subsisting, fattening, stimulating resources from Freesoildom just think a moment and it is ruined. In this terrible plight Freesoildom finds herself without any Federal organization. Having been peculiarly dependent upon the Federal Government, that Government will suddenly have vanished like a ghost. Perhaps not. Well, admit that Freesoildom may hold to

---

She was the daughter of Harriet M. Murray, who later remarried Newton Sessions of Sabine Parish in 1860. Judith married Louis Stanton on September 9, 1864, at age eighteen. She died on May 1, 1868, in New Orleans where they had moved. In their four-year marriage they had two children.

312. *Times Picayune*, July 25, 1854, pg. 2.

313. *The Louisiana Democrat* published the article and story of the shooting in its July 5, 1854, edition. It was reprinted in the *Times Picayune* on July 11, 1854, on page 2.

314. From the *Bienville Times* on July 14, recorded in the *Times Picayune*, July 24, 1854, pg. 2.

the old constitution and laws and insist that she is the Government. Still most unquestionably the main resources of that Government will be gone and still worse, gone to strengthen and encourage the energy "The Government" will be a heavy weight for Freesoildom to bear when her nourishment is lost.

Though the population of the Northern States for political effect, by the action of majorities stand as united against the South: still it is a fact of great significance that the minorities everywhere are strong in numbers, earnest and hostile to the majorities. As a natural consequence of the dreadful situation in which the whole population will be thrown by reason of the events we have been contemplating, especially when no one considers that thousands of the poor will be in of poverty and starvation- the political parties will become active hostile elements and will wholly disorganize society, and rend the foundations of Government and order. Freesoildom will be powerless for aggression.[315]

Waddill also noted that North Carolina chose not to replace the U.S. Senator Willie Mangum, a Whig who had served since 1841. The term ended on March 3, 1853. The state legislature did not appoint a replacement. The office was vacant until December 6, 1854, when the legislature of North Carolina appointed a Democrat, David Reid.

---

315. DJW, July 1854, pgs. 172–73.

CHAPTER 55

THE LAST LEGAL FILING AND
DEATH OF JOHN P. WADDILL

On June 23, 1855, John P. Waddill filed on behalf of the estate of Claude Ricouly, who left three children, namely Louise, Narcisse, and Eugene. The widow was Elizabeth Fauquier. The property was a tract along the Red River and livestock. The order of transfer was signed June 25, 1855.

After Waddill's death, September 26, 1855, his brother, who had practiced law for a few years, filed the estate proceedings for the deceased, John Pamplin Waddill. His last will and testament had been written months before the date of his death. He simply wrote, "I will to my wife all that the law permits." Julia became the sole tutrix of the children, and William and Julia were co-executors. He also wrote that his desire was that "My property be kept together as long as suitable." He handwrote his will in olographic form.

Seth Lewis Taylor, O. M. Donald, and Edward DeGeirisie executed the affidavits of death. The succession was finished on January 18, 1856. The family held quite a large land hold on the fertile soils of the Red River until 1866. It was at that point that Julia and W. W. Waddill petitioned the court to sell the two tracts of land that served as a second home place and final resting place of John P. Waddill. The tract closest to the river brought $8,250, and the second tract of two hundred acres brought $7,000.00.

The *Louisiana Democrat* of Alexandria noted that the succession sale would take place to sell property of John P. Waddill, comprising 475 acres on the Red River. The paper described the property as "On the North Bank of Red River, bounded North by the heirs of Fountain Barlow, the lowerline by William Voorhies, on the Front by Red River and back line by Pierre Ricouly." This property was adjacent to Julia Waddill's family property. The advertisement included the fact that 115 acres were that year in cultivation, "well secured by levees and free from overflow on account of said levees protecting the same."[316]

There is a small cemetery in Marksville known as the Waddill Cemetery, where John P. Waddill and Julia M. Barlow Waddill are buried.[317] His death occurred on September 26, 1855 from yellow fever. His burial was not far from his home place in the town of Marksville. W. W. Waddill moved back to his adopted home of Marksville and handled the estate. In 1861, he became mayor of Marksville and is also buried in this cemetery. It appears that John's daughter, Florence Waddill, married Adolphe Lafargue's son, A. D. Lafargue. She was born in 1852 and died in 1937. Thomas Hickman Waddill served in the Confederacy as a lieutenant. He was wounded during the Second Battle of Bull Run (Second Battle of Manassas) and died from the wounds on August 31, 1862. He was twenty years old. He is buried at St. Paul's Episcopal Church in Prince William County, Virginia.

Before his death, Waddill continued to write poetry. He wrote in late August 1853 of international politics in the following:

Far eastward where the Black sea waves
Encircles Crimia's Classic shores
Earth's mightiest Empires armed and brave
Now drench the land with human gore.
Britania's Meteor Cross is seen
To blend with France's tri color

Whilst Turkey's Crescent's bloody shine
Lights them to slaughter and to war
opposed to these in bold defense
of hearts and altars, homes and wives.
The Russians mighty battlements.

Waddill's wife, Julia, noted in the diary: "Line written by my dear husband. John P. Waddill a short time previous to his death in August 1855 it is unfinished."[318]

---

316. *The Louisiana Democrat*, November 14, 1866, pg. 3.

317. The Waddill Cemetery is on a small lane in present day Marksville.

318. DJW, August 1855, vol. 3, pg. 29.

Death of John P. Waddill

Marksville experienced a horrible epidemic of yellow fever during the summer of 1855. Many thought that it was a contagious disease, yet not even isolation seemed to prevent it from spreading. No one was aware that mosquitoes spread the infection. Waddill's long time friend and colleague, Judge Ralph Cushman, followed his death of only a month later.

Approximately 10 percent of Marksville's town population died from this 1855 epidemic. The population was between 1,500 and 1,800 in the incorporated area of one square mile. Just there, not the outlying area, approximately 160 to 180 citizens died. It was a gloomy time for the young town. Yellow fever knew no bounds, rich or poor, black or white, and the dreaded disease would take fourteen to eighteen days to die from the black vomit. The effect of so many deaths during a time of growth in central Louisiana prohibited what would have been much progress.

The New Orleans *Picayune* reported on October 6, 1855, that the *Alexandria Republican* newspaper ran a story on yellow fever in Rapides and Avoyelles parishes.

> We hear that the fever is raging fearfully in our sister parish of Avoyelles. At Marksville, Snaggy Point, where there are some boats laid up; and in Pointe Maigre we learn there are proportionately as many cases as there (are) here, and that the disease is more fatal. The Hon. John P. Waddill died at Marksville, a day or two since, and his family, it is said, are down with it. Business is at a perfect standstill. Many of four stores are closed one half of the time. The river is falling.

This story ran on page 1 of the edition. No other Waddill family member contracted the yellow fever, but it was prevalent in the community.

W. W. Waddill moved back and continued to live in Marksville until his death in September 1882. He became a prominent attorney and politician. He was elected alderman in Marksville in 1858, and after serving as mayor for one term, in 1865, he was again elected alderman.

John P. Waddill left a will in olographic form (which he wrote and signed) dated January 18, 1855. This was about eight months before his death. He willed to his wife all that the law allowed. He appointed Julia Barlow, his wife, as sole tutrix of their children. He also wrote that he wanted his "property to remain together" and the "planting partnerships to be kept together as long as suitable." He asked that William W. Waddill handle his estate affairs. W. W. and Julia petitioned the court to be co-executors of the estate. W. W. filed as the attorney for the estate. These pleadings to probate the will were filed in January 1856. Several sales of property and management of Waddill's estate were handled by W. W. Waddill.

Waddill's daughter, Ida, who was born in 1847, died an early death. Laura Elizabeth, born in 1845, later married Thomas Overton, who served as a judge in Avoyelles Parish. He attended law school at Louisiana University, now Tulane. He served in the Confederacy during the Civil War and moved to Avoyelles Parish to practice law after the war ended. In 1869, he and Laura married.[319] She had three sons, the youngest of whom was John H. Overton, who became a lawyer and lived in Rapides Parish, where Laura and Thomas had moved. Julia lived until 1896. Laura died on October 27, 1937, and stayed with her mother until her death.

John H. Overton, born September 17, 1875, in Marksville, became a U.S. Senator for the State of Louisiana. He graduated from LSU in 1895 and Tulane Law School in 1897. He began his practice in Alexandria and allowed his mother, Laura, to live with him until her death. He became a staunch supporter of Huey P. Long and served as his counsel during his impeachment proceedings in 1929. He was elected U.S. Senator in 1932 and re-elected in 1938 and 1944. He died during his last term on May 14, 1948.[320] One of his children, Mary Elizabeth Overton, married Elbert C. Brazelton. They are the parents of Elizabeth Brazelton, who possesses the original diaries of John P. Waddill.

John P. Waddill had an impact on those around him in his early family life, his college years, his time with the Hickman Brothers, in the community of Avoyelles, and in his political career. His legal practice led to the release of the wrongfully enslaved Solomon Northup. The community of Marksville lost a prominent citizen in 1855.

---

319. *Biographical and Historical Memoirs*, 645.

320. John H. Overton, Wikipedia, https://en.wikipedia.org/wiki/John_H._Overton.

EPILOGUE

New Orleans, April 12, 2014

Solomon Northup never heard from nor contacted John P. Waddill again. This must have caused some wonderment between the two of them. One wonders if Waddill ever read the *New York Times* article printed on January 20, 1853, pertaining to Northup's release. Part of it read:

> From Washington, Mr. N. (Henry Northup) went, by the way of Pittsburg and the Ohio and Mississippi rivers, to the mouth of the Red River, and thence up that river to Marksville, in the parish of Avoyelles, where he employed Hon, JOHN P. WADDILL, an eminent lawyer of that place, and consulted with him as to the best means of finding and obtaining possession of the man. He soon ascertained that there was no such man at Marksville, or in that vicinity. Bayou Beouf, the place where the letter was dated, was twenty-three miles distant, at its nearest point, and is seventy miles in length. For reasons which it is unnecessary to give, the very providential manner in which the residence of the man was ascertained cannot now be given, although the circumstances would add much to the interest of the narrative.[321]

Of course, the fact that John P. Waddill, the "eminent lawyer," just so happened to know Sam Bass, and his beliefs about slavery that ultimately led Waddill to Bass, which led them to Northup, were the circumstances that the *New York Times* did not have.

As to Samuel Bass, Northup assumed that he left the Marksville area, as did others. He stayed, and his legacy lived on in his children and grandchildren.

---

321. *The New York Times*, January 20, 1853.

Loyola University, April 12, 2014

The sound of music emanated from the orchestra with a deep resonating harmony. One piece after another cascaded through and to the walls, pouring over the audience. Loyola University hosted a concert to celebrate the music of Solomon Northup's time in Louisiana. The Avoyelles Tourism Commission helped to sponsor this, and a group of citizens interested in the Northup story were invited for this one-day trip.

The Loyola University New Orleans Chamber Orchestra performed in Roussel Hall located in the Communications/Music Complex on the University's main campus. This was presented in partnership with the Afro-Louisiana Historical and Genealogical Society and featured violinist and Loyola Student Amahl Hodge, symbolically representing Solomon Northup, who also played the violin.

It was at the Loyola reception, after the concert, in the lobby area, when the descendants of John P. Waddill first met the descendants of Solomon Northup. Eileen Jackson and Evelyn Jackson, who were great-great-great granddaughters of Northup, were present, as well as Elizabeth Brazelton, the great-great granddaughter of John P. Waddill. It was an emotional visit. Descendants of Samuel Bass were also present at the event.[322]

Interestingly, many people, including Solomon Northup, never found out what happened to Samuel Bass. Many thought he had moved back to Canada, however, he died about eight months after the freeing of Northup. Waddill was with him the night before his death finalizing his last will. Bass's daughter, Ellen Bass, and her husband, John Cass of Marksville, lived near Waddill in the town.[323] Ellen was apparently born of the union between Justine Tournier and Samuel Bass, though out of wedlock. Their great-grandson was H. Claude Hudson, who was born in Marksville and later was educated at Howard University. He was active in the Niagara Movement with W.E.B. Du Bois, which was a precursor to the National Association for the Advancement of Colored People (NAACP).[324] As the Niagra Movement died out in

---

322. http://www.loyno.edu/news/laag/20140411/5099

323. Northup, *12 Years a Slave*, illustrated edition (Randy Decuir, January 2013), 210.

324. Burt A. Folkart, "H. Claude Hudson Dies at 102; Helped Found NAACP," *Los Angeles Times*, http://articles.latimes.com/1989-01-28/news/mn-1131_1_h-claude-hudson See also: https://en.wikipedia.org/wiki/H._Claude_Hudson

1908, many of the active members helped form the NAACP in 1910. Hudson died in 1989 at age 102.

Many of the people that Waddill met and knew had a great influence on the history of the United States during the antebellum period, the Civil War, and after. Waddill affected many people. Perhaps Waddill's greatest act was his method of finding Samuel Bass, his friend and business associate, which led to freeing Solomon Northup, the free man who lived twelve years as a slave.

APPENDIX

What Can Immortalize a Name?
April 15, 1837

What can immortalize a name,
Or make it dearly prized on earth,
Apart from martial deeds of fame
Or the proud claim to lifted worth?
What save it from the eternal doom
Or death's oblivion in the tomb?
    2nd
Is it not friendship? Or is Love
The mighty vivifying power
That breaks the spell which fate has wove,
And builds aloth the eternal tower,
Whose giant form and heightened sublime
Will send a shadow through all time?
    3rd
If it be friendship, let my soul
Be found in adamantine bands,
With some firm hearts: as ages roll
Alternate through the dropping sands
Of time, they, be only serve to wear
The wreathed links more bright and pain!
    4th
But if it be Love, let some fond heart,
Which independent hearts inspire,
Its feeling into mine impart; ---
For a congenial spirit's fire
Will give it welcome there; nor age,
Nor death, shall blot it from the pages
    5th
Then oh! Let Love or Friendship twine,
Around my name upon this page
A wreath whose glittering braids shall shine;
Undimmed through youth and trembling age;
And when cold death has sealed my eyes
Trill here my name immortalize!

Memory – an Essayical Retrospection

How sweet is the feeling, produced by looking back through the vista of years that are gone, upon those scenes which were once spread before our eyes in all the identity of reality. How sweet to read over the records of memory, in which are registered the events of our lives, and the lives of those with whom we were intimately connected by the tender ties of love, or of friendship, yet this sweet feeling while we are thus engaged is tinged with a soft melancholy! And why? It is because we are invading the Cemetery of buried thoughts, hopes, and fond endearments: of scenes in which we are mingled, joyed, when our lives wore a different coloring, to that, with which they are now shaded; and when surround by other friends than those that now gladden our hearts with their attentions. While enjoying the friendships of those that are gone, and whose faith had been tried and found unwavering, with every test, we could have wishes, had not the thought been impious, that the Almighty disposer of all things, had granted us the boon of eternal youth and health and that we should have dwelt together through the unknown extension of boundless eternity.

Though we are deprived of immortality here, and have been prohibited the privilege of penetrating the unborn ages of the future; yet, a benevolent creator has given us one faculty, by the aid of which we are enabled to look back upon the past and call up every scene of endearment, every pleasure and enjoyment, in all the beauty and splendor with which they first greeted our senses. By the power of memory we are carried back to the Elysian fields of infancy: We wander amid the flowery landscapes of our childhood, and revel upon the banks of those sparkling streams that first kindled in our bosoms an admiration for the wonderful, and beauteous works of the Creator. Every feeling of the soul that has animated us, again returns; and filled with the same buoyant spirit and love for adventure, we seem to plunge into the deep makes of the almost impenetrable forest, seeking in its primitive wilds, something that will satisfy the burnings of an ardent, and youthful imagination.

Again we seem to scale the mountain's side whose towering summits breaks through the fleecy clouds ethereal ships sail round its sides, carrying their bosoms the awful lightings of the skies, and the rending tempest which desolates the earth. Again we seem to stand upon the summit of the mountain; and while gazing upon the expanse below, the beauteous and variegated landscapes bursts upon our sights with all the splendor and magnificence of former time. In truth, such power has memory over thine that the lapse of years, aided by the beasom of destroying time, cannot brush the slightest dewdrop from her vernal map!

Age cannot affect it: many of its scenes may have been engraven in the halcyon days of boyhood, and though 70 years may have rolled over its pages, yet we can turn to them and find the precious gems of yore sparkling with their pristine radiance: lightning with their hallowed rays the dreary gloom of life and teaching us that mind must be immortal.

How exquisite, then must be our feelings, when life has been worn to the last shreds of existence, to cast a retrospective glance to the past, and behold all the endearments of youth, and manhood arrayed in the habiliments in their own native loveliness? Though they departed from us, and ascended into the tomb, yet they were buried in memory, and their embalmed, they seem to be living still softening the pillow of pain, and soothing the cares of age.

The World

Some men by nature formed are wise
And some by schools and good advice
While others plod with the make
Of dolt like folly all their days;
Nor can they ride above the grade
In which by dullness they're arrayed
No more than bears can mount and fly
Like eagles though the ethereal sky.
Some men there are who misconstrue
Their wisdom and their learning too,
And think all the other fools who go
Contrary to the forms they know.
These are, of all the human race
The kind most wrights in wisdom's chase
And halt and hobble on their way
To every plodding thought of prey,
And in the scale keep sinking down
Into the follies of the Clown,
Nor perceive with what an air
They play the gambles of the bear,
And what to make their case still worse
Is, that within their groveling course
They try to quiz, mock, or deride
Their betters upon every side,
And in the pride of ignorance pour
Their spumy sets from door, to door,
As wit of sterling value froth
 With wisdom, our exalted though
And fit to be recorded even
Upon the portals of high Heaven.
The fool perhaps through wick or chance
Has learned in life a need to dance,
Or to pour out in sobs and sighs
His love to some weak girl, whose eyes
With scorching heat, he does make known
Has burnt his belly to the bone!
And doomed him all his days to stray

Through realms unknown, to love a prey.
And those who do not act like he
In each particular degree
Must be compelled to grim and bear
His gibe, and snarl his whining sneer
As punishment which clowns deserve
Who do not fashions laws observe.

Song
Sunday, April 23, 1837, 9 o'clock AM

How sweet it is for those who love
To know they are beloved again
That she who is with life is wove
Joys to relieve the tender pain.
Yea! When each bosom burns to pour
Its feelings in the other's heart
And revel on the word "no more
In life shall we be doomed to part."
Oh, then this bliss! Tis heaven on earth,
When thus the mortal promises made
Breaks not, till both from life go forth
To sleep in the death's eternal shade
But oh how cursed through life is he,
Who forced to hide the blame he feels
And to the forest flower, and tree
Alone, his burning thoughts reveal
Peace from his bosom flies, and there
Are planted by the hand of fate
The goading thorns of life which tear
A way each thrill of joy elates.
Death the grim monster whose cold hand
Makes mortals tremble in despair

Written in Despondency
July 16, 1837

And all is night; even life's bright morn
    With midnight gloom is overcast,
    And hope of every beam is shorn,
That glowed so brightly through the past.
    And my soul's gloom glows darker still,
    Portending some disastrous fate,
    That hangs unseen above me still,
    And does the will of heaven await
    To fall and crush the furrowed heart,
Which now is torn and racked with cares,
    Ready from life's last sands to part,
    And end in death its woes and fears.
    It has withstood the tug of strife,
    And joyed to meet the scorn of man;
    It proudly strode o'er ills of life
Nor deemed them scarcely worth a band.
    But now in bleeding fragments broke
    Upon the hidden rocks of fate;
    It staggers from the iron stroke
    Aimed by misfortunes furious hate
    But still whilst its life pulse's beat
    Though whirling in chaotic wreck,
    It shall in contest boldly meet,
    And give the opposing force a check.
    It has in former times been strung,
    With nerve of iron strength to bear
The sternest storm, though lightning swung
    And rolling thunders of despair;
    It shall again be armed to meet
    All ills, as it in time hath done;
    Advancing onward, nor retreat
Till heaven shall will its race is run.

----||----

Upon the same occasion
And I am one, whom fortune's frown
    Has tried to whither to the dust;

Yet all its thunders flashing down
Fall harmless; and forever must.
Fate seems at war with me and mine;
For on my peril broken way,
Few beams of weal have deigned, to shine
As beacon of a better day
Yet heaven so formed me at my birth
That I "soul, and sense" should dare
To battle with the woes of earth
And hurt defiance at despair,
Then come what will in weal or woe
This spirit which has brook'd the past,
Shall meet the fiercest storms that blow,
And move impending to the last!

Legend of the Yaho
Told by William J. Elam

In the summer of 1820---- Moss, Esqr of the then territory of Arkansas, together with several of his friends, formed a resolution to explore the regions on, and adjacent to the Red River above Pecan Point. They accordingly sat out in the month of July, well equipped for a long journey in the dangerous backwoods country. After many days travel they arrived I the region which they wished to explore. The country was very picturesque; it being somewhat mountainous, with large verdant valleys lying between the mountains, some of the plains, being prairies upon which grazed large herds of Buffalos, and deer. The explorers, towards noon, one day, had got into a region so wild in appearance, that it bordered upon the Terrific. While wondering about, gazing at the scenery, they came upon the remains of a buffalo—upon examining the mutilated carcass, they found that it had been killed by large animals; but a short time before their arrival, probably some two or three hours. They searched around for the tracks of the hostile animals, but could find none, with the exception of a deep indenture, in the shape of a smoothing iron. These appeared to be distant from each other, about 12 or 13 feet, and were about 18 inches in length, by 10 inches in breadth at the broadest point, having at the extremity of the smallest point, a deep impression, which appeared to have been made by an enormous claw.

It was sometime before they could bring themselves to the belief that it was the footstep of some strange and enormous animal which inhabited the Rocky Mountains and had hitherto escaped the observation of naturalists. But the truth of its being the track of some animal was now too plain to admit of any doubt; and they being well armed, each with a rifle, tomahawk, and bowie knife, resolved to follow it, and if possible kill it. They immediately went into pursuit and having proceeded a few hundred yards from the place of their departure, they discovered a large beam about 15 feet in length, by 10 inches in diameter, much worn, and to all appearances served the animal as a whacking club, or walking stick. The followed on through dark forests and rocky ravines during the remainder of the day without being able, as they imagined, to gain any on their object. Night coming along, they trammeled their horses in prairie, and lay down, without kindling any fire for fear of being discovered. Early the next morning they arose, breakfasted, and went forward with all the possible dispatch in pursuit of the animal. Towards noon they came across a small creek with rushed down between two lofty hills; its banks on each side being 25 to 30 feet high, and nearly perpendicular. They found that it was impossible for them to get their horses across the creek; where upon they again trammeled them, determining to follow on foot. They examined the banks carefully, and found that the animal in climbing the bank on the opposite side, had at each step, went up 7 or 8 feet. So soon that they had gotten fairly on the top of the bank, they discovered that another animal of the same species had joined the, of which they were in pursuit. They had now pursued the track upwards of 60 miles and to all appearances had gained nothing on the chase. The country wore a remarkably dread appearance. Lofty mountains towered one above the other, as far as the eye could reach; and every step they advanced appeared more pregnant with danger than the last. Some of the company becoming alarmed at their situation, and believing that if they should overtake the animals, that it would perilous in the extreme to attack them, refused to proceed any further. They communicated their fears to the rest, and after a short council agreed to retrace their steps, and forever keep secret what they had discovered. But some 5 or six months later after their return home one of the company divulged under the following circumstances.

In a large company assembled at an Inn was an old man, who was one of the first pioneers to the state, (or their territory) of Arkansas. He was relating his old hunter's stories to the company; and among them he unraveled one to the following effect. " In early times a famous hunter, and his son, who resided in the state of Kentucky, in one of their rambles to prove their love for adventure, had crossed the Mississippi, and Arkansas Rivers, entered the region of the Rocky Mountains. They selected a suitable place and erected a camp, and hunted for several days with great success. One evening as the hunter was wandering his way down an intricate pass of a mountain he heard his son's gun fire, at about the distance of a mile from him. He paid but little or no attention to the circumstance, and pursued his toilsome way towards the camp, at which he arrived near sundown. He prepared supper for himself and sun, and throwing himself down upon a bed of bearskins, resolved to take a little repose, before he supped, and also to await his son's return as company at the evening meal.

He now concluded that his son has killed some large animal, and being unable to skin until late, had resolved to remain by it all night, and return in the morning. The hunter upon this conclusion supped and betook himself to repose, yet not without some evil forebodings as to the fate of his son. The next morning the old man remain in his camp for several hours, but his son not returning, he resolved to go in pursuit of him. He went to the place where he had heard his son shoot the evening before, and (Mirabile Dictu)[1] he found his carcass horribly mangled lying near a fallen tree. The old man, though unpracticed in the noisy wailings of polished society, felt all that a father could feel on the occasion, and vowed to be avenged.

He discovered an imprint in the earth, of uncommon shape and dimension, and justly supposed that it was the destroyer of his child. He has primed his pan afresh, prepared his flint, and warily began his pursuit. He had proceeded but a short distance before he discovered a monster, seated upon a rock, and wiping his breast with a bunch of leaves and moss which he held in his hand. He soon found that it had discovered him and was beckoning him to approach. Steadily, and strictly upon his guard the old man advanced, until he arrived within a hundred paces of his foe. He then rested the muzzle of his gun to the side of a small tree, and fired at the breast of the animal. He had no sooner fired and the animal springing upon the rock which it sat, began to hurl enormous fragments of rocks at him, which cracked among the branches of the trees over his head, with Terrific violence. The hunter immediately commenced a retreat, and as he fled reloaded his rifle. So soon as he found a situation among the rocks that somewhat protected him from the missiles of the enemy, he halted to give battle—The animal observed this movement, and seemed fearful to approach as if it had learned from the recent encounter, that it had grappled with a powerful antagonist,-- But arming itself with two huge stones it cautiously advanced, to until within 80 yards of the hunter, when he fired at its head, upon which it bounded form the earth to the height of near 15 feet, giving a tremendous scream somewhat resembling the human voice, and falling prostrate upon the earth appearing dead. The hunter recharged his gun, and drawing his tomahawk approached the monster. When he arrived at it, he found that the last shot had taken effect in the brain, and that it was quite dead.

He discovered that two shots had been lodged in its breast, one he justly supposed was from the rifle of his lamented son. The figure of the animal, in nearly every respect, was that of a man of the most giant-like dimensions, being between 18 and 20 feet in height, and proportionately made at that. The hunter after viewing it until he was satisfied, left it, buried the bones of his son, and returned to his camp, revolving instantly to depart from the region, that had been the scene of so great a misfortune to him."

When the old man had finished this narrative, his hearers unanimously with the exaction of one of Moss' companions, agreed that the narration was

---

1. Wonderful to relate or to report.

all a fiction. But he gave it as his unqualified opinion that it was true, and that if he was not under promise otherwise, that he could confirm it by undisputable evidence. After much persuasion from the company he gave a narrative of what he and his companions had seen, and they being interrogated, unanimously confirmed the report----

Friendship and Love
For R.K.M. (R. K. Meade – fellow Student)
November 22, 1837

Tis said that friendship's but a word
A wave of air, an empty name,
And Love, the fond affections, Lord,
Is but an evanescent flame
That flickers but a moment, then
"Delivers to empty air again"
      2nd
But where? Oh where? Now dwells the sage,
With bosom of Siberian snow,
Whose frigid tongue would teach this age
That all we feel, that all we know
Is like the twinkling rays that rise
From fields of ice in northern skies?
      3rd
If there be such upon the earth,
Who feel for all mankind alike,
Like woman never gave them birth;
For she a softer soul would strike
Even into the forms of steel, or stone
And make the earth born marble own
      4th
That Love and Friendship is the breath,
The life, the light, the sense, and soul
Of all mankind; nor even death
Has power these feelings can control;
For tis decreed when hence wage,
Friendship and Love, no end shall know!

John P. Waddill
&
Julia M. Barlow
Marriage
26th November 1840.

Marriage License of John and Julia Waddill

438

State of Louisiana } Know all men by these presents that we John Parish of Avoyelles } Pamplin Waddill of the Parish of Avoyelles and State aforesaid as principal and John L. Garrett also of the Parish of Avoyelles & State aforesaid as security are held and bound unto Gervais Baillio Parish Judge in and for the Parish of Avoyelles and his successors in Office in the sum of Two Hundred Dollars for the true and faithful payment whereof we bind ourselves our Heirs, Executors, Administrators and assigns firmly by these presents Signed with our hands at Hydropolis Avoyelles on this twenty fifth day of November Anno Domini Eighteen Hundred and forty. The Condition of the above obligation is Such that whereas the above bounden John Pamplin Waddill has this day applied to the aforesaid Parish Judge to Celebrate the bonds of matrimony between him and Miss Julia Melvina Barlow of this Parish.

Now therefore if there should hereafter appear to exist no legal impediment to the said marriage then the above obligation to be null and void otherwise to remain in full force and effect.

Signed and delivered at Hydropolis Avoyelles & State aforesaid in the presence of John W. B. Hens and D que Coco —

Witnesses —
Jno W. Hens
D que
" Coco

John P Waddill
John L. Garrett

438

State of Louisiana } Be it known that on this twenty sixth day
Parish of Avoyelles } of November Anno Domini eighteen hundred
and forty before me Gervais Baillio Parish Judge in and for the Parish
aforesaid and in presence of the witnesses hereinafter named and under-
-signed
    Personally came and appeared Mr. John Pamplin Waddill
of the Parish and State aforesaid of the one part and Miss Julia
Malvina Barlow also of the Parish and State aforesaid of the
other part who having fulfilled the formalities in such cases
required were by me at their request united in the Holy Estate
of Matrimony.
    In testimony whereof the said appearers have hereunto
affixed their names at the residence of Widow Fountain Barlow
on Red River in this Parish in presence of Messrs. Charles D. Brash-
-ear, William Edwards and William H. Duvall witnesses of full
age and domiciliated in this Parish who have signed with the said
appearers and me Judge aforesaid after lecture.
Witnesses
C. D. Brashear
Wm Edwards
Wm H. Duvall

John P. Waddill
J. M. Barlow

Gervais Baillio Par.
Judge

Marriage License of John and Julia Waddill

438

I hereby give my consent and approbation to the marriage contemplated between Mr. John P. Waddill and Miss Julia Malvina Barlow my minor daughter. In testimony whereof I hereunto affix my name at Avoyelles on this 26th day of November A. D. 1840.

E. Barlow

The first courthouse in Avoyelles

The Waddill Home

Estate of
Samuel Bass dec?

Proof of Last will
& testament—

Filed the 21st of Sept
1853.
J. M. Parker
C. M.

State of Louisiana }
Parish of Avoyelles }

Be it remembered that on this twenty first day of September Anno Domini One thousand Eight hundred and fifty three, pursuant to an order of the district Court in and for the aforesaid parish & State, based upon the petition for the probate of the last will and testament of Samuel Bass deceased.

I James H. Parker Clerk of the district Court in and for the said parish of Avoyelles, proceeded to take the proof of the death of said testator & of his last will and testament,

Whereupon came and appeared Mess.rs Alcibiade Derivas, John P. Waddill & Donat McEnery, as witnesses, whose testimony I have taken as follows to wit:

Alcibiade Derivas, being first duly Sworn, Says that he saw the testator Samuel Bass lay out dead, that he recognizes the testament presented to him as being the same which was written in his presence by John P. Waddill Esq. by the direction of the said testator, & which he declared to him contained his last will; that he recognizes his signature & that of the testator at the foot of said testament, & also those of the other subscribing witnesses, Said testament was read in an audible voice by the said John P. Waddill to the testator in presence of the witness & the other Subscribing witness was then Signed by said testator, by the witness himself & the other witnesses. The dictation, writing, reading and signing of said testament, were all done without interruption or turning aside to other acts.

The Said testator was at the time in the full enjoyment of his Senses

Sworn to & Subscribed before me on this 21st of September 1853
Ale(Derivas
J. H. Parbin
Ch. M.

John P. Waddill being next duly Sworn, deposeth & Saith, that he went to the burial of the testator Samuel Bass, That he recognizes the testament presented to him as being the same which he wrote out by the direction of said testator and which he declared to him contained his last will. He also recognizes his signature and that of the testator at the foot of the testament & also those of the subscribing witnesses. Said testament was then read by the witness to the testator & the other Subscribing witnesses, then signed by said testator, the witness himself & the other witnesses. The dictation, writing, reading and Signing, were all done without any interruption or turning aside to other acts. Said testator was at the time in the full enjoyment of his Senses.

Sworn to & Subscribed before me on the 21st of September 1853
John P. Waddill
J. H. Parbin
Ch. M.

And lastly came and appeared Donat
McEnery, who being duly sworn deposeth
& saith that Samuel Bass the testator is
dead, that he saw him lay out dead.
Witness further states that he recognizes
the testament presented to him as being the
same that was written in his presence by
John P. Waddill Esq. by the direction of
the said testator, & which he declared to
witness contained his last will, he also
recognizes his signature, that of the testator
& those of the other subscribing witnesses.
Said testament was read by the said
John P. Waddill to said testator in the presence
of the witness & the other subscribing witnesses
then signed by the testator, by the witness
& the other subscribing witnesses. The dictation
writing reading and signing were all
done without any interruption or turning
aside to other acts. Said testator was at
the time in the full enjoyment of his
senses.

Sworn to & subscribed before
me on this 21st of Septr.
1853.

Donat Mac Enery

J. H. Barbin
Clerk

And the said last will and testament having
been produced before me and the death of
Samuel Bass the testator being proved and the
execution of the said testament being also proved
by proof had of the signature of the deceased
& testator, to said will (being a nuncupative
one under private signature) by the deposition

of Macheade Dérivas, John P. Waddill & Donat McEnery, under oath all domiciliated in this parish and witnesses of full age, I proceed to read and did read the said testament in an audible and distinct voice to the said witnesses and other persons present and have signed it "Ne Varietur" at the beginning and end of each page.

It is therefore ordered and decreed that the said last will and testament be deposited in the office of the clerk of the district Court in and for the parish of Avoyelles that it be recorded & that the same be executed by William Sloat named therein as testamentary executor of said last will & testament.

Done and Signed at Marksville Avoyelles Louisiana, on the 21st day of September A.D. 1853

J. H. Barbin
Clerk

No. 2712.
Solomon Northup &c. &c.
Henry B Northup agent
vs
Edwin Epps.

Memorial Book C p. 274.

To the Honorable the Judge of the Thirteenth Judicial District Court holding sessions in and for the Parish of Avoyelles and State of Louisiana.

The petition of Solomon Northup a Citizen of Warren County and State of New York, & who is herein aided and assisted by Henry B. Northup, a Citizen of Washington County, State of New York, for said purpose duly appointed Agent on behalf of the People of said State of New York, as the law directs, by his Excellency Washinton Hunt, ~~Governor~~ Governor of the State of New York, which appointment is hereto annexed and referred to, most respectfully represents that said plaintiff Solomon Northup, is a free Mulator, Griffe or Colored person, about forty five years of age, born of free parents in the County of Washington and State of New York, one of the United States of America in which slavery at the time of the birth ~~nor ever~~ of said Solomon, nor since, did not exist, it being what is called a free State. Your petitioner the said Solomon alleges that about the year A.D. 1841 — being on business at the City of Washington District of Columbia, he was violently & fraudulently kidnapped and forced into the State of Louisiana against his will and consent, and there held in slavery, or to service as a Slave, wrongfully and fraudulently & contrary to law. ~~your petitioners further represent~~. Your petitioners further represent that since the year A.D. 1844 or thereabouts, one Edwin Epps a resident and Citizen of the Parish of Avoyelles has fraudulently & forcibly detained your petitioner the said Soloman Northup, in Servitude as a Slave, knowing him to be free, and said Epps has endeavoured to fraudulently conceal the name of the said Soloman one of your petitioner's by calling said Soloman, by the name of "platt". Your petitioners further represent that since the said Epps has had your petitioner so in his service, your petitioner's services are worth two thousand dollars, which your said petitioner Claim as wages and Damages, and two hundred dollars per month, or at that rate, for services and damages, until the said Soloman is decreed, & set free, from the time this suit is served. Your petitioner's further represent that they fear that the said Soloman one of these petitioners will be, by the Defendant, the said Epps concealed, parted with, disposed of, or misused, or sent out of the Jurisdiction of the Court, during the pendency of this suit, unless sequestered judicially and retained in the hands and possession of the Sheriff, until this suit is decided. They allege amicable demand without effect.

Wherefore the premises considered your petitioners pray that Edwin Epps the said Defendant be legally cited to answer hereto, and after legal proceeding had that your petitioner the said Solomon Northup, be legally ~~citen to~~ decreed to be a free and independant person and discharged from the control of said Defendant; and further that he have judgment against said Epps for the said sum of two thousand Dollars for his services, and as damages, up to the filing of this Suit, and judgment at the rate of two hundred Dollars per month from the filing hereof until said Soloman is releaded, or declared free by the judgment of the court. & They pray your Honorable court for judgment for costs, & for general relief &c. ~~And they said Henry B Northup further prays that And~~ they further pray that the said Soloman be judicially sequestered and held within the possession of the sheriff, until the decission of this suit, as the law directs

John P. & W Waddill
Attornies for petitioners

I am security for costs
John P Waddill

State of Louisiana } Soloman & Henry B
Parish of Avoyelles } Northup vs Edwin Epps

Personally before me the undersigned authority came, Henry B Northup a plaintiff in the above entitled suit, who being duly sworn declares he fears and believes that Edwin Epps the defendant in this Suit, will conceal, part with, or dispose of, or abuse, or send out of the Jurisdiction of the Court the said Solomon, (who has in this Suit, claimed his freedom from Slavery,) before this said Suit can be determined, and during the pendency thereof; and he further deposes that he do desires the said Solomon to be Sequestered and held in the possession of the Sheriff until duly discharged by the court as the law directs.

Henry B Northup

Sworn to and subscribed before me this 3d day of January 1853. Ralph Cushman Judge 13th District.

Upon reading the foregoing petition and the law authorizing the same. Let a sequestration issue as prayed for the plaintiff giving bond and good security in the sum of five hundred dollars conditioned according to law   Done & signed at chambers at Avoyelles La this 3d January 1853

Ralph Cushman Judge 13th District

Solomon Northup f.m.c. & } 13th Judicial District
Henry B. Northup agent&c } Court
vs } Parish of Avoyelles
Edwin Epps } Apl term 1853.

In the above entitled suit the plaintiffs by their Counsel, having moved the Court for a dismissal alleging that the matter in dispute had been settled; It is, by reason thereof, ordered adjudged & decreed, that the same be dismissed at plaintiffs Costs.

Done and Signed in open Court on this 22nd day of April A.D. 1853.

Ralph Cushman
Judge 13th District

Filed the 22nd of April 1853.

The State of Louisiana
To the Sheriff of the Parish of Avoyelles

Greeting

Whereas Solomon Northup a citizen of Warren County and State of New York and who is herein aided and assisted by Henry B. Northup, agent, a citizen of Washington County, State of New York, has filed in the office of the Clerk of the District Court in and for the Parish of Avoyelles his certain petition of complaint against Edwin Epps praying, among other things, that an order of Sequestration may issue for himself the said Solomon Northup

And whereas the said Solomon Northup by the said Henry B. Northup has filed his bond and complied with the formalities of the law in such cases

Now therefore you the said Sheriff are hereby commanded to seize and sequester the said Solomon Northup and him safely keep in your custody until further orders by said Court.

Given under my hand and official seal at Marksville Avoyelles this 3rd day of January 1853

J. H. Parker
Clerk

Received 3rd January 1853 and on the same day month and year, after serving a copy of the petition and citation and a copy hereof on Edwin Epps, I sequestered and took into my possession a mulatto (or Griff) named Solomon Northrop aged about Forty five years

G. P. Voorhies Sh'ff

Solomon Northrop
Henry B. Northrop agt
Dr. S. Sequestrato
Edwin Epps

Original Petition to Free Soloman Northup

THE STATE OF LOUISIANA.

Solomon Northup and
Henry B. Northup *agent*
vs
Edwin Epps

13th **Judicial District Court,**
Parish of Avoyelles.

To Edwin Epps, of the Parish of Avoyelles:

YOU are hereby summoned to comply with the demand contained in the petition, of which a copy accompanies this citation, or deliver your answer thereto in the office of the Clerk of the District Court, in and for the Parish of Avoyelles, at Marksville, in *twelve* days after the service hereof. WITNESS the Honorable Ralph Cushman, Judge of the said Court, this *third* day of *January* A. D. 1852.

J. W. B. Barbin
Clerk.

The "Banner" is published every Saturday in French and English by Robert Wilson, in Franklin, Parish of St. Mary. (La.)

Terms:—Four Dollars payable in advance; Four Dollars and a half at the end of six months; Five Dollars at the expiration of the year.

AMBROISE LACOUR,
Agent for Avoyelles Parish.

Runaway in Jail.—Was committed to the jail of the Parish of Avoyelles, on the 17th inst, two negro men, who says they belong to a Mr. Charles Mulhollen, living near Bayou Bœf in the Parish of Rapide, viz:

JOHN—aged about 35 years, dark complexion, 5 feet 7 or 8 inches high.

ABRAHAM—aged about 26 years, light complexion, 5 feet 7 or 8 inches high.

The owner of said slaves is requested to come forward prove property, pay charges and take them out of jail, or they will be disposed of according to law.

F. EDWARDS, Jailor.
Marksville, Sept. 23, 1843.

NOTICE.—Parish of Avoyells, Court of Probates.—*Succession of Marie Dupuy deceased.*—Notice is hereby given to all heirs, claimants and other persons interested, to show cause within ten days from this publication, why the account of administration of said estate filed in said court of Probates by Laurent Dupuis ad-

WILL attend to all business ed to their care in the Courts of this and the adjoining Parishes—the Supreme Court at Alexandria, and the United States District Court at Opelousas. Office at Marksville.

JOHN P. WADDILL,
Attorney and Counsellor at Law.
OFFICE AT MARKSVILLE.

WILLIAM BISHOP,
Attorney and Counsellor at Law,
MARKSVILLE, AVOYELLES.

EDELEN & BRIGGS,
ATTORNIES AT LAW.

THE undersigned have entered into partnership, and will practice their profession in Rapides, Avoyelles, and the adjoining Parishes.

JAMES S. EDELEN,
Office at Alexandria.
SAMUEL W. BRIGGS.
Office at Marksville.

H. BAGARLY,
U. STATES DEPUTY SURVEYOR
RESIDENCE—Bordeaux Post Office, Avoyelles, La.

SEABORN D. JONES,
PARISH AND UNITED

INDEX

A

Adams, John Quincy, 43, 171
Adams, Thomas C., 236, 260
Adolph (Waddill slave), 214
Afro-Louisiana Historical and Genealogical Society, 318
Alexander, Solomon, 260
Alexander, Mrs. (Julia Waddill's mother), 191, 221, 259, 309. *See also* Duke, Mrs. E.
Alexander, William A., 218, 221–23, 232–33, 237, 247–48, 259, 265, 290, 300–2, 304
Alexandria, La., 64–65, 115, 245; post office, 121–22
Alfred Kearney & Co., 237
Algiers, La., 172
Ardry, Leander F., 249
Arista, Gen. Mariano, 138–39
A. Rivarde & Co., 135
Armstrong, A. C., 127, 223
Atchafalaya River, 5, 122–23, 159
Augusta College, xi, 7, 58, 66; B.F. Power Home, 66; debates at, 23, 26, 39, 75, 83; Echo Hall, 66; end of Waddill's education, 55; founding of, 7–9; politics, 34; recreation, 22, 41, 44; religion, 29, 47
Avery, D., 272
Avoyelles Parish, 91, 159, 300; Anglo population, 118; Archives, xii, 113; and Mexican War, 136; transportation, 117; Tourism Commission, 318
Ayish Bayou, 73, 208
Aymond, John Pierre, 206
Aymond, P. J., 302

B

Backer, W. 194
Baillio, Gervais, 96, 99, 102, 128, 223
Ball, J. W., 221
Barbin, Aristide, 127, 205–6, 220, 233, 304
Barbin, F. B., 156, 221
Barbin, James H., 127, 137, 297
Barbin, Marie Angela, 103
Barlow, Fountain, 99
Barlow, Henerie L., 197
Barlow, James H. C., 133, 156, 201, 206, 209, 214, 222, 236, 290
Barlow, Julia Malvina, 99, 249. *See also* Waddill, Julia Malvina Barlow
Barlow, Mary Jane, 233, 259, 262, 272, 290
Barnard, Elizabeth Jane Brand, 194
Barnard, J. G., 246
Barron, George, 159–60, 243, 289
Barry, Patrick, 191
Bartell, Augustus, 232, 235–36, 260
Bass, Catherine, 276
Bass, Ellen, 318
Bass, Martha, 276
Bass, Samuel: death, 276, 293; friendship with Waddill, 216–17, 269; and slavery, 216, 250, 270, 274; Northup case, 273–74, 277–81; work on Waddill home, 213, 220, 229, 238, 269; will, 275–76, 293
Bassett, William H., 270
Baton Rouge Advocate newspaper, 205
Battle of New Orleans, 199
Bayou Boeuf, 109–10, 119, 190, 192, 247, 273, 278–79, 285
Bayou Boutte, 138, 140; floods, 207

Bayou Clair, 111, 117
Bayou Courtableau, 5
Bayou des Glaises, 150, 187, 218, 247, 250, 288, 297, 301; flooding, 148, 241; naviagion of, 170; plantations, 106, 119, 296; Waddill property, 176, 192, 208
Bayou du Lac, 113, 223, 253
Bayou Huffpauir, 274, 286
Bayou Rouge, 119, 148, 189, 217, 224, 243, 257, 262, 286, 303–4; Baptist Church, 286
Bayou Sara, 202, 220
Bee newspaper (New Orleans), 145, 173
Bellevue Plantation, 92. *See also* Fairmount Plantation
Bell, James M., 196
Bell, John M., 170
Bell, Joseph W., 117
Bell Tavern, 127
Bell, Thomas, 213
Benjamin, J. P., 242
Benoist, Frels, 144
Benton, Thomas H., 71
Beridon, Louis, 203
Berlin, George, 294, 297
Bingham, Gideon, 209
Bishop, William M., 96, 98, 117–18, 137, 159–60, 212
Black Hawk War, 64
Blackwood's Magazine, 266–67
Blagrave, Elizabeth, 72
Blair, Francis, 69
Bland, Maxwell W., 58
Bledsoe, James T., 2, 4
Boifsielle, Pam, 129
Bonnett, Joseph, 224
Bonnett, Louis, 117, 297
Borde, F., 307
Bordelon, Adelaide, 289
Bordelon, Appolinair, 222
Bordelon, Gilbert, 159–60
Bordelon, Louis, 169, 187, 272

Bordelon, Marcelin, 205, 214, 243
Bordelon, Norbert, 232
Bordelon, St. James, 289
Bordelon, Sylvert, 243
Bordelon, Valery, Jr., 220
Bordelon, Victorin, Jr., 214
Bordelonville, La., 103
Botts, Maj. John, 119, 219–20
Botts, Mary, 219
Bouner, Willis, 294
Boutte-de-Bayou, 138, 140. *See also* Bayou Boutte
Bowman, Robert, 287
Boyce, Henry, 129
Boyer, Jacques Amedee, 194
Boyer, John H,. 253, 272, 287
Branch, Leroy K., 103, 145
Brand, Anna, 147–48
Brand, Anne G. Browder, 194
Brand, Frederick, 148
Brand, Jane E., 148, 246
Brand, William, 147–48, 194, 246
Brashear, Charles Duval (C. D.), 99–100, 102, 118, 127, 129, 160, 191, 213, 232–33
Brashear, Eliza Caroline Pearce, 118, 191
Brashear, W., 170
Brazelton, Elbert C., 316
Brazelton, Elizabeth, xvi, 316, 318
Bress Frellsen & Co., 249
Brewski, James, 94
Briggs, E. L., 128, 150, 191; death, 138–40, 143–44, 149
Briggs, Samuel W., 99–100, 150–51
British Imperial Act (1833), 216
Broussard, Valery, 213–14
Broussard, Mahali, 214
Browder, Anne G., 148, 194
Browder, Bartlett Milton, 147
Browder, Elizabeth Pamplin, 1
Browder, Frederick Avery, 1, 147
Browder, J. J., 147
Browder, Narcissa J. Hewelette, 147

Index 357

Brown, William, 287
Bryce, L. G., 170
Bryce, J. Y., 190
Buena Vista, Mexico, 165
Burroughs, James, 94
Butler, William O., 183
Bynum, Jessee A., 294

C

Caillteau, Eugene, 102
Calhoun, John C., 27, 38, 122
California, 143, 191, 233
Callegari, Jerome, 206
Callihan, Young, 117
Cappel, Agnes, 308
Cappel, Jaques Aristide, 308
Cappell, Charles, 119
Carmouche, Clement, 221
Carrigan, James N., 272
Carroll, Timothy, 287
Carrollton Bank, 98, 128, 300–301
Cartwright, John, 208
Cartwright, Polly Cruchfield, 208
Casou, Caroline C., 241
Casou, Fanntarie W., 241
Casou, Francis Marthas, 241
Casou, Susan Elizabeth, 241
Casou, W. L., 241–42
The Caspian (steamboat), 255
Cass, Ellen Bass, 276
Cass, John, 318
Cass, Lewis, 183, 242
Catahoula Parish, 5, 72
Catalpa Grove Plantation, 190
Cazabat, Alphonse, 217
Chabert, Leon, 145, 208
Chalybeate Springs, 223
Chambers, Robert, 181
Chapman, Joseph, 125
Chapman, Mary Ann, 125–26
Charrier, Louis, 206
Chaze, Emile, 198
Cheneyville, La., 110, 190, 286

Childress, Anna, 222
Childress, Berlin, 222
Childress, Minerva, 222
Childress, Nancy, 222
Choate, Nancy Ann, 209
cholera, 198, 263, 291
Cilley, Jonathan, 70
The Citizen newspaper (New York), 308
Civil Code of Louisiana, 92
Clapp, Theodore, 216
Clark, Daniel, 94, 98
Clay, Clement Comer, 71
Clay, Henry, 42–43, 184
Clayton, John M., 193
Cleona (steamboat), 257
Clopton, William, 111, 138, 243
Cocke, Joseph Addison, 109
Coco, Adolph D., 206, 272, 297
Coco, Aurelien B. Dominique, 220, 248, 293; election, 163, 174, 205–6, 227, 235; funeral, 236; land, 117; murder, 235–35, 238, 259–60, 263, 287
Coco, Eugenie, 293
Coco, Ferdinand B., 206
Coco, Julianna, 262
Coco, Lucien D., 262
Collamer, Jacob, 193
Comanche Indians, 135
Combe, George, 24, 181
Common Law, 92
Compromise of 1850, 96
Connell, Terrence O., 197
Conner, William, 225
The Constitution of Man (Combe), 24
Constitutional Convention: of 1845, 242, 254, 256–57, 265; election, 126–27
Cooley, Thomas J., 199
Cooper & Co., 223
corn, 3, 5, 125, 133, 145, 148, 176, 192, 198, 213–15, 218, 221, 237, 243–44, 247, 249

Cosden, J. H., 96
cotton, xi, 3, 5, 78, 148, 176, 198, 207–8, 213, 219, 232, 238, 276, 285, 305
Cotton, John B., 255
Cottonport, La., 127
Couvillion, Adrienne, 289
Couvillion, Arsenne, 289
Couvillion, Augustin, 289
Couvillion, Edmond, 263
Couvillion, Gregoire, 289
Couvillion, L. H., 304
Couvillion, Marie, 241
Couvillion, Marin, 235
Couvillion, Marrinett Mayeux, 289
Couvillion, Martin, 227, 297
Couvillion, Olive, 289
Couvillion, Olivier, 289
Couvillion, Gen. Pierre, 95, 122, 126, 134, 161, 173, 232, 237, 241–42, 262, 289
Couvillion, Rose, 289
Couvillion, Sosthene, 227, 235
Couvillion, Sylvert, 289
C. Pasquier & Co., 257
Crawford, George H., 193
Crawford, James E.: suit, 116
Creole, 136, 155; in Avoyelles, 136, 159, 162, 262; Catholics, 160
Crittenden, John Jordan, 71
Cross, Elizabeth, 271
Cross, William, 271
Crouch, Winder, 195
Cuba, 228
Culbertson, Thomas "Doc," Jr., 309–10
Cullom, E. N., 263
Cullom, Francis, 117, 148, 231, 263
Cullom, Mary, 231
Cumberland: College in Kentucky, 64; Presbyterian Church, 64
Cushman and Waddill firm, 95, 97–98
Cushman, Marjorie, 247
Cushman, Ralph, 135–36, 160, 231, 247, 267, 315; as judge, 154, 191, 214, 277, 282; lawyer, 94, 98, 128; in politics, 122, 295–97; as Waddill law partner, 95–97, 118
Cushman, Walter, 247
Custard, Mary, 219

D

Daily True Delta newspaper (New Orleans), 197
Daily Union newspaper (Washington, D.C.), 197
Dauzat, Raphael, 170
Dauzat, Valaire, 170, 263
Davezac, Auguste, 199
Davies, M., 141
Davis, H. Colombe, 168
Davis, Horatio, 168
Davis, William E., 305
Davis, Sophronia, 305
Deaver, John N., 217
DeBellvue, François B., 95, 97, 113, 118, 133, 195
Debouche, Joseph, 119
DeClouet, Alexandre Etienne, 208
Decuir, François, 128
Decuir, Marcelline, 218
deGeirisie, Edward, 313
Dellman (steamboat), 287
Democratic: Association for the Parish of Avoyelles, 173; Convention, 223, 227; party of Avoyelles, xii, 121, 189, 205; Regular Party, 265–66
Democratic Review, 201, 271
Derivas, Alcibiade, 197, 267, 276, 297
Descant, Sean, 303–4
Deshautelle, Julien, 137, 163, 174, 206, 267
Desoto Parish, La., 115
Desselle, Basil, 206
Dever, David, 150
Devers, J. B., 137

Donald, O. M., 313
Downs, Solomon W., 241–42
Dubroc, François, 232
Dugouf, John, 242
Duke, Bailey C., 192
Duke, E. Jane, 215, 218, 259
Duke, Mrs. E. (Julia Waddill's mother), 135, 191, 207, 218, 221. *See also* Alexander, Mrs.
Duke, Spencer Mayo, 259
Duke, W., 135
Dulany, Benjamin Tasker, 105, 198
Dupuy, Belizuire, 297
Dupuy, Laudrent, 119
Durand, A., 307
Durand, Nelson, 128, 248
Durell, Edward H., 245
Duvall, William H., 99, 118, 189, 195, 249

E

Eakin, Sue, xvi
East Carroll Parish, La., 147
Edelen & Briggs, 118
Edelen, James L., 224
Edelen, James S., 96, 249
Edgar, Hugh W., 135, 137
Edinburgh Review, 266–67
education: in Avoyelles Parish, 110, 127, 185, 232–33, 246, 299–300; manual labor system, 65; Waddill's early, 2, 4, 7, 12. *See also* Augusta College
Edwards and Conner sawmill, 213
Edwards, Fielding, 191, 195, 231, 261; as alderman, 118; as business partner, 129, 154, 224; as courier, 189–90, 195, 215, 220, 222, 249–50
Edwards, Hayden, 235
Edwards, Henrietta, 191
Edwards, William, 99, 113, 144, 176, 197, 203, 225, 263; and Gorton murder, 154–55; as sheriff, 102; Whig party, 296
Egana, Juan Y. de, 190
Egan, Eugene, 174
Elam, Edward, 72
Elam, John Pamplin, 5, 7, 71–72
Elam, John Waddill, 115–16
Elam, Joseph Barton, 115, 128
Elam, William Jefferson, 71, 73, 115
Eldred, Daniel R., 111, 243, 259, 288, 300–301
Eleventh Brigade, 95
Elgee, John K., 144–45, 190–91
Ellinckuysen, Angelina, 195
Ellinckuysen, Pierre, 195
Elmer, G. E., 103–4, 231, 233, 250, 301, 305–6
Elred, Daniel R., 110
Ely, Mary, 247
Epps, Edwin, 111, 273, 281–82, 285
Eustis, George, 228
Evans, H. B., 214
Ewell, John, 288
Ewing, Thomas H., 71, 193
Expositor newspaper (Marksville), xvii, 117–18

F

Fairmount Plantation, 5
Farmer, W. W., 272
Farrar, Preston W., 167, 169, 214
Fauquier, Elizabeth, 313
Ferguson, James, 183
Ferguson, Roderic, 261
Fillmore, Millard, 184, 189
Fisher, Amos, 243
Flag Land Plantation, 5, 91–92
Flint, E. H., 223
Flint, James F., 229
Flint, James T., 272, 294
Fogelman, Michael, 151
Fort Jesup, 73, 115
Fortier, Alcée, 254

Foster, E. Lumins, 197, 201
Foster, William H., 306
Foulk's Landing, 135, 290, 302
Frank, Adolph, 286
Franklin, Benjamin, 42
Frazee, Calvin A., 307
Free Soil Party, 193, 310–11
French, David, 250
Frith, John E., 117, 215, 235–36, 260, 263, 287
Fugitive Slave Law, 96

G

Galligher, William, 248
Garcon, John Bon, 174
Gaspard, Baptiste, 117
Gauthier, Leon, 297
Gauthier, Marius, 195
Gayarré, Charles Étienne Arthur, 265–67
Generes, Ed, 127
Generis, John L., 154, 156, 222, 233
Glass, Frances, 241
Glaze, Gideon M., 197
Gober, William, 290
Gollighar, William, 137
Goodwin, Sally, 249
Gorgey, Arthur, 206
Gorton, Lewis, 115, 119–20, 122, 128, 213; murder, 153–56
Gorton's Landing, 119, 121–22, 148, 153, 213, 249–50, 261, 276, 288, 309
Goudeau, Don Louis, 232
Goudeau, Henrietta Edwards, 218
Goudeau, Julien Jules, 217–18, 262
Gould, Victor, 94
Goux, Clair, 206
Goux, John B., 215, 288
Goux, S. N., 286
Graham, William A., 267
Grand Bend Plantation. *See* Fairmount Plantation

Graves, Jane Brockenbrough, 75
Graves, William, 70
Gray, Abraham M., 272
Gray's Creek, La., 237
Gremillion, Valerien, 117
Greneaux, Charles E., 272
Griffin, Amanda: suit, 116
Griffin, James B., 111
Griffin, Mary A., 111
Griffin, Thomas M., 288
Griffin, William F., 111, 115, 194, 286–87; election, 163, 174, 206, 227, 235, 272, 291; land, 216; politics, 295–97, 305; slaves, 243; sugarcane, 176, 301
Grimball, Johnson P., 248
Guillot, George, 133
Guillot, Joseph, 145, 233
Guillot, Zenon G., 267
Guviller, Alexander, 169

H

Hadspeth, Joel, 128
Hadspetth, Samuel W., 128
Hagains, H. M., 229
Hallberg, Rev. Charles J., 271, 246, 250, 288
Hannegan, Edward A., 196
Haralson, Archibald D. M., 197
Harmanson, John Henry, 122, 175, 183, 198, 201, 213, 227, 289
Harper's Magazine, 262
Harvey, Hiram, 287
Hatcher, Charles F., 306
Havard, Elizabeth V., 259
Havard, Henry Monroe, 202–3
Havard, John A., 202, 214
Havard, Louisa, 203
Havard, Monroe, 117
Hebert, Gov. Paul O., 272, 285, 300
Hegel's Science of Logic, 66
Heliopolis (boat), 95
Henarie, Samuel King, 209

Henarie, Samuel W., 98, 221, 245, 259, 300
Henarie, William, 209
Heron, A. L., 272
H. Frellsen & Co., 189–90, 194, 237, 249
Hickman brothers, 5, 12, 92, 209
Hickman, Peter, 5
Hickman, Terry, 5
Hickman, Thomas J., 50, 56, 73, 87, 93–94, 173, 209, 246; death, 295; plantation, 5, 7; suits, 149; as Waddill benefactor, 12, 91–92, 131, 220
Hickman, William P., 5, 92; Hickman and Martin partnership, 94
The History of Avoyelles Parish (Saucier), xvi
History of Louisiana (Gayarré), 254, 265
Hitchborn, Freeman P., 135–37, 176, 182–83, 192, 288–91, 300
Hodge, Amahl, 318
Hollenback, John G., 137
Holmesville, La., 119, 281
Howard, James Elihu, 100, 161–62
Howard, Joyce Holmes, 162
Hudson, H. Claude, 276, 318
Hudson, Thadius, 276
Huie, Green, 272, 290, 309
Huish, Robert, 49
Humphreys, Samuel I., 41
Hurricane Creek, 110
Hydropolis, La., 122, 133, 223, 247, 292–93

I

Iberville Parish, La., 7
Indian population, 222
Ireland, 96
Irma (Waddill slave), 214
Isaacs, Andrew J., 236, 254, 290

J

Jackson, Andrew, xii, 27, 69, 71, 199, 302; administration, 42, 84–86; Democrat, 265; Expunging Resolution, 27
Jackson, Eileen, 318
Jackson, Evelyn, 318
Jackson, Thomas, 137
Jacquelin, Pierre, 129
Jefferson College, 127
Jefferson Literary Society, 23
Joffrion, Joseph, 160–61, 213, 253, 294, 297
Joffrion, Olympe, 194
John, G., 302
Johnson, Cave, 193
Johnson, Barnard, 125
Johnson, Reverdy, 193
Jones, Samuel, 117
Junto Club, 42–43

K

Kavenaugh, Hubbard H., 50
Kay, Benoist W., 228, 237
Kay, Charles, 263
Kay, Cordelia, 263
Kay, Leona, 263
Kay, Mary, 263
Kay, Pamela, 263
Kay, R. W., 174, 261, 263, 288
Keary, Hugh M., 190–91, 194
Keary, W. V., 190
Keller, George, 117
Kenner, Duncan F., 169–70, 172–73, 255
Ker, Robert J., 168
Kilpatrick, Andrew R., 104
Kimball, Alexander, 137
Kimball, Ann A., 224
Kimball, Thomas H., 205–6, 223–24
King, Edward, 94
King, John E., 297

King, W. R., 250
Kirk, J. B., 307
Kirk, John, 221, 269
Kirk, Joseph, 211
Kirkwood Plantation, 211
Kossuth, Louis, 206

L

Labadie, Jean, 129
Labadie, John, 129
Lafargue, Adolphe D., 127–28, 235, 267, 304, 307, 314
Lake Pearl, 170
Lambeth, William M., 289
LaMothe, Jeannette Poiret, 249
Landry, Frasimond, 170
Lane, Lydia Catlin, 275–76
Leake, John A., 41
Leckie Robert & Co., 215
Leckie, W. R., 300
Ledoux, Asmaron, 97–98
Lee, John, 94–95
Leglise, Pierre, 248
Lemoine, Zenon, 121
Lerethe, John, 224
Le Villagois newspaper (Marksville), 118. *See also The Villager*
Lewis, A. G., 95
Lippard, George, 144
Little River, 72, 292
Little Tour (steamboat), 233
Livingston, Edward, 199
Logsdon, Joseph, xvii
Louisiana Constitutional Convention, xii, 126–27, 238, 242, 253, 260, 269
Louisiana Democrat, 296, 313
Louisiana Militia, 95, 106, 134, 156, 254
Louisiana State Seminary of Learning and Military Academy, 300
Loyola University, 318
L. Sperier Hardware, 129

Lyceum Movement, 8
Lynch, William, 113

M

MacEnery, Donat, xix, 107, 196, 215, 218, 222, 237, 267, 276, 293, 302
MacEnery, James, 195–96, 233
MacEnery, Lucetta, 107
Madam Maillet's Corner, 137
Maillet, Julien Baptiste, 206, 259
Mangum, Willie, 311
Mansfield, La., 116
Mansura, La., 138, 159, 205–6, 227, 267, 294, 296–97
Marcelle, Enoch, 248
Marcottt, Margueritte, 99
Marcy, W. L., 193
Marge, A., 137
Marksville, La.: Academy, 217–18, 299; City Council, xii, xv, 127; commerce, 56, 95; incorporation, 101, 118–19; mail delivery, 121–22, 174–75, 197, 201; Protestant Church, 248, 266; Volunteers, 182
Marshall, Brant, 222
Marshall, James Horace, 249
Marshall, Eliza Eugenia Pearce, 249
Marsolla, Josephine Coral, 105
Martin, Aunis, 276
Martin, David, 294, 296
Mary (Waddill slave), 237, 306–7
Masons, 237–38, 245–46
Mason, John Y., 193
Matamoras, Mexico, 132–33, 136, 139, 143, 149
Matthew, Cartwright, 208
Mayeaux, Louis H., 205–7
Mayer, Alfred, 233
Mayeux, Celeste, 289
Mayeux, Louis H., 227
Mayeux, Joseph, 289
Mayeux, Marienett, 242, 289

Index 363

Mayeux, Pierre, 289
McCall, Daniel, 137
McCauley, James, 243
McClintick, W. J., 63
McCown, Burr H., 50
McDonald, George T., 75
McDowell, John, 217, 228, 299–300; School, 228, 232–33, 246
McDowell, William, 296
McElroy, James, 218
McElroy, William W., 218
McEnery, James, 107
McEnery, Samuel Douglas, 107
McMahon, Thomas, 242
McWhorter, George C., 173, 272
Meade, Richard Kidder "R. K.," 75
measles, 214, 307
Mechanic's Bank, 98
Medical Institute of Louisville, 103
Meindillon, Jacques, 197
Meridith, William, 193
Methodist, 7–8, 58, 216, 247, 290
Meuillon, Enemund, 249
Mexican-American War, xii, 106, 133–35, 138–40, 143, 149, 166–67, 170, 182
Mexico, 80, 131, 172, 183; Army of, 139, 166
Miles, Lemuel, 183
Miles, Nancy, 241
Miley (Augusta student), 76, 79–80, 83
Millen, J., 195
Milligan, Angelina, 195
Milligan, Russell, 195
Milligan, Stephen Franklin, 191, 233
Milligan, Stephen H., 137
Milligan, William, 137
Mills, Clemment, 137
Mississippi River, 122, 198
Missouri Compromise, 229
Mitchel, John, 308
Mock, Oliver, 250, 259
Moncla, Joseph, 106

Moncla, L., 248
Montanye, A.: suit, 115
Moore, Thomas O., 235, 294
Morde, Isaac E., 272
Moreau, August, 117
Moreau, C., 156
Morris, Mahali, 213–14
Morrow, A. G., 297
Morrow, John, 98
Murdock, David M., 106, 196
Murray, James F., 309
Myrtle Grove Plantation, 290

N

Nashville Female Seminary, 65
Neal, Meriday, 294
Neal, Mitchell, 272, 296
Nelson, Hugh, 241
Nestor, Aaron S., 97
New Hope Plantation, 5
New Orleans & Carrollton Rail Road Co., 128–29, 150
New Orleans Canal and Banking, 190
New Orleans, La., 172; convention, 100, 122, 126–27; mercantile trade, 135; population, 96; Port, 228
newspapers, 183, 185, 201, 205; Waddill advertising, 119
Normand, John Pierre, 249
Normand, Oliver, 198
Normand, Pierre, 99–100, 128, 153
Normand's Landing, 195, 231, 237
Norment, Cooper & Co., 223
North Bend Plantation. *See* Fairmount Plantation
North British Review, 266
North Carolina Railroad, 306
Northup, Henry, 273–74, 277–78, 281
Northup, Solomon, xii, 273, 279, 316–18; freeing, 168, 275–78, 281, 283, 319; kidnapping, 274
Norwich University, 147

O

Oakwold Plantation, 96, 117, 224, 274, 285–86
Ogden, R. N., 272
Ohio River, xi, 31, 41
Oliver Lodge (Alexandria, La.), 237, 245
O'Neal, Louis M., 205–6
Opelousas, La., 106, 247; district court, 118; mail, 122; Methodist Church, 224; Railroad, 262
O'Quin, John, 294, 297
Oregon, 143, 193
Orr, Daniel T., 119–20, 128; plantation, 117
Overton, John H., 262, 316
Overton, Mary Elizabeth, 316
Overton, Thomas, 316

P

Paine, Thomas, 144
Pamplin, Jane, 72
Pamplin, Robert, 72
Parker, Cephas, 277
Patrick Henry Junto Club, 42, 75–76. *See also* Junto Club
Paxton, Elenzer G., 113
Payne and Harrison merchants, 291–92
Pearce, Alanson Green, 96–97, 117, 224, 249, 285–86, 288, 308; as planter, 96; and Northup, 274; as tutor, 110–11, 217
Pearce, Joshua, 196, 249
Pearce, Malvina, 249
Pearce Plantation, 274
Pearce, Sally Goodwin, 195
Pearce, Sidney Elizabeth Kay, 249
Pearce, Stephen, 195, 249
Pearce, Susan Heddingrant, 195
Pearce, William, 111, 117, 274, 286
Penn, Alexander G., 224, 227, 235
Perades, Mariano, 139, 143
Perkins, Septhinus M., 111
Perry, William, 277
Phillip, Louis, 171
Phillips, Eliza, 215
Phillips, Henry, 169
Phillips, John M., 137, 154
Phillips, Monroe, 153–54, 156
phrenology, 17, 25, 181
Picayune newspaper (New Orleans), 122, 129, 153, 186
Pierce, Franklin, 250, 267
Pista (steamboat), 309
Pittman, Lemuel, 285
Pittman, Susan M., 285
Pitts, Frances Bernard, 289
Plain Dealing, La., 223
Platt, 273, 277, 279, 281. *See also* Northup, Soloman
Pluncket, John, 135, 137
Point Maigre, La., 118–19, 207, 267
Polk, James K., 193, 196
Pond, Preston, 297
Porter, Thomas C., 170, 228, 235
Post Boy (steamboat), 245
Poster, E. J., 185
Prairie Star newspaper (Marksville), 185, 201
Prescott, Willis B., 126
Preston, Judge Isaac Trimble, 229, 262
Preston, William B., 70, 193
Princeton Theological Seminary, 64
Prostdamme, J. O., 307
Protestant, 159–60, 245, 299

R

Rabalais, Evariste, 121–22, 148
Rabalais, Martin, 236, 297
Rabalais, Rose, 128
Ralph, Thomas L., 239
Randolph Colomb Plantation, 5
Ransdell, J., 95
Ray, John, 272
Rebouché, Victor, 135–37
Recoully, Pierre, 304

Redmond, David J., 135, 137
Red River, 91, 95, 121–22, 159, 207; flooding, 118, 123, 133; plantations, xi
Reid, David, 311
Rey, James, Jr., 97, 101, 113, 118, 133, 262, 308
Reynaud, E., 218, 286
Reynolds, M. M., 170
Richard (Waddill slave), 192, 215, 221, 237, 260–61, 276, 287
Riche, Sosthene, 205–6
Ricord, Fabius, 122, 127, 155, 182, 192, 195, 227, 249, 286, 297
Ricoulie, Pierre, 302
Ricouly, Claude, 313
Ricouly, Eugene, 313
Ricouly, Louise 313
Ricouly, Narcisse, 313
Rio Bravo. *See* Rio Grande
Rio Grande, 134–36, 138, 183
Rives, Francis, 69–70
Robert, Franklin Agrippa, 109–11, 300–301
Robert, Grimball Addison, 286
Robert, Joseph B., 109–11
Robert, Leckie, 221
Robert, Mary A. Griffin, 109
Robert, Sarah A., 217, 301
Robert, Sarah Evolina, 109–11
Robert, Sarah Jane, 224
Robert, Wilson C., 111
Roberts, Mary, 99
Robertson, Edward White, 7
Robincott, C. N., 137
Robinson, John, 135, 137, 231
Robinson, Laura M., 202
Robinson, Mary Jane, 191
Robinson, Margarette, 191
Robinson, Orin, 196
Robinson, Rowland, 115, 231, 248
Robinson, William, 301
Rockaway #2 (steamboat), 220

Romeo (steamboat), 224
Rose, David, 287
Rost, Pierre A., 229
Roy, Leandre, 159–60
Roy, L. F., 307
Rust, Jeremiah T., 2
Ryan, Michael, 110, 254, 294–97

S

Sabine Parish, La., 115–16
Sadler, G., 286
Sanders, G. N., 271
Sanders, William S. H., 91
Santa Anna, 80, 139, 143, 150, 165–66
Sasser, Whitely M., 245
Satterfield, Edward Henderson, 248, 307
Satterfield, Tammy, 248
Saturday Evening Post, 262
Saunders, L., 134–35
Saunders, Neal Lafayette, 199
Scallan, Ellen, 206
Schoolfield, W., 58
Scott, George, 213–14
Scott, Leonard, 294
Scott, Thomas L., 145
Scott, Windfield, 267
Scott, William A., 64–65, 213
Second Seminole War (1835–1842), 39
Selser, N. R., 176
Selser, Rachael, 199
Seminary for Young Ladies at Winchester, 64
Servius, A., 136
Seventeenth U.S. Infantry, 156
Sevier, Ambrose Hundley, 172
Sherman, William Tecumseh, 300
Shreve, Henry, 95
Shreve's Cut Off, 211
Sibley, R. H., 253
Simmes, Bennett Barton, 95, 98, 100, 117, 159–60, 210, 254
Simmesport, La., 159

Simmons, Lucinda, 232
Simms, Philip, 224
Sindry, A. Rivarde, 245
Slaughter, Richard L., 138
slave: anti-, 14, 216, 229; laws, 96, 255; market, xii, 213–14, 278; murders, 126, 212; Red River, 106, 145, 208, 255, 289; Waddill's, 72, 113, 192, 214, 221, 224, 237, 287; Waddill free a, 221, 273. *See also* Northup, Soloman
Slidell, Thomas, 172–73, 229
Sloat, William, 276
Sons of Temperance, 191, 195
Soule, Joseph A., 7, 58–60, 76–77, 79, 83
Soule, Joshua, 58
Soulé, Pierre, 167–68, 173
Spring Creek, La., 110; Academy, 110, 254
Spurlock, Thomas J., 117
Stafford, Leroy, 135
Starnes, Joshua, 137
St. Charles Hotel, 215
St. Edinburgh Review, 294
steamboats, 95, 190, 255, 262
Steinman, Henry C., 221, 224, 286
Stemman, Thomas, 213
Sterling, Anna, 215
Stevens, George A., 118, 145, 191
Stirling, John, 133
Stirling, Susan B., 222
sugar, xi, 5, 79, 148–49, 176, 198, 203, 213, 215, 243, 289, 291, 296, 301

T

Tanner, Lodowick, 148
Tanner, Peter, 189, 286
Tanner, R. J., 290
Taylor, A. J., 291
Taylor, Clara C., 307
Taylor, Ellen, 248

Taylor, Henderson, 99–100, 223, 243, 247–48, 271, 282, 285, 291, 307; as lawyer, 96–97, 150, 191, 195–96, 198, 229, 263; as politician, 136
Taylor, John J., 227
Taylor, John L., 232, 235, 242, 307
Taylor, Lewis S., 137, 198
Taylor, Oilo Sophia, 243
Taylor, Seth Lewis, 247, 313
Taylor, Gen. Zachary, 133–36, 138–39, 165, 183–84; inauguration, 192–93
temperance, 176, 179
Tennessee, 1, 64, 72, 103
Texada, Lewis E., 294–96
Texas, 79–81, 131, 139, 183; admission of, 75–76, 78–79, 132, 193; frontier, 135; Rangers, 132, 183; Supreme Court, 208
Thorpe, T. B., 267, 272
Three Pioneer Rapides Families (Stafford), xvi
Tiller, T. B., 127, 153–156, 212–13, 215–16, 261, 263, 291
Toler, Eliza, 286, 308
Toler, Joel, 214–15, 242, 286, 308
Toler, Patrick Henry, 214, 222, 286, 290, 300
Toler, Thomas T., 296
Tomlinson, Joseph S., v, 13–14, 21–22, 33, 66, 76, 81, 83
Tom (slave named), 269, 279
Torras, Michael, 211
Torras, Joseph, 211
Tournier, Helena, 276
Tournier, Justine, 275–76, 318
Transylvania University (Morrison College), 12
Trimble, Joseph M., 50
Trinity River, 232
Trist, N. P., 167, 172
Tristram Shandy (Sterne), 24
turpentine, 305

Twelve Years a Slave (Northup), xvi, 277, 279; film, xii, xv
Twenty-Second Regiment, 95
Tyrell, James, 137–38

U

Union and Democratic Review, 242
Union Literary Society, 64
United States Magazine, 271
Universalist Church, 190
U.S. Corps of Engineers, 246

V

Vanwickle, Stephen, 254
Vega, Rómulo Díaz de la, 139
Vernon, William, 224, 301
The Villager newspaper (Marksville), xvii, 118, 121–22, 145, 153, 197
Vitrac, Rosaline, 292
Voinche, Auguste, 129, 218, 224, 243
Voorhies, Cornelius, 216
Voorhies, Gradenigo P., 195–96, 205–6, 212, 270
Voorhies, William, 313

W

Waddill, Elizabeth Blagrave (JPW mother), 1, 72
Waddill, Frederick Browder (JPW brother), 1, 4, 37, 91
Waddill, Henarie Browder (JPW son), 214, 247, 290
Waddill, Ida Amelia (JPW daughter) 173, 203, 214, 218, 316
Waddill, James R., 183
Waddill, John Pamplin: as alderman, 118, 127, 131; death of, xix–xx, 313–15; as farmer, xi, 133; education, 2, 7, 10, 17, 92. *See also* Augusta; freeing of Northup, 273, 275–78, 281, 283; land purchases, 113, 288, 303–4; law, 66, 94, 117–21, 153; marriage, 101–3; move to Louisiana, 4–5, 87, 91, 94; politics, 28, 100, 118, 122, 208–11, 253–57, 271; religion, 30, 47, 52, 83, 203; as senator, xii, 118, 159, 161, 163–67, 170, 187, 211; slaves, 113, 192, 214, 237, 255, 260, 269, 287, 306
Waddill, Julia Malvina Barlow (JPW wife), xx, 103, 131, 135, 173, 191, 198, 221–22, 242, 246, 272, 313
Waddill, Laura Elizabeth (JPW daughter), 173, 316, 214
Waddill, Martha Jane (JPW sister), 1, 91
Waddill, Mary Ann (JPW sister), 1
Waddill, Mary Florence (JPW daughter), 242, 272, 290, 314
Waddill, Narcissa Browder (JPW sister), 1
Waddill, Rachel Elizabeth (JPW sister), 1
Waddill, Samuel D. (JPW father), 1–2, 72
Waddill, Samuel Rittenhouse (JPW brother), 1
Waddill, Seth Quee, (JPW brother) 1, 183
Waddill, Thomas Hickman (JPW son), 131, 173, 221, 246, 314
Waddill, William Wallace (JPW brother), 1, 4, 37, 191, 196–97, 205, 208, 211, 276–77, 281, 286; as attorney, 209, 221–22, 225, 231; education, 131, 217–20, 224–25; left Marksville, 309, 314
Wagner, Peter K., 173
Walker, Gen. Joseph, 168, 173, 198, 208
Walker, Robert L., 193
"Wandering Piper," 11
War of 1812, 219
Washington, William H., 305
Waters, Dr. Thomas, 272

Waters, George R., v, 12, 17, 25, 43, 50–51, 63, 69, 76, 83, 91, 144; trip to D.C., 70–71
Webster, Daniel, 69, 71
Weekly Deltas newspaper (New Orleans), 201, 205
Wells, James M., 272, 296–97
Wells, W. E. Mitford, 195–96
Whetstone, Thomas H., 64, 76, 83
Whig party, 167–68, 172, 205; losing strength, 310; in St. Landry, 169
White, Lewis, 198
White, Maunsel, 169
White Sulphur Springs, La., 259, 292, 294
Whittington, W. W., 254
Wickliff, Robert, 41
Wild Cat Bayou, 302
Williams, Levi W., 176
Williamston County, Tennessee, xi, 1, 72
Wills & Peak, 250
Wilson, Peter, 263
Winaris, Rev. W., 172
Wise, Henry A., 70
Woodlock, Freeman, 276
Woodruff, Turner, 98
Wright, Dr. Jesse D., 110

Y

Yale University, 110
Van Buren, Pres. Martin, 199
Yazoo County, Ms., 58
yellow fever, xix, 293–95, 308, 314–15
Yellow Stone (steamboat), 5

Z

Zeline, John, 232